Mountain State Stories of the People

Celebrating West Virginia

Populore

Populore Publishing Company
Morgantown, West Virginia

Edited by
Amy A. Stevenson
Rae Jean V. Sielen

Foreword by Gaston Caperton

Mountain State Stories of the People. Copyright © 1997 by Populore Publishing Company. Printed and bound in the United States of America. All rights reserved. No part of this publication may be reproduced, stored in a retrieval system, or transmitted in any form or by any means, electronic, mechanical, photocopying, recording or otherwise without the prior written permission from the publisher, except by a reviewer, who may quote brief passages in a review. Published by Populore Publishing Company, PO Box 4382, Morgantown, WV 26504. First edition. Second printing.

ISBN 0-9652699-1-4

Library of Congress Catalog Card Number: 97-065941

Each Populore narrative in *Mountain State Stories of the People* has been assigned an identification code. The code is found at the end of the narrative with the following six components: *Narrative Number — Country — Series (General) – Series (Specific) — Volume Number — Year*. For example the first narrative by Barbara Smith in Chapter 1 is coded *1-001-ST-WV-001-1997*. Individual narratives will be stored in the Populore Database according to Narrative Numbers, e.g., "No. 1" for Barbara Smith's narrative. Requests for reprints should include the author's name and the one-digit to three-digit narrative number.

Reference to any narratives from *Mountain State Stories of the People* in other works should cite the author and year within the text, e.g., (Smith, 1997). Footnotes, end notes, and/or bibliographic references should include author, year, narrative title, narrative number, editors, book title, publisher, and page(s). For example: Smith, Barbara. 1997. Jean Wagner, Miner's Widow, Miner's Wife. Narrative No. 1. In A.A. Stevenson and R.J.V. Sielen (Eds.). *Mountain State Stories of the People*. Morgantown, WV: Populore Publishing Company, pp. 5-7.

*Dedicated to all
who call
West Virginia home*

Acknowledgments

First and foremost, this book would not be a reality without the trust, talent, patience, and enthusiasm of the authors. They dared to do something new; sent us — essentially strangers — precious photos and memories; and stuck with us through forms, mailings, updates, proofs, and what must have seemed to be a never-ending process. There are no words to express our gratitude.

We'd like to thank our families for their help in project promotion; their critiques and suggestions; their cheerleading and support services; and their devotion and love. Rae Jean particularly thanks her mother, Beverly Farfsing, and her husband Ken St. Louis. Ken has been much more than a supportive husband in the background; rather, he played a key role in project conception, and his involvement has been extensive. Both Amy and Rae Jean appreciate all he has done, all his ideas, and all the time he has devoted to problem solving, festivals, and meetings.

Several folks deserve mention for spreading the word, hosting workshops, and helping out in other ways. Colene Heim, for hosting a workshop and being a generally superb person; Joy Gilchrist and Harry Davis, for sharing their wonderfully entertaining stories during workshops; Carolyn Mathena, Maxine Corbett, and Ann Grimm, who quickly spread the word in their neck of the woods and beyond; Debbie and Larry Escue, who got kin from several states involved and recruited for the young authors' section; and Teresa Dingess and other teachers at Chapmanville and Sissonville Middle Schools. Also, members of the local and wider writing community: Sandra Wales, George Lies, Gerald Swick, Sandy Hopkins, Nan Lewis, Carla McClure, and Anne Johnson. Col. Pauline Shaver, was especially inspirational and helpful as the first one to give us a story.

We appreciate the support of various West Virginia state individuals. Thank you Gaston Caperton, Carolyn Curry and Robert Gassner. And from the Homecoming '96 office, Sam Sutton and Harriet Casto. Martha Barnitt also deserves thanks for her interest and encouragement. And, we appreciate the help and encouragement of our local Small Business Development Center and the Center in Charleston.

Pioneer Press of Terra Alta and MountainNet of Morgantown deserve mention for providing valuable products and technical support.

Francoise Stauber, Joyce Coombs, and interns Stephen Vandevander, Melissa Thornhill, and Sarah Bracy provided ideas and hours to make the project successful.

The media played a key role in informing the public of the project. Special thanks to West Virginia Public Radio for two excellent pieces, and those columnists and newspaper editors who recognized the importance of story preservation.

Finally, a big thanks goes to Angela Caudill — our master of production — for her superior graphics and design work. We're awed, as usual. For safeguarding the photos, for working into the wee hours of the night, and for working with file after file, our gratitude is immense.

Preface

If you love West Virginia, you're invited…

That invitation was extended to *everyone* with a story to share about this wonderful state. The purpose of the invitation was to collect true, short stories and memories about West Virginia's people, places, heritage, traditions, events, and accomplishments. In the end, dozens of people responded, and 207 of their narratives are presented in *Mountain State Stories of the People*.

The stories in this book range from one paragraph to several pages in length; many include photos. The topics are varied. Authors reminisce about childhood friends and loved ones, family traditions, and a sense of security. Many people wrote tributes to loved ones, often deceased and dearly missed. Humorous anecdotes mingle with bittersweet memories of bygone eras. Some authors felt that the book provided an ideal chance to thank the people who had influenced and improved their lives. Young and old voices combine to provide a collage of stories from different generations of a rapidly changing, evolving state; this is a time when memories of dirt roads and horses and buggies are as vivid to many as the highways that now connect us for transportation and information. Traditions, technology, and industry are changing, but a spirit remains. Documenting and preserving this indomitable spirit is one reason why this book is important.

Many experiences that were once common to life in West Virginia are disappearing. Mining camps, cake walks, box socials, wedding serenades, molasses making, and mail carriers on horseback defined rural living and socializing in the state. Some traditions remain, and, as the student contributions to this book show, new ones are evolving. West Virginia's young people, new residents, and even natives will find the book an entertaining and educational look into a part of life that shapes the image and the world's perception of the state and its residents.

Throughout this project, our guiding principle was that a good story does not necessarily come from an accomplished writer; it comes from an experience. The stories contained in this book are not meant to be literary masterpieces, although we happen to think some are close. Participants needed only a willingness to write or tell the stories in their own words, their own style. Most stories are from everyday folks who work, live, love, and raise families in West Virginia. Some narratives come from expatriate Mountaineers who have left the state for one reason or another. All the stories, however, have one thing in common: the story is a glimpse into what is near to the heart of the author.

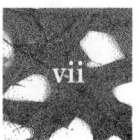

The narratives in this collection may include dialectical or grammatical inconsistencies that some people might consider "errors." However, we do not believe that they are intrusive to the reader's understanding or enjoyment of each narrative. Rather, they serve to bring forth the personality and "voice" of the individual author. It is with this viewpoint that we decided to make minimal changes to the original manuscripts.

Students of history and English, teachers, historians, genealogists, folks who love a good story or turn of phrase, new residents, expatriates, retirees, and the just plain curious will all enjoy revisiting or learning about the "good ol' days," hearing the voices of newer generations, and appreciating the hospitality and wisdom of the Mountain State. So we now invite *you* to get to know some of us who call West Virginia home.

Foreword

From the beginning, Homecoming '96, West Virginia's yearlong celebration of its history and heritage, has relied on grassroots interest. Throughout the state, 1996 was a time of community celebrations, family reunions, and visits home by those who have left our hills over the years. During these events and visits, memories and stories were shared, laughed about, and sometimes cried over.

These stories are the essence of West Virginia. They are history, development, and change as experienced by our friends, families, and neighbors — everyday folks who call West Virginia home and make it such a welcoming place.

I am delighted that out of the spirit of Homecoming '96 should emerge the *Mountain State Stories of the People* project. By recognizing that every person has significant memories to share, that every life is extraordinary, we are sending an important message, facilitating and reinforcing family bonds.

This book contains stories from all parts of West Virginia. Also included are special contributions from some of our state's young residents, many of whom provided their own reflections on growing up. Others chose to interview older West Virginians. All of these young authors have developed a stronger sense of belonging, of history, and have improved their writing ability through an enjoyable, interactive educational activity.

It is my sincere hope that stories such as these continue to be recorded, archived, and appreciated for their contribution to our state's popular history, the history of the people. What rich stories we have, with timeless and universal messages and themes of courage, resourcefulness, caring, determination, and light-hearted fun. Let them serve as an uplifting example, inspiring people to take the initiative and put their stories in writing.

Gaston Caperton
Governor
January, 1997

Contents

CHAPTER 1: INTRODUCTION AND INVITED NARRATIVE 1
Introduction 3
Jean Wagner, Miner's Widow, Miner's Wife • *Barbara Smith* 5

CHAPTER 2: NORTHERN PANHANDLE 9
And Her Children Will Rise Up
 And Call Her Blessed • *Ruth Phillips* 11
Preacher's Portrait • *Debbie Van Schaik* 12
Memorial Service For Charles Kuhens • *Karen Kuhens* 12
More Than Just A Newspaper • *Mary Voltz* 12
A Harvest Of Memories • *Juanita Fitzsimmons* 13
Memories Of Family Life • *John Samuel Smith* 13

CHAPTER 3: MID-OHIO VALLEY 17
Home To His West Virginia Hills • *Evelyn R. B. Carr* 19
Picnics And 'Portant Stuff • *Deborah Escue* 19
The Sweet Water Spring • *Thelma Davis Nolan* 19
Mudlick School Memories • *Edith Parker Griffith* 20
Prayer Of My Five-Year-Old Son • *Mildred Marshall* 21
I Watched My Father Die • *Kay Young Hill* 22
Dump Truck Escapades • *Robyn Lindamood* 22
The Coming Rain • *Robyn Lindamood* 23
The Brownie Camp Road • *Robyn Lindamood* 23
A Hunter's Tall Tale • *Danny R. Osborne* 23
The Road Brought Me Happiness • *Ruth Ann Nida* 24
Baptism At Reedy Creek • *William R. Waterman* 24
Those Were The Days • *Polly Shepherd* 25
The Maytag Man • *Herbert L. Roush, Sr.* 25
Women Doing More Than Tending Hearth
 And Home • *Ann Sams Grimm* 26
Our Simple Freedoms • *Colene Heim* 27
Memories Of Grandpa Parker • *Donna E. S. Davis* 27

CHAPTER 4: METRO VALLEY 29
1920s Adventure • *Gene Cox* 31
Brawley's Hollow • *Margaret Bowden* 31
The Rummage Club • *Kathryn Campbell* 31
Wild Creature • *Kathryn Campbell* 32
Nora Rood's Lost Legacy • *Richard Marks* 32
The Influence Of My Life • *Lucille Monfradi Beck* 33
My Mother's Stories • *Richard C. Bainbridge* 33
Reading, Writing, And Arithmetic:
    Family Matters • *Gaston Caperton* 34
A Brief Tribute To My Dad • *Frances Meredith* 35
Childhood Playhouse • *Roberta E. A. Escue* 36
Horse Quip • *L. A. SQ* 36
Thank Goodness For Cans • *Donald Williams* 37
That's Just The Way It Was • *Lorena M. R. Siders* 37
Sisters • *Carla Thomas McClure* 38
My First Look At History • *Martha Gregory* 38
Picking Up Coal • *Catherine Sue Frye* 39
Home Sweet Home • *Malcolm "Pat" Patterson* 39
Be Home 'Fore Dark • *Zella Jarrett* 40
An Awkward Age • *Katie Pratt* 41
When Grandpa Was Growing Up • *Stacey Vande Linde* 41
Corn Cob Baseball At Millertown • *Harold L. Stump* 42
The Future Is Our Children • *Sally L. Patterson* 42
A Nice Guy • *Ralph Williams* 43
The One-Room Schoolhouse • *Pearl Todd Miller* 43
The Gift Of Hope • *Katherine P. Manley* 43
Susan's Blouse • *Katherine P. Manley* 44
A Legendary Legacy • *Rebecca Miceli* 44
Window Birth • *Priscilla H. E. Brace* 45
The West Virginia Army National Guard
    Yesterday And Today • *Kenneth Bailey* 45
A Good Life In West Virginia • *Phyllis Williams Jarvis* 48
The Road To West Virginia • *Jay Rockefeller* 48
Paw Paw • *William T. McKeny* 49
Triplett • *Barbara Parkins Mallett* 50
A Rich Heritage • *Phyllis Williams Jarvis* 51

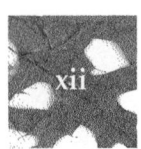

A Gift Of Remembrance • *Carrie Eldridge* 51
My Father, The Teacher • *Denver C. Yoho* 52

CHAPTER 5: MOUNTAIN LAKES 53
Job's Temple Homecoming • *Charles E. Arbanas* 55
Samuel Bennett, Union Soldier, 1840-1930 • *Billy Bennett* 55
Now I Am A Right-Handed Writer • *Eloise Davis Warfield* 56
Have You Seen Icabod Crane Lately? • *Carla Coffman* 56
A Mother's Love • *Colene Heim* 57
Blackberries And Bears • *James B. King* 57
Phillips Run, Nicholas County • *Mary S. T. Cottle* 58
Our Family Strength • *Alice Brown Juergens* 59
Painful Lesson On Baptism • *Elizabeth Murray Deitz* 60
Molasses Makin' • *Patricia Samples Workman* 60
Birthday Home • *Nancy A. H. Bryant* 61
Old Treasure Trunk • *Carol Warren* 62
Rich In History — Rich In People — Richwood • *Maxine Corbett* 62
A Lasting Paradise • *Maxine Corbett* 64
The Schoolteacher • *Mildred Marshall* 65
Love Created This Community • *Mary Ann Radabaugh* 65
Addie Dawson: Clay County Storyteller • *Evelyn Eagle McLaughlin* 69
Grandad And Old Sam • *Barbara Mullins Parsons* 69
The Barn • *Preston Fitzwater* 70
Making Music • *Phyllis Jarvis* 71
The Blizzard Of 1993 Brings Life • *Damon Hanshaw* 71
The Making Of The Mill • *Joy Gilchrist* 72

CHAPTER 6: NEW RIVER / GREENBRIER VALLEY 75
Granny • *David Austin Rodes* 77
Homecoming For Mrs. Basham • *Wilma Lilly Rodes* 77
Thinking Of Appalachia • *Wilma Lilly Rodes* 78
The Story Of Alta, Fayette County • *Richard C. Bainbridge* 78
Sweet Kiss Of Blackdamp • *Glenna Carroll* 79
The Simple Pleasure Of Being A West Virginian • *Robert Overbey* 79
How I Conned Movie Fare • *William C. McGhee* 80
The Phantom Cat: A True Story • *Nell C. Corkrean* 80
The Risen Dead • *Virginia Forren Hudson* 81

The Little Pump Organ • *Virginia Forren Hudson* 81
Barefoot Mountaineers • *J. D. Moore* 82
Liver For Thanksgiving • *Carolyn Mathena* 82
The Christmas Tree • *Lois Maxey Rosenow* 82
"Flimflam" • *James R. Pettry* 83
Aunt Pheobe And Uncle Ike • *Cathy A. S. Helms* 83
The Year Was 1937; The Month Was
    September • *Lucille Litz Walthall* 84
My First Mallet Steam Engine • *Richard C. Bainbridge* 84
Papa Jim • *Gayle Walthall Wise* 85
The War On Two Fronts • *Michael Hughes* 85
Pearl Buck Of West Virginia • *Geneva Anderson Wynne* 86

CHAPTER 7: POTOMAC HIGHLANDS 87
The Vegetable Vendor • *Barbra Borror* 89
The Outhouse • *Edward Hartman* 89
Pure West Virginian • *Freeda Davy* 89
The Meaning Of A Photograph • *Amy Stevenson* 90
The Smoking Smokehouse • *Sally A. Phares* 91
Early Stitches • *Sally A. Phares* 91
Surprised By Joelle • *Renaud Stauber* 92
Gramma's Day Out • *Beverly Sue Ketterman* 93
What Grandma Said • *Macel G. Gear* 93
Tales And Mountain Philosophy • *Macel G. Gear* 94
Papaw's Bike • *Erica L. Stratton* 95
General Lee In Slatyfork And Linwood • *Luther David Sharp, Jr.* 95

CHAPTER 8: EASTERN PANHANDLE 97
The Face Of America: From Tyler Texas, 1936 To
    Martinsburg, West Virginia, 1996 • *Riccardo Accurso* 99
Come Home To West Virginia • *N. J. Lewis* 99

CHAPTER 9: MOUNTAINEER COUNTRY 101
Of Memories, Magic, And Mulberries • *JoAnn Danks Dadisman* 103
A Country Serenade • *Mary L. S. Matlick* 103
Shaw's Run • *Phyllis J. Carpenter* 104

Teaching In The High Lonesome • *Alice Bickford Farley* 104
Rose Bud • *Sandra Bunner* 105
Kohl Lined With Coal Dust • *Aida J. M. Everhart* 105
A Tribute • *Aida J. M. Everhart* 106
Memories • *Judith Drumpus Bennett* 107
I Love West Virginia Auctions • *Kenneth St. Louis* 108
Tribute To Blanche Geary • *Melinda St. Louis* 109
The Forgotten Shotgun • *James Edward Nedrow* 110
Lillie's Legacy • *Haley Elizabeth Garwood* 110
Television With Granny And Poppy • *Leslie F. M. Downey* 111
A Country Church Celebration • *Evelyn T. Kennedy* 111
Mountains In My Horizon • *Rae Jean Sielen* 112
You Never Know Who You'll Meet
    At The "Y" • *Howard Cobb* 114
Life's Photographs • *Claris Mitchell McDaniel* 114
Remembering What Used To Be • *Tawny Layman Hoxter* 115
Defy The Storm • *Gerald D. Swick* 116
The Fuller Brush Man • *David Darwin Calvert* 117
The Purple Heart • *Ethel Louise Righman* 117
The Grand Old Lady Of Morgantown • *Bettijane Burger* 118
Happy Memories Of Long Ago • *Dana A. S. Righman* 119
My Father's Bootstrap Education • *Dale Heaster* 119
Cove District High School • *Agnes Dennison Haller* 120
Excerpts From My Journal • *Dorothea C. R. King* 120
Growing Up In Memorial City • *Louis W. Smith* 122
Long Ago But Not Forgotten • *Norabelle Shuman Corra* 123
The Keeper Of The History • *Patricia Kiger Morgan* 123
Without History • *Patricia Kiger Morgan* 124
Rationed Candy / Rationed Gum • *Charleen Evans-Thomas* 125
Memories Of The Rural Mail Carrier • *Loutellus Stout* 125
The Simpson Hotel • *William H. D. Shelton* 126
Losing My Mamaw • *Jennifer Nicole Whyte* 126
What Ever Task Lies To Your Hand Do It With All
    Your Might • *Dorothy Moore* 127
Home Brew And Ice Wagons • *Jessie Volk* 129
A Comforting Change • *Sarah Bracy* 129

Home Is West Virginia And West Virginia
   Is Home • *Pauline Wilson Shaver* 130
A Favorite Time Of The Year • *Melissa Thornhill* 131
Grand Are The Grandchildren • *Edith Ware* 132
Generations • *Ray Pefley Hutchinson and Sylvia E. Parker* 132
Nestorville United Methodist Church • *Betty Marsh* 138

CHAPTER 10: YOUNG AUTHORS 141
Introduction 143
My Grandmother And Lye Soap • *Brittany Nicole Adkins* 145
A Winter To Remember • *Eamon Barker* 145
Papaw Edd • *Amanda Ann Aldridge* 145
Growing Up In The 1940s • *Kristin Farley* 145
The Early Life Of Dianna Adams • *Clarissa Nicole Fekete* 146
Grandma's Good Old Days • *Jennifer Bryant* 146
A Day in the Life Of My Grandfather • *Jilleyn Gabrielle Gore* 146
Polly Hall And Harvey Gore • *Ashley D. Gore* 147
Making Lye Soap • *Crystal Dawn Spangler* 147
Molliemunchers • *Shelly M. B. Carter* 147
Soccer Kid • *Zachary Damon Hanshaw* 148
My Grandma • *Amanda Kay Dingess* 148
The Mountain Lion • *Joshua William Jones* 148
The Greenbrier River Trail • *Jeffery Duffield* 149
Interview With Mabel Lucas • *Matt Lucas* 149
A Peaceful Picnic • *Malindia Hensley* 149
When Great-Grandma Was Little • *Ashley Adkins* 150
The Devil Made Him Do It • *Daniel Whittington Baldwin* 150
An Average Day For My Grandparents • *Seth Cyfers* 150
Mountains • *Jennifer Dingess* 151
Making Molasses • *John David Dingess* 151
One Of The Best Days Of My Life • *Jeremy Wells* 151
Fox Hunting • *Alicia Workman* 152
My Mountain Grandma • *Mesha Maren-Hogan* 152
Grandma Emmie Remembers War • *Casey Maran Bowling* 152
My Grandparents' House • *Christina Kessell* 153
The Cow On Coco Road • *Amber Smith* 153
The War • *Jacob Smith* 153

How Pecks Mill Go Its Name • *Jennifer Smith* 154
Hidden Objects • *Erica Johnson* 154
A Town's Loss • *Brandon John Picklesimer* 154
My Grandmother • *Kara Brooke Meeks* 154
Working In The Coal Mines • *Matthew Foster* 155
Growing Up On My Farm • *Matthew Mullins* 155
Hurt And Scared • *Andrew Mullins* 156
Life In The Past • *Gary Lee Jeffrey* 156
My Granny • *Ashley Jeanette Varney* 156
My Grandma Bryant • *Jarrod Russell Bryant* 156
Camping At Pipestem • *John Gancs* 157
When My Grandmother Was Little • *Alisha Dawn Sparks* 157
A Man Named Rabbit • *Jonathan Edgar Anthony* 157
When Ruthie Was Young • *Kathryn Leigh Erb* 158
The Huge Sandbox • *Kendra Burgess* 158
My Family • *Andy Henson* 158
Beethoven • *Anthony Dale Collins* 159
The Big Garden • *Michael Smutko* 159
Uncle Fain • *William Crichton Miller, III* 159
West Virginian Through
    And Through • *Bridgett Alexandra McNeely* 160
Christmas Traditions • *Emily Gray Walters* 160

Appendix 1: The Project 161

Appendix 2: Ideas And Resources 165

Appendix 3: Who's Who - Family Tree Form 169

Index 173

About The Editors 185

West Virginia Map 186

Chapter 1

Introduction

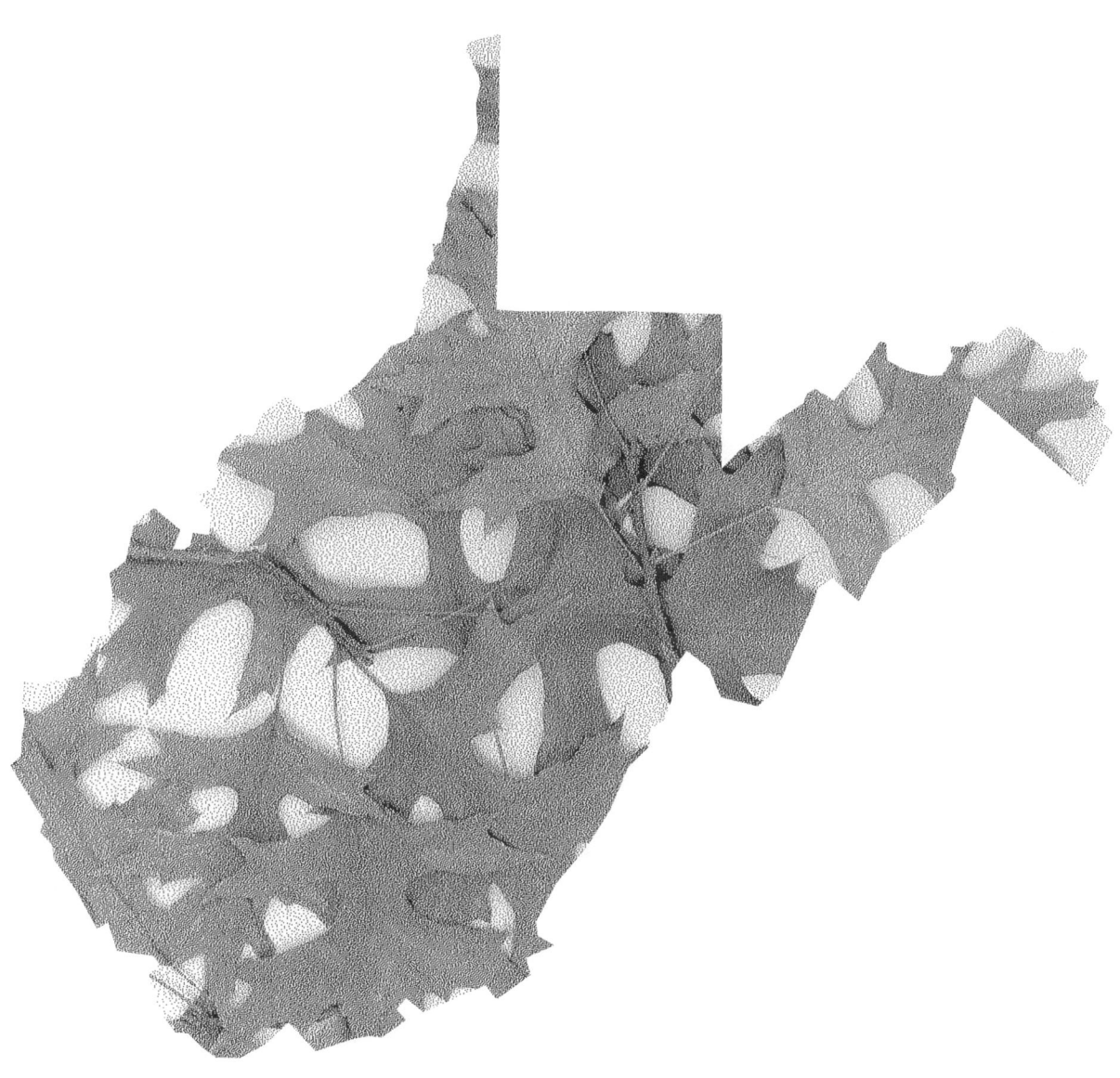

CHAPTER 1: INTRODUCTION AND INVITED NARRATIVE

Introduction

West Virginia's history is inseparably twined with industry, mountains, and rural culture. Words like family, community, handmade, homemade, and home-grown evoke a sense of pride in accomplishment, heritage, and tradition. Home-spun tales and mountain music come forth naturally, to be soaked up by appreciative ears. Just like the coal that runs through the hills and valleys, stories about life in the Mountain State course in seemingly endless veins through its residents — past and present — reflecting a vast array of unique experiences, ideas, attitudes, and perceptions.

Mountain State Stories of the People is a collection of West Virginians' narratives, sent to us in response to an invitation to preserve true stories of personal significance. From experience, we had a good idea about the types of stories we would receive. Nevertheless, we worried about "balance." What if we received a hundred stories about one community, all focusing on the same topic? What would we do then? Happily, however, that never became an issue. The mix of narratives was just right and we were pleasantly surprised by each one. We are delighted to be able to include various writing styles from folks of all walks of life. Inquiries came in from some elementary and middle school teachers, and although not part of our original plan, we decided to include a special section in the book of contributions from our state's youngsters. The remainder of the stories are divided into eight regions, as defined by the state's Division of Tourism, each encompassing various West Virginia counties. The county designation for each story was chosen by the author. Stories have been included from thirty-seven counties, and eleven states.

Narratives are arranged such that the reader can skip around, enjoying them in any order. For readers looking for a specific topic, place, person, or author, a comprehensive index has been included, making the book a valuable reference for students, historians, genealogists, and others. In the index, the page numbers for topics featured in the narratives are shown in bold print. Authors' names are listed in bold print, and pages numbers are underlined for those index entries including a photograph.

This book project was undertaken in an effort to honor all voices, regardless of writing skill or experience. Yet, as you will read in this book, there are some very talented writers among us. Additionally, West Virginia as a whole has produced writers of much acclaim. We wanted to acknowledge this with a special invited piece to begin the book. We chose "Jean Wagner, Miner's Widow, Miner's Wife" written by Barbara Smith. Mrs. Smith has served on the executive committee of West Virginia Writers, Inc., almost since its inception in 1977. She is also a member of the Appalachian Writers' Association, the Southern Appalachian Writers' Cooperative, the Society for Technical Communication, and several other writers' organizations. She serves annually as a workshop leader at the Appalachian Writers' Workshop in Hindman, Kentucky, and the Writers' Conference in Green Lake, Wisconsin. Formerly Chair of the Division of the

Humanities and Professor of Literature and Writing at Alderson-Broaddus College, she is now a free-lance writer and editor. With over two hundred published poems, short stories, and journal articles to her credit, she has also published seven books of fiction and non-fiction.

The story of Jean Wagner is particularly appropriate to begin this book. Coal is a major theme of the story. Coal built the community, employed the families, determined the course of their lives. It could be considered a representative story; although entirely personal, the story can be related to by many residents of declining mining or industrial towns. Like coal, other West Virginia industries have seen better days. This book is full of examples of ingenuity, resourcefulness, perseverance, and a sense of entrepreneurship that help people face the hurdles and go on. Family and community bind them together, forging a spirit that prevails and endures all.

West Virginia's history has its somber moments. But the underlying humor and inner strength of its people is something to celebrate. Laugh with us at the mischief and antics of "Old Sam." Relive the days of one-room schools and "The Outhouse." Revel in the spirit at the "Baptism at Reedy Creek," and take a refreshing dip in "A Lasting Paradise." Some stories will pull at your heart strings and you'll mourn the loss of someone you will wish you had known. "The Maytag Man" is one such person. Visit simple places like "Triplett" that have inspired and nurtured love and family. Get to know your neighbors, and you might even run across a long-lost relative or two. Turn the pages and discover the true stories of West Virginia.

Jean Wagner, Miner's Widow, Miner's Wife

The focal point in Galloway, the community in which Jean Wagner has lived almost all of her life, is an enormous slag pile. It dwarfs and serves as a backdrop for the tiny town created when the mines went in. It has been only within the last two years that the slag has finally been reclaimed, and the hundred or so families who remain in Galloway still have to look twice to realize what has happened. The abandoned machinery is finally gone, the old tipple has been torn down, the eternal smoke from the burning slag pile has dissipated. The hills are finally green again instead of red and brown and gray and black.

No coal has been produced in Galloway in well over twenty-five years. The company houses have been replaced or at least repainted so that only a few still look just alike. The location of the company store, which remained the local post office for years after the store itself was closed, has to be pointed out to strangers. The railroad tracks that carried the coal are rusty with disuse. The only new business in years was a nightclub which advertised in the local papers its most attractive activity — male strippers on special weekends. Even that nightclub has, however, disappeared.

Jean has always lived with coal. Her father was a miner at Camp Run Hollow. He worked for the Simpson Creek Collieries, then located between Philippi and Galloway. Andy, Jean's first husband, was also from a coal family. He worked — and died — at the Sardis mine owned by Clinchfield. Andy and his brothers followed tradition, going into the mines to handload coal when they were only thirteen or fourteen years old. They have spent almost their entire working lives in the mines.

Jean is a proud, handsome woman, red-haired and wearing black slacks and a silky lavender blouse. Her ruddy coloring makes her dark eyes bold, and her thick-muscled shoulders tell the story of her life. She is a worker, a Cleavenger by birth, who married another hard worker. Her first husband was from a Hungarian background. It is his name, Kurucz, that her children still bear, though Jean remarried ten years ago. Her second husband is a foreman for Martinka Coal Company in Marion County. He, too, was born and raised in Barbour County.

Jean tells of the day when Andy Kurucz died. Earlier he had decided to get out of the mines and had gone to Cleveland to work for GMAC. A new mine opened at Sardis, however, and Andy's former boss begged him to come back. He did, only a short time before the fatal accident. A fire broke out, and Andy and six others were trapped behind the fire. They all died.

It was an off-day, a Saturday, October 16, 1965, and Andy had been working the second shift. Jean was in the habit of waiting for him to come home, but it was about 3 A.M., and Jean had fallen asleep watching a movie on television. "I don't know why — I have no idea why — I hadn't fixed him anything to eat. I always fixed him something to eat when he got home.

Jean Wagner, 1986.

But I didn't that night. I just fell asleep in front of the TV." Then two of Jean's sisters-in-law were pounding on the front door. They had been called from the mine office. There was a fire in the mine, the sleepy women were told, and Andy was inside.

She thought she had dreamed it, but when Jean looked out the window at the middle-of-the-night town, there were lights on in all of the in-laws' houses. Jean's mother-in-law offered to stay with Jean's children. Andy, Jr., was then thirteen. Deborah Lynn was almost twelve. Donna Jean was eight.

And so there was the traditional scene — the mine whistle blowing, every light in the community shining, the miners' wives and relatives and, indeed, the whole community standing around and waiting. They could do nothing but wait.

And then they could do nothing but go home. Word was official: the fire had, as mine fires almost inevitably do, used up all the oxygen. Poisonous gases had spread. None of the men would come out alive.

Andy's body was not found until Monday morning. He died with another miner, Isaac Moats. Andy was buried on Deborah Lynn's twelfth birthday. He had gotten her a wristwatch on the day he was killed. She still has it.

Jean apologizes now for crying. "I don't know why I still do this," she says. She uses a tissue to wipe her eyes, then folds her hands back in her lap where they had been.

"That wasn't the only accident that Andy was involved in," Jean reports. "He and his brothers used to get together and talk about the mines, and sometimes I'd overhear. They'd never tell us directly. Once, for instance, I heard them talking about all the new young miners who had been put on. Andy told me when he came home that night that he had caught a bad cold. But then I overheard him and his brothers talking, and what had really happened was that they were running a continuous miner, and a cable sparked and started a fire. Andy had to fight it all alone because those new young miners just ran out on him. I remember Andy or one of his brothers saying, 'Those damned kids are going to kill some of us.' That was just about two weeks before the fire when Andy was killed. But," she hastens to add, "I don't know that any of those younger men were involved in it one way or the other. What happened was that they were moving some big machine — the miner or something — and it wasn't padded, and it rubbed up against some electrical wires, and that started the fire." She smiles slightly. "And not even Andy could put it out."

Jean's two older children took Andy's death hard. Their son, Jean observes, has never been inside a mine, and he swears he never will be. He makes his living driving a truck. Deborah Lynn is a respiratory therapist at the local hospital. Donna Jean married a strip miner and has two children. Neither of the girls has ever talked much about how they feel about the mines. Jean knows, however, that Donna has always been strongly opposed to her husband, Todd, going underground.

All three of her children, Jean states, went to grade school there in Galloway. Then they went to the high school in Philippi. Discrimination, Jean believes, was not so much against the coal miners' children as it was against the children from any outlying community, regardless of how their parents made their living. "Galloway may have had a burning gob pile, and it may have had some run-down houses, but by golly it also produced the best football players in the county. The athletic teams at the high school would have been hurting if it hadn't been for Galloway and Brownton. And they knew it.

"I've always said that the best people in the world live in Galloway," she continues. "They're genuine. If anybody is in trouble, any kind of trouble, the whole community pitches in to help. Bob Getschman was the minister for a recent funeral, for instance, and he said there were eighty-two cars there. I don't know how he knew, but it was a really big funeral. And it wasn't just the funeral. Everybody helped right along afterwards, too.

"I didn't get anything at all from the company, just Workmen's Compensation and Social Security, but the men took up a collection for us, and everybody kept bringing us food and offering to help in lots of other ways.

"That's the way it's always been," Jean continues. "It was that way even when I was a very little girl. We lived so close to the mine where my daddy worked that I could look from our house right into the mine. He worked as a ditcher." She explains. "There was a lot of water in that mine, and his job was to dig ditches to carry the water out." She smiles. "His clothes were absolutely filthy, but my mother took it all in stride. I think she just took it for granted that she was supposed to. All the women did. They knew that their job was to raise the kids and keep their husbands happy and healthy so that they could work. I never had to wash on a washboard myself, but my mother and mother-in-law sure did. And they raised gardens and hogs and chickens, and they swept their yards. That's because the ground was so poor and there were so many kids playing around that there never was any grass. We never even knew that there was supposed to be.

"And I can remember my mother-in-law telling about heating bath water on a torchlight stove out in the bathhouse. There weren't any showers in the mines in those days, so people had bathhouses — or at least we did. Then Andy built a shower, not a toilet or anything, just a shower, in the basement so that the men coming from the mines could get clean before they came upstairs."

She changes the subject. "We had different ways of having fun. Not toys or anything. I can remember — I must have been around ten or eleven years old — playing in the woods a lot. And we had a playhouse in the pasture." She laughs. "Oh, boy, do I remember. We had this playhouse, and we had built the chimney out of the cardboard from a roll of linoleum, and of course we set it on fire.

"We used to play a lot around the creeks, too. And we'd go hunting, but without any guns. Just playing in the woods, really. And on Sundays we'd go to the Pt. Pleasant Baptist Church. There wasn't any church in town then. And then, much later but still on Sundays, we'd walk in to Galloway itself — that's when we were living up the hollow — to the movie. That was about seven miles altogether, each way. We'd get home real late, or what seemed real late then."

She remembers even more. "The miners used to listen to the radio a lot, too. I remember when the neighbor was the first to get electricity and everybody gathered at his house to listen to 'Baby Snooks' and 'Amos and Andy' and Edward R. Morrow. That was a really big deal because before that, before electricity, all we could listen to was crystal sets, and we had to take turns, and the sound kept coming and going.

"We didn't really have it too bad, though. We got by pretty well. There may be better homes, more modern now, and the paychecks are sure a lot bigger, but we always had plenty to eat. Plenty. In fact, I remember people saying, 'You can always go to a coal miner's house and find a good meal.'"

Jean pauses for a moment, reflecting. Then she says, "It's true. Miners' families do really well now, when they're working, but there's just no future any more in mining. The strikes and lay-offs wipe out everything anybody can save. I just hope boys like my grandson can find something better. There's nothing wrong with mining, but there's just no future in it. No future at all."

Author: Barbara Smith

1-001-ST-WV-001-1997

Chapter 2

Northern Panhandle

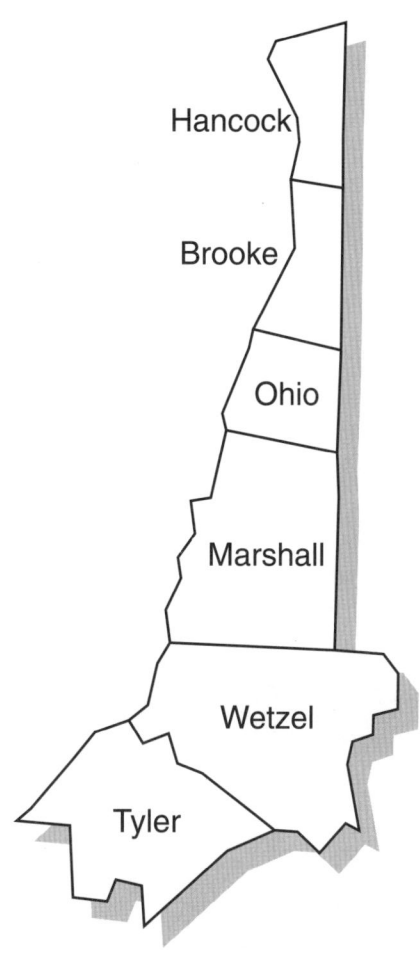

And Her Children Will Rise Up And Call Her Blessed.
— Proverbs 31:28

Ruth Gaynell Morgan George, better known as Gay, was a direct descendant of Morgan Morgan, being of the sixth generation, daughter of Jeremiah and Mary Waters Morgan. She was the epitome of a virtuous woman as described in Proverbs 31:10-31. Her life was a love of God and fellow man. "Gay, can you come?" was a frequent question. Whether it was to stay with an expectant mother until the doctor came, an illness, or to help with a wedding, birthday celebration or funeral, people seemed to draw comfort from her presence. She seemed to have a proverb or saying for every occasion.

Gay with brothers Jerry and Evan Morgan.

She and my father bought a farm at Hastings during the Depression. In 1938, Dad died and the responsibility of a home, farm, and four children fell on my mother. Mom eked out a living on this hillside farm without any income other than what she earned by selling butter, eggs, and occasional cans of cream. She had two cows to milk, a couple of hogs, and a flock of chickens.

The few groceries she bought had to be carried three miles from Pine Grove, the last half-mile straight up. Flour was bought in twenty-five pound sacks and sugar in ten pound bags. My mother made light bread every Saturday to last the week and she made "schmeircase" (cottage cheese) from the clabber left after the cream was skimmed off the milk.

In the spring my mother planted a garden, a potato patch, and a field of sweet corn plus field corn for the animals. She canned hundreds of quarts of vegetables and fruits to tide us through the winter, as well as many jars of jelly, jam, apple butter, pickles, and preserves. She made crocks of sauerkraut, green tomato ketchup, and pickle beans as only West Virginians know how to make. Green beans were also dried, also known as fodder beans or leather britches, and were so good cooked with a ham bone in the winter.

In November the hogs were butchered. We ate the spareribs, back bones, liver, and sidemeat first, as we didn't have refrigeration. This meat was also shared with the neighbors who helped with the butchering. Mother sugar-cured the hams, shoulder and sidemeat, made sausage and canned it, rendered the fat for lard, made mincemeat from the meat on the head, and pickled the feet and ears. Nothing went to waste. What a busy and messy time it was!

My mother's reputation as a good cook was widely known and we often had twenty people for Sunday dinner. We didn't have many clothes, but had a clean house and lots of good food Mom was always pleased to share. At various times relatives and friends down on their luck found refuge in our home.

One of the biggest worries my mother had was getting the money to pay taxes. She hoed the neighbor's corn field for a dollar a day, and sometimes had to borrow money at ten percent interest to pay her taxes.

My mother depended on home remedies to alleviate the distress of many illnesses. As a child it seemed every cold I got turned into asthma. Knowing this, every fall she made pokeberry jelly and gathered "fields blossom" for tea to treat it. How she determined the dosage, I don't know.

One remedy I remember well. Aunt Tillie Wilson — she wasn't a blood relative but it was the custom in my home to call older folk "Aunt," "Uncle," "Grandma," or "Grandpa" — always came from her two-story log cabin on Lower Run for buttermilk when Mom churned. Once when I had an earache, she went home and returned with oil for my ear. I later learned it was rendered from polecat fat.

Author: Ruth Phillips. Mrs. Phillips is a retired executive secretary, wife of an Air Force retiree, and mother of three daughters, Patricia, Debra, and Sharon. The family has lived in Florida, California, Ohio, and Okinawa, Japan.

2-001-ST-WV-001-1997

Mountain State Stories Of The People

Preacher's Portrait

My neighbor's hound "Preacher" was shot and killed, so Billy's father commissioned me to do a portrait.

One dreary morning, I ran across Billy hunting near my pastures. Keeping the painting a secret, I listened as he spoke with a tear in his eye about his beloved family pet and hunting companion of eleven years. He leaned on his rifle as if for moral support, and my heart went out to him.

Billy's father brought me pictures which I studied, noting Preacher's markings — the brown and black bandit mask on his face and the speckles and patches on his flanks. One pose was a classic pointing stance. Another showed the dog standing proudly over a row of dead rabbits, his hunting trophies. The face was best portrayed in a touching pose with little Aly, Billy's daughter, hugging the dog. All these I used to create a good likeness.

Preacher, a dearly missed hunting companion.

When I delivered the painting to Bill senior, I was nervous. He excused himself to show it to his bedridden wife, and came back saying it made her cry. "He's going to love it," he said. Already I felt the comfort of knowing my work was appreciated.

As I was leaving, Billy's family arrived! Convincing me to stay, Bill proudly presented the painting to his son. My heart stood still as Billy recognized his dog and quietly murmured, "Hey there, buddy." As his wife smiled warmly, Billy showed the painting to little Aly who squealed, "It's Preacher, Daddy!"

I left that day with a strong feeling of connection with my neighbors. My monetary compensation was still to come, yet I already felt I had been paid. I'm gratified to know my "Preacher" portrait hangs on a wall, a visual image which warms the heart of another human being.

AUTHOR: Debbie Van Schaik. Debbie is a freelance artist who lives with her husband, horses, dogs, and cats on a farm near New Martinsville.

3-001-ST-WV-001-1997

Memorial Service For Charles Kuhens

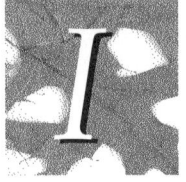

I am Charles Kuhens's daughter, Karen. I want to tell you about a conversation between my dad and me. It was sometime in the past year or two that I was visiting and my dad and I were sitting around the kitchen table talking long into the night as we had done so often over the years. And there was a pause in the conversation. My dad said, "There's something I want you to read." He handed me a magazine and said, "Here, read this article. It's short. Go ahead. Read it."

So I looked at the magazine article; it was less than a page in length and it was entitled, "Where to Bury a Good Dog." Now, if you knew my dad, you knew he always had a good dog. So I read the article and the advice went something like this:

Do you bury a good dog under the big oak tree where it can lie and watch the world go by? Or do you bury a good dog high on the hill where a fresh wind always blows? Or do you bury a good dog down by the creek where the sound of the water carries its troubles away? These are all fine places to bury a good dog, but the best place of all to bury a good dog is *in your heart*.

So I looked up from the magazine article at my dad sitting across the table from me and he said, "That's not a bad place to be buried, is it?"

So, for me, that's where I've buried my father — in my heart. And maybe for you, you have made the same decision.

AUTHOR: Karen Kuhens. As spoken by Karen March 5, 1995. Karen and her two sisters Charlotte and Vicki loved their father and have buried him in their hearts.

4-001-ST-WV-001-1997

More Than Just A Newspaper

Even though I haven't been around for the entire 101 years that the Shaw-owned *Moundsville Daily Echo* has been serving Marshall County, West Virginia, its influence has followed me and many others throughout our lives.

Growing up in the isolation of Blair's Ridge in the 1920s and 1930s, the highlight of my day was the daily trip to the mailbox for the paper. It was my link to the community and beyond.

My horizons expanded, and I joined the WAVES in WWII. While stationed in Hawaii where my bundle of *Echos* continued to arrive, others from big cities were fascinated by such a personalized paper. Obituaries on the front page without regard to one's status in the community, detailed personal items on the life in a small community, reporting of club and church events in minute detail — it was here that I realized the uniqueness of my hometown paper.

Returning home after college (journalism, of course), marriage, and raising a family, the call came from the owner, Sam Shaw. "Will you come and take over for two weeks while I'm away?" Need I say more?!

My two-week stint turned into a four-year experience. I learned the full extent of Sam's brilliant mind and eccentric personality as he looked at things in a somewhat different way. And as so many before me learned, working for the *Echo* is a total experience in the newspaper business.

The *Echo* and I have a long relationship — it's still the first piece of mail taken from my mailbox.

Sam is gone but the *Echo* remains the same. Ownership was left in the capable hands of Charles and Marian Walton, faithful friends and loyal employees of the late Sam Shaw.

Author: Mary Voltz. Submitted by Marian Walton.

5-001-ST-WV-001-1997

A Harvest Of Memories

As you travel along West Virginia highways, it is a common sight to see farmers putting up hay. The huge tractors lumber along, spitting out compact square bales, or huge round bales, of sweet smelling hay. There is no fragrance in the world like the smell of well cured hay!

Putting up hay was quite different when I was growing up in the late 1930s. All the work was done with horses. Daddy would mow the hay with the mowin' machine. When it reached just the right degree of dryness, he would hitch the horses to the dump rake and rake it into windrows. After allowing it to dry a bit more, the windrows were piled into hay shocks and hauled into the barn on wagons or sleds.

Once the hay was hauled to the barn, it was packed tightly into the hay mow and stored for winter feeding. When the mow was filled, the remainder of the hay crop was put into haystacks. Making a haystack that would "turn water" was no small feat, but if done properly the hay in the haystack would still be fresh looking when the last of it was fed in the spring.

A man could be identified by the shape of the haystack he made. Daddy's were square at the bottom, then gradually they became smaller and smaller until he "topped it out." Each layer of hay had to be placed "just so" and tramped down tightly before the next layer was added. A haystack made by my father Archie Stewart was easy to recognize.

I miss the sight of the haystacks as I travel the country roads in Marshall County. With their passing we have lost an entire era of rural Americana. All the farmers helped each other at harvest time; they knew that each was dependent upon the other. The process was painfully slow, and much harder than today's method, but you know, there is something to be said for the "old fashioned" way of doing things. You could say that it was the "stuff" of which memories were made!

Today's methods are definitely easier and quicker. But I'm not so sure that the youngsters of today will have the nostalgic memories of "haying time" tucked away into the inner-most chambers of their hearts, as I have been able to tuck away into mine. I often recall those "Good Old Days" with a smile. And yes, sometimes a tear.

Modern technology is mind boggling...But you know, I would love to stand back and admire one of Daddy's haystacks one more time — in awe of HIS TECHNOLOGY. It, too, was mind boggling. A lifetime of memories are nestled in these West Virginia hills. They are worth more to me than silver or gold.

I love you Daddy...Thanks for the memories!

Author: Juanita Fitzsimmons. Mrs. Fitzsimmons was born and raised in rural Marshall County, near historic Fort Beeler. She still owns acreage from her family's "homeplace."

6-001-ST-WV-001-1997

Memories Of Family Life

My maternal grandparents Sam Ferrell (1882 - 1965) and his wife Ottie May (1887 - 1965) were exceptional people for their time.

They grew up in Tyler County, around Bearsville and Iuka, outside Middleborne near the western side of the county line. In those days, most folks in that area were finished with school after the sixth grade. High schools were only in the county seats, and young people traveled dirt roads to attend. If you

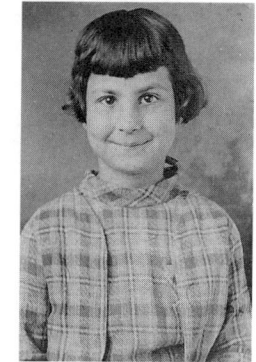

Peggy June Ferrell, circa 1937.

Peggy June Ferrell, circa 1947.

went to high school, you paid for room and board. Sam and Ottie May, like most children, stayed home and worked. But my grandparents had good minds and great handwriting!

Throughout the years, and in recent conversations with my mother, Peggy June (Ferrell) Smith, and father Craig Ancel Smith, I have been able to collect bits and pieces about the lives of family close to me, especially my mother, her parents, and her brothers and sisters, George, Bruce, Eythel, Stanley, Maude, and Betty.

Grandfather would drink liquor during Prohibition and went on an occasional binge. After a good one, Grandmother would make him sign a pledge that he would not drink for six months. He usually consented and signed his name on top of a Bible. One winter day he was late coming home. The family could see his wobbly lantern from a distance in the dusk. He was apparently soused and had broken the pledge! During Prohibition, liquor stills were hidden from federal revenuers who combed the area for illegal operations. The stills typically were mash barrels, and were sometimes buried. However, Grandpa claimed he had not touched a drop, but had fallen into one of these stills and the liquor saturated his skin. A "likely story," according to the family.

My grandparents loved to sing hymns. They sang a lot, especially in the winter when everyone stayed inside. Their favorite songs were *Amazing Grace, Come to the Garden,* and *Old Rugged Cross.* There was no television for folks to watch in the early 1920s and 1930s, although they had a radio. They also had a Victrola they could wind up and sing along with. Grandpa had a beautiful baritone voice, and Grandma sang alto.

The kids couldn't play the radio too much because the batteries would die and Grandpa couldn't hear how the stock market did that day after he came home from work. Important stocks were: Montgomery Ward, Sears & Roebuck, Socony Vacuum (an oil stock in New Jersey), and Sun Oil. He bought his stocks during the Depression when stock prices were low. He made about $90 a month and supported seven kids, and put two of them in college. His estate was valued at about $70,000 in the 1950s, including property in Alma, and savings bonds.

Later, in Alma, Grandma had a television in both the kitchen and the living room. That was living good.

The family left Davis Run around 1940 and moved to Flint. In 1943 they moved again, buying a home out-

Maude and Peggy Ferrell, circa 1948. (Now the late Maude McMillan of West Union, and Peggy Smith of Paden City, Wetzel County.)

side West Union, Doddridge County. They purchased the beer joint across old Route 50 as well. Grandpa bought the home as a retirement property and the beer joint to keep Grandma busy.

Growing up back then, dress for my mother consisted of items made from printed "feed sacks" put out during the war for cows and horses. Underwear was made of flour and sugar sacks. The family washed clothes on a board until they

Craig Ancel Smith of West Union, Doddridge County, circa 1952.

got a gasoline-powered washing machine. They ironed their clothes with a "sad" iron which was heated on the stove.

Later, Mom was able to make money by mowing the lawn. She would get a quarter each time, and in three weeks she had enough money to buy material for a dress. Grandma helped her sew. Mom actually made a "doll quilt" when she was only six years old. It was known as a Dresden plate pattern. Since Grandma thought she was doing so well, it eventually grew into a full-size quilt, and she still has it.

The family received gas for free because Grandpa was a pumper for Murphy Oil in Davis. There was no electricity or refrigerators. They used gas lights. Wealthier folks had gas refrigerators. Meat, if available, was smoked or cold-packed, as was sausage. They had chickens, and on special occasions they would have one prepared for dinner. Grace wasn't spoken before dinner, but everyone sat at the table together. Breakfast was usually pancakes and/or eggs. Everyone rose by 6 A.M.

In the 1930s, when the family lived up Davis Run, Eythel took the kids to the mouth of George's Run where the school bus route started, then another mile to Shirley, where the three-room schoolhouse was. If the roads were rutted out, they had to walk much of the way. If they were late and missed the bus, they walked the entire route.

During this time the state sent vitamins to the school. Everyone took cod liver oil from the same spoon!

My Aunt Eythel, the eldest child, kept a shanty right in Davis because it was closer to school. She was a teacher and children boarded with her. I guess they had a good time with no parents around. Mom said they wouldn't let her come around because she was the youngest. For fun, Mom enjoyed community Play Parties or corn and potato roasts that were held in Davis. About thirty or forty people of all ages usually attended and they would play games and dance.

The kids liked to sled ride during the winter. Once, my Uncle Stanley was sleighriding and ran into a barbed wire fence! He cut his chin, but it was bleeding badly and my Aunt Maude thought he had cut his throat. She had him drink a glass of water to see if the water would flow through the cut!

When Uncle Stanley was about sixteen years old, Grandma bought him a car, and he would drive the kids to school. He courted (and eventually married) a girl named Billie Fluharty, and he liked to drive her around on dates. Billie, however, would make bring his sisters (Maude and Betty) to "kee straight" and they would sit in the ru He didn't appreciate his sisters' co to show it, each time the run c he would speed up and get t

Peggy June Ferrell, circa 1948.

Holidays were special times. At Christmas the family used old green and red roping for decorations. They also used icicles and stringed popcorn and cranberries. The children did not receive many presents. Grandma would have a little bit of money to divide between the children and would have them choose what they liked in the Sears, Alden, or Montgomery Ward catalogs. My mother always got a doll and doll dishes. According to Mom, it must have hurt my grandmother so if she wasn't able to buy the kids everything they marked in the catalogs.

Easter presents were usually boxed chocolate bunnies, hollow in the middle, with candy and artificial grass. They were purchased from Alden's catalog and mailed in time for Easter Sunday. One year the package didn't arrive and the Post Office was closed on the Saturday before Easter. However, the Postmistress in Shirley "sent word" that the package came and opened the Post Office for Grandpa to pick up the presents that evening, just in time for Easter Sunday.

In 1947, it was at the home in Avondale outside West Union, where Craig (my father) met Peggy (my mother). Just after mom's family moved there, a wreck occurred near their new home and Papa lived just a few houses down. Today Mom calls that "the wreck of my life!" But Papa says "it was a more like a collision!"

Author: John Samuel Smith. Sam is a civil engineer with the US Army Corp of Engineers and resides in Pittsburgh, Pennsylvania. He grew up in Paden City, Wetzel County, and graduated in 1981 from West Virginia University.

7-001-ST-WV-001-1997

Chapter 3
Mid-Ohio Valley

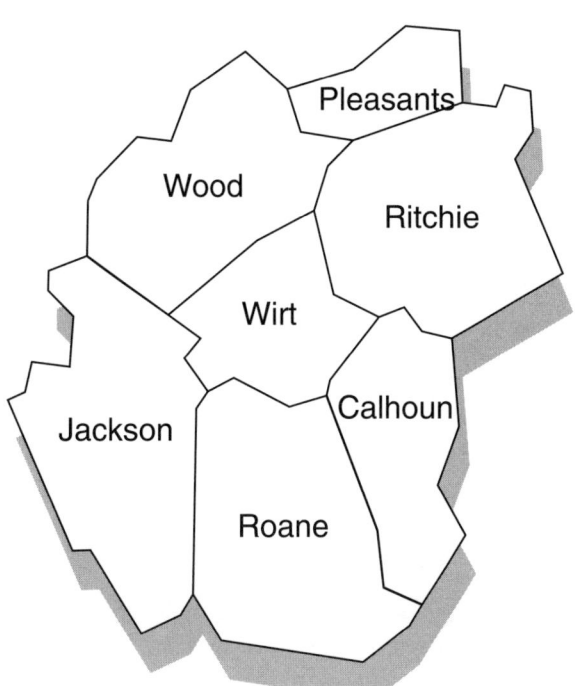

Home To His West Virginia Hills

When my father was growing up, families were often large. My father, George F. Reynolds, was the youngest of Christiana and Charles Bonar Reynolds's twelve children. He was born January 3, 1892.

Dad and some of his brothers left West Virginia looking for work, just like many of our young people are doing today. Dad met my mother in Harrisburg, Pennsylvania, married her and stayed, but he talked constantly about his beloved West Virginia hills.

He talked about how most times people doctored their own with old-time remedies. When very serious illness came, they went for the doctor either on foot or horseback. The doctor would arrive in his Sears Roebuck automobile with its wagon-like high wheels. One time when my grandma was very ill, the doctor ordered for her first meal a boiled squirrel's head. The boys rushed squirrel hunting to fill the doctor's prescription.

Walkers Crick near Eatons was where the family was raised. The house still stands today but is used as a barn. The crick supplied a good supply of fish, frogs, and turtles to supplement the foods they raised in their gardens, and there were wild berries, nuts, and greens. In addition to wild game, their farm animals supplied meat, milk, eggs, and butter. Because canning hadn't become a well known thing, many foods were dried, smoked, or put down in crocks in a heavy salt brine for the winter.

Life outside the home centered around the church and school or visiting family and friends. Dad talked of the debates that were held which became very lively at times. He quoted some of the poems he learned in school. He was so proud of his photo of the Eatons Baseball team. He and several brothers, a cousin, two Sprout boys, two Spears brothers, and a coach were the team.

On Labor Day 1976, I brought my dad back to West Virginia to a farm close to his home. He died on Veterans Day, November 11, 1976. I buried him on the family plot next to his parents as was his wish. He had finally come home to his beloved West Virginia hills.

Author: Evelyn Reynolds Breitmeier Carr. Born in 1924 in Harrisburg, Evelyn moved to West Virginia in 1976. She is the mother of John, David, and Thomas Breitmeier. She was the 1996 Wood County Belle for Extension Homemakers.

8-001-ST-WV-001-1997

Picnics And 'Portant Stuff

I have many memories of my maternal grandparents Butsy and Daddy Bob Jackson. I spent a great deal of time with them because Mother had to work. I was with them most weekdays until I was nine or ten years old. The following are a couple of those memories.

Butsy had picnics for just the two of us. She prepared homemade vegetable soup, grilled cheese sandwiches, and chocolate chip cookies. She spread a blanket on the front lawn, picked some pansies from her small flower garden in front of the basement window and placed them in a glass of water for a centerpiece. We spent a good hour or two sitting, eating and talking. She always had time for me when I was lonely or bored. To this day I love pansies and try to grow them every year in remembrance of our picnics.

Daddy Bob built their Spring Hill home himself when I was two years old. I don't really remember this experience, but he told me many times about teaching me to use a hammer and allowing me to help him pound some nails.

When he came home after work, Daddy Bob would take me on his lap while Butsy got supper ready and teach me lots of 'portant stuff. He used his large, silver wrist watch to teach me how to tell time, and his work shoes to teach me how to tie shoes. He even taught me how to shuffle and deal cards while sitting across from me at the coffee table. That's why I deal cards left handed.

Butsy has been gone since 1986 and Daddy Bob since 1995. I'm very lucky to have had such wonderful grandparents for most of the first fifty years of my life. I miss them immensely.

Author: Deborah Escue. Deborah is a native of Romance, where she resides.

9-001-ST-WV-001-1997

The Sweet Water Spring

I was born in 1929, the daughter of Arthur and Alma Davis, in a little shack in a hollow down from Farrow Hill in Murphytown, approximately six miles east of Parkersburg off Route 50. My family had no gas, electric, or water in the house, but we had a spring that had the sweetest water in the whole area. Everybody around drank "sweet water" from our spring. I was told that my grandfather used to say that

Mudlick School Memories

The sweet water spring in Murphytown, Wood County.

Mudlick School was a one-room school located on Mudlick road in Wood County, West Virginia, and covered grades one through eight. My family and I lived about one-half of a mile from the school. Of course we walked to school and usually we returned home for lunch. I and my two brothers and one sister all attended Mudlick until we graduated from the eighth grade.

In this part of Wood County during the late 1930s and early 1940s, there was no electric service, no natural gas service, and no telephones. Our school had no lights except the natural light which filtered through the windows. Many times on cloudy days the light was very poor. Our heat was provided by a pot-bellied coal stove, located in the center of the room. On days when the weather did not allow us to go outside to play, our teacher would conduct cyphering matches and spelling bees. These were simply competitions in arithmetic and spelling skills. We enjoyed this pastime while we were learning.

The chalkboard (called the blackboard) was located on the wall opposite the windows, which were all on one side of the room. The students were seated, usually in double desks, with their backs to the windows, facing the blackboard. The teacher's desk was in front of the blackboard, facing the students. Somewhere between the teacher and the students was a long bench, known as the "recitation bench." When the teacher called the first grade reading class, all the first graders would be seated on the recitation bench for their reading class. While a class was in session, the rest of the students were expected to continue with their own lessons and pay no attention to the action on the recitation bench. And this worked.

During my early years at Mudlick I was extremely shy. On one occasion the teacher had given us a lecture on leaving the room unnecessarily. She said, "I'm going to notice who is leaving the room during class time." A short time later I had to go to the outside toilet, but I was afraid to ask to leave since the teacher's words were still ringing in my ears. While standing by my desk for spelling class, I wet my pants! I wanted to die! When the teacher saw the water on the floor she asked, "Has someone taken water to their desk again and spilled it?" I immediately raised my hand, eagerly accepting this infraction of school policy, as opposed to admitting what I had done. I was instructed to wipe up the floor and never to take water to my desk again. Was I ever glad to go home for lunch so I could change clothes!

Mudlick School had a rough pine,

the water was so sweet it would make a sick man well.

My father died when I was five years old. Mother raised all seven of us children in Christian love and taught us to be there for each other. My sisters are Elsie, Marjorie, Betty, and Mary. My brothers, Edwin and Harry. We didn't have much in the way of worldly goods, but we had a lot of love. We had neighborhood parties every Saturday night. Neighbors played music; we roasted wieners over a fire by the creek; everyone sang songs and played games in the field across the creek. Some of the parents played dominoes.

During the summer of 1995, my brother and sisters and I all revisited that hollow. The area where the house had been is now covered by a big lake with a boat-dock, boats, and a large covered picnic shelter. We walked around the lake looking for landmarks, and we found the most important one of all: the spring that we all loved so much. It was covered with trees and bushes, but the owner agreed to take care of that, and maybe we will get to taste the sweet water again someday. We gathered under the shelter and sang some of our favorite songs and remembered the good times we had there as children.

Brother Harry is passed on now; Edwin has been a church song leader for fifty-six years. We sisters are all Christians and have "slumber parties" once a month to talk, eat, sing, and sometimes cry and pray together. We have all been involved in various phases of nursing, and are all still there for each other, as Mother taught us to be.

AUTHOR: *Thelma Davis Nolan. Mrs. Nolan married her husband Mervin in 1948. After traveling extensively with the United States Air Force for twenty-eight years, they came home to Parkersburg with their six children.*

unpainted, uncovered floor. To keep the dust down the floor was periodically "oiled." This was done by simply pouring crude oil on the floor, spreading it around, and allowing it to soak into the wood. My two brothers were janitors of the school and after they graduated my sister and I took over. We often used this floor oil to start a fire in the pot-bellied stove. We definitely were not supposed to do that. I often wonder how we kept from burning the building down. This janitor's position paid twenty-five dollars a school year, and our duties consisted of sweeping the floor, erasing and washing the blackboard, and a general straightening up. Also, when needed, we were expected to wash the windows and oil the floor.

I remember one particularly bad winter day when the roads were impassable and the teacher could not get to the school. My brother had built a fire in keeping with his janitorial duties, but since no one showed up for school he wrote the following message on the blackboard before going home: "I built a fire, no one came, so I have gone home." I carefully studied the message and decided in my wisdom, or lack thereof, that it was grammatically correct to say "have went home." The following day the teacher reprimanded Dave for using poor English. Ironically, Dave didn't realize he had written it correctly and I had changed it.

After my father's death in 1943, my mother, Isa James Somerville, became the teacher at Mudlick School, and was my teacher for one term. While my mother was at Mudlick School she succeeded in securing the hot lunch program, which not only assured all students of one nourishing meal a day, but also provided employment for a cook. If some item was needed for the school my mother did not wait for the school board to provide it; she simply planned a fund raiser. These events were usually "pie socials" or "box socials." The girls would bring a box lunch or a pie to be auctioned off. The boys bid on these, hoping to get a special one, because the boy was expected to eat the lunch or pie with the girl who had brought it. Many romances flourished over the sharing of "boxes." The socials were the highlight of the school year, since they not only provided much needed revenue but also a great deal of fun.

Mudlick School no longer exists. But for many former students, scattered far and wide, the many memories remain.

Author: Edith Parker Griffith. Mrs. Griffith is a retired Internal Revenue Service officer. She is the mother of two daughters, Susan Morris and Linda Roberts.

11-001-ST-WV-001-1997

Prayer Of My Five-Year-Old Son

I entered the room of my five-year-old son tonight, to hear his prayers and tuck him into bed. He was lying there, all scrubbed and shiny, with his usual happy grin splashed across his face, one blue pajama-clad leg lying on top of the covers, the other making a small mound underneath. I could see evidence of three trucks sticking out here and there, one with traces of mud on the wheels. And at the bottom of his bed I could see the tip of a forbidden dog's tail, wagging furiously.

Resisting my impulse to expose all of these undesirables, I sat down on the edge of his bed and waited for his prayer. Expecting to hear his usual "Now I lay me down to sleep," I was surprised to hear him say, "Mom, I think I'll say my own prayer tonight."

I said, "Good! and remember you're saying it to God and not to me."

"I know that," he answered, a slight frown indicating that he did not need to be reminded.

Then his happy look returned and he said, "God is great, God is good. I thank you for the birds; and the grass; and the trees; and my dog (here he opened one eye to see if his mention of the dog gave away his secret at the bottom of the bed); and Grandma — and I thank you for my fine dad, my big brothers, and all that."

Then in a rush, he said, "And I pray this in Christ's name. Amen."

I echoed his "Amen" and kissed him quickly on the forehead, because already he thinks he's too big for all that "baby stuff" from his mother. In one big lunge he was under the covers, a truck under one arm and his head buried in the pillow. I knew it would be only moments until he was sound asleep.

I stood in the doorway a minute and said a prayer of my own which included, "Thank you God, for a fine little boy who already knows that prayers should be mostly for praising and thanking You."

As I walked downstairs, a smile trembled on my lips as I hoped ruefully that in his heart he included me in his "Thank You for my fine dad, my big brothers, and all that."

Author: Mildred Marshall. This scene occurred in Mrs. Marshall's home in 1963. She is the mother of three sons, grandmother of six, and wife of fifty-three years to husband Harold.

12-001-ST-WV-001-1997

I Watched My Father Die

He was one of nine children, desperately poor, whose own father had not cared for education. He found the means to acquire two Master's degrees and taught school for forty-two years. As a grandfather he established a fund sufficient to pay for the education of his grandchildren and great-grandchildren.

I watched my father die.

New Era School, Wood County. Given Mr. Young's firm belief in education, his family held their memorial service in this building, similar to that in which he began teaching in 1930 in Sandyville, Jackson County.

He was strong. Physically small, he had held in his hands the power of a team of horses, had swum the Ohio River. At the end, those same hands were less capable of handling a cup of milk than those of a fourteen-month-old great-granddaughter.

He was weak. Though a student of the mind, he was unable to fathom the emotional needs of his own wife and children. The last of the few hugs he ever gave was in the manner of a child who had been told to return that which was being given to him.

I watched my father die.

That scholar's mind, the convoluted thought procedures, had succumbed to old age. He who had trekked for hours in the woods with grandchildren in search of hickory nuts and pawpaws could no longer find the zipper for his pants. He who had once been able to recall conversations years old could no longer remember to take off his boots to go to bed.

I watched my father die.

AUTHOR: Kay Young Hill. Mrs. Hill wrote this tribute January 10, 1996, the morning of her father's death. It was finished shortly before 7 A.M. At 8:20 A.M., she received a phone call; her father had passed away at 7:05 A.M. Her father was Lewis Otho Young of Ripley.

13-001-ST-WV-001-1997

He died imprisoned, his mind in his body, curled in a bed with rails, like a child's. The bed in a "home" where strangers lovingly mothered him. The bed and the body inside brick walls protecting him from the snowstorm without.

He died imprisoned, his mind in his body. He had memorized classic poetry as a lad, had discoursed for hours over Shakespeare to anyone who would listen. Near death, barely able to answer "yes" or "no," he could still recite *Invictus* as it was read aloud to him, and he could still sing *The West Virginia Hills* with his daughter.

I watched my father die.

He was strong. He believed in hard work. A stoic who missed not one day's work at the death of either of his parents, yet he shed tears when a son "borrowed" a car from an auto dealer.

Dump Truck Escapades

I remember many fun escapades that I, age five, my sister Jane, age eight, and the Jackson girls next door, Margaret, age seven, and Marsha, age six, would get into while growing up in Harrisville, Ritchie County. Margaret and Marsha's father Doug owned and operated the local Western Auto store. On occasions when he would be hauling home gravel for our long driveway, we would meet him at the bottom of the drive.

He would usually give in to our combined pleas to ride the dump truck to the top of the steep drive. He would good-heartedly hand us up into the bed of the truck and warn us to "hang on." When he got to the top of the drive he would push the

button to lift up the bed of the truck and we would roll like logs onto the pile of gravel. Boy, did we ever get dirty!

Our game was over when one day Marsha grabbed onto a branch of a big tree and swung out of the bed of the truck. Boy, did she ever get into trouble!

Front (L-R), Marsha Jackson, age six, Robyn Elliott, age five. Back (L-R), Margaret Jackson, age eight, Jane Elliott, age nine, Darlene Moore, age ten.

AUTHOR: *Robyn Lindamood. Robyn is a registered nurse. She was born in Dr. Coplin's office in Elizabeth, in 1953. She currently resides in Morgantown with her husband Alan. They have two daughters, Nikki and Becki.*

14-001-ST-WV-001-1997

The Coming Rain

I have many fond memories from when I was a youngster of visits to my Grandmother Elliott's in Brohard.

One particular memory is of a rain storm. My grandmother took my sister Jane and me up on a hill. She told us to be very quiet and listen to the coming rain. She showed us to look toward the other hillside in the distance. We were amazed that we could actually see the rain coming, hear it, and even smell it! She told us to wait until it was almost to our hill and run to the house as fast as we could so as not to get wet! We didn't make the house in time.

AUTHOR: *Robyn Lindamood*

15-001-ST-WV-001-1997

The Brownie Camp Road

Our home in Harrisville, Ritchie County was on the outskirts of town leading to North Bend State Park. In those days (1958-1960) the road to our brownie camp was gravel, single lane, and steep with no guardrails. My mother, being all of 4'8" tall, sat on two pillows in order to see over the steering wheel. She was so afraid that while going around a turn she might slip off those pillows and lose control of the car. There had been some accidents on that road when cars went off the steep drop-offs and over the hill.

My mother's solution, prior to the coming of seatbelts, was to make my sister Jane and me crouch on the floor of the back seat all the way out the road. My mother's rationale, was that if the car would drop and go over the hill, we would be safe! My sister and I, not knowing any better, thought that our trip to camp was very different and exciting!

AUTHOR: *Robyn Lindamood*

16-001-ST-WV-001-1997

A Hunter's Tall Tale

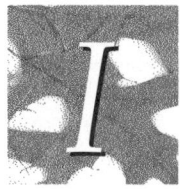

I remember a story that was told to me by my grandfather when I was a small child. My grandfather was Henry C. Boggs, and he lived in an old house up a long, deep hollow between the tall mountains in Roane County near the town of Newton, West Virginia.

As the story goes, my grandfather was a great hunter, and he would kill many game. He would go for days trying to make that kill. One day he was deer hunting and not having much luck. He hunted all day and into the late evening, when out from behind a tree stepped a trophy-size buck. He got all excited about his find and jammed his hand into his pocket for his last mini-ball. He loaded it into his rifle; deer for supper he thought.

Danny Osborne, age 42.

He took aim and pulled the trigger, but the ball lodged deep into a tree. He missed the deer completely, but he was not one to give up. He picked up a dried peach seed from the ground and loaded it in his gun. This time, with careful aim, he pulled the trigger. In the deer's snout the peach seed sunk, and the deer took off running as fast as he could go. He did not know what hit him, but I'm sure it hurt from his nose to his toes.

Grandfather was sad for his misfortune, and home he went. The days passed by quickly, weeks into months. Finally, a year had passed, and with Grandfather still being spry, deer hunting he must go.

He came upon the same spot he was the year before. He couldn't see a thing from where he was standing, so up a tree to the top he climbed. To his surprise the tree took off running. Grandfather soon figured out why. The tree he was in had sprouted from the seed he had shot into the old buck's snout. The seed had grown a peach tree in the form of antlers, so my grandfather said.

AUTHOR: Danny R. Osborne. Danny was born in Ronceverte, Greenbrier County. He moved to Florida in 1974. His hobbies include oil painting, pencil sketching, photography, and port and scuba diving.

17-001-ST-WV-001-1997

The Road Brought Me Happiness

As my knees were knocking, I lifted my hand to knock on a stranger's door. "Hi, my name is Ruth Ann, and I am here to talk to you about the disease we hear so much about, cancer." As the door opened wider, I walked right in and shared my information.

That's all there was to it, unless you counted the miles and hours spent on the road. "We're on the road this week," my manager would say. This meant motels and money. I enjoyed working the road as it took me away from a bad situation at home. Plus, people in West Virginia are extremely friendly. I worked in Clay, Mason, Cabell, Wayne, Jackson, Pleasants, Ritchie, Wood, Kanawha, Braxton, Webster, and finally Roane Counties. Most of the time I spent two weeks in each county along with a team of agents and managers.

I have special memories from each county. I took pictures almost every day. Sheep, geese, trophy kills hanging on walls, streams, mountains, tiny post offices, and the eagle monument in a high school field are just a few of the snapshots in my picture album. This job gave me opportunities to see our beautiful state. And the money was good.

Women can shine in the insurance field. I worked hard each day to sell all I could. I knew that I would soon be on my own, as the man who once provided for me would soon be taken to his grave.

I hit the road again after his death and a few weeks of adjustment. There were days I would just talk to people. I met folks with the same type of problems I once had, and I knew they needed to talk. I was a good listener.

My favorite county has to be Roane. I made some lifelong friends there. I also met a very kind gentleman. It was like a fairytale come true. We met in February, 1991, while I was talking to him about updating his insurance policy. We married on March 9, 1991. Although I was diagnosed with Parkinson's Disease a few months into my new marriage, I can truly say that, "we all lived happily ever after."

Part of a chant we learned in training goes:

I was walking down the street, with a book in my hand;
I'm the best darn salesman in the whole darn land;
If I had a hundred people lined up against the wall,
I'd take two steps back and sell them all.
I am somebody; I can do anything.

I did feel I was somebody, but not just for the money. I knew I was really helping families meet some of the financial losses that cancer could bring.

AUTHOR: Ruth Ann Nida. Ruth Ann is a native of Crosslanes. She has two sons, Scott and James, and one daughter, Angie. Ruth Ann now resides with her husband Ross in Roane County.

18-001-ST-WV-001-1997

Baptism At Reedy Creek

"Praise God forever!" someone said,
"At last old Clement's sins are dead.
Praise God, his sins are washed away;
A child of God, baptized today."

Old preacher said, "We've God to thank."
"Amen!" they shouted from the bank.
"The Holy Ghost came down today,
And washed this brother's sins away."

"My friends, behold!" the preacher cried,
"Old Satan failed, although he tried,
To steal the soul of this poor child."
And on the bank, the folks went wild.

Old sister Smith, whose hair came down
And very nearly touched the ground,
With both eyes closed tight as could be,
Danced in the Spirit, don't you see!

And Bobby Rogers standing by,
I noticed had begun to cry.
And Bobby's knees had never bowed;
But now he knelt and cried out loud.

And Tressie Mae and Becky Sue
Had spoken not since fifty-two,
When Tressie married Billy Joe;
And Becky claimed he'd been her beau.

But now with all their anger spent,
Together to the water went.
And sister Smith with shining face
Began to sing, "Amazing Grace."

Then as the sun was sinking low,
The preacher said was time to go.
And thus they closed revival week,
With baptizing in Reedy Creek.

Author: William R. Waterman. This poem was written based upon William's experience as an evangelist in the early 1960s. Baptisms were conducted after conversion in Reedy Creek following a week of revival in a small community near Spencer. The names in the poem are representative, but fictitious. William lives in Marion, Ohio.

19-001-ST-WV-001-1997

ersburg for groceries and ice cream cones.
Home has always been amidst the West Virginia hills.

Author: Polly Shepherd. Mrs. Shepherd is a native of Parkersburg. She has been married forty-three years, has five children and nine grandchildren. She enjoys family, reading, writing, sewing, crafts, and gardening.

20-001-ST-WV-001-1997

Those Were The Days

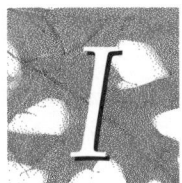

I grew up in the 1940s on Montgomery Hill off Route 50 in Wood County. Each spring while the trees were still bare, my family used an ax and hoe to clear brush, roots, and rocks to make a garden. We burned the roots for heat and used the rocks to repair our road. I enjoyed watching the trees turn green and the garden grow.

The summertime was spent hoeing the hillside gardens or picking blackberries. Each morning and evening we fed pigs and chickens. While gathering eggs, I used a pitchfork to fend off a rooster with two-inch leg spurs. I carried spring water to do laundry and helped cut winter firewood with a crosscut saw. My brother Bob Nutter and I swam in the creek or watched the oil well pump. When it was too hot to sleep we sat watching the stars twinkle.

Tree leaves turned beautiful shades of red, orange, and yellow in the fall. We pulled turnips, onions and dug potatoes for the root cellar. We stuffed red clay mud between the logs of our house.

In winter the wind blew through the valley and over the hills making the tree limbs sing. The snow fell, covering everything with a blanket of white, causing the trees to bend and shape a canopy of white over the road. Sometimes swirling snow drifted several feet deep. Oh, what fun to sled ride down a mile-long hill!

Those were the days when children walked two miles just to catch a school bus. All the neighbors helped each other. There were outhouses with Sears Roebuck or Spiegel wishbooks in the corner. Nobody had to lock their doors.

Saturday was the day we drove to Park-

The Maytag Man

An elfin-like man with an easy grin,
He faced each day and its strife,
In a manner so bold he seemed never to
    grow old,
And a heart that was bigger than life.

He'd open your door, track mud on your floor,
With a shout that would waken the dead;
Crying, "The Maytag man's here.
Your washer just died, but I'll leave you a new one
    instead."

With his hat cocked on the back of his head,
His clothes all covered with grime,
His cheerful grin would get him in,
Any place, anywhere, anytime.

He dealt with life with a hand that was firm,
Determined to make his own way.
If men forbid it, he generally did it,
And left them with nothing to say.

No mountain too steep, no road too long.
No river too deep to be crossed;
The challenge of life was a game that he played,
And seldom it was that he lost.

It seemed to his family he'd always be here,
To love them and stand by their side;
Like a great forest tree with roots that were deep;
A safe place where they could hide.

Without warning it came, bringing its pain,
And weakness began to plague him.
He tried to ignore it, in silence he bore it,
As hope grew exceedingly dim.

Consulting with men who study such things,
    They told him the most terrible news;
    The thing was too strong and the fight would
        be long,
    Their treatment he should not refuse.

Mountain State Stories Of The People

George O. "Pappy" Davis, a man from the old school of hard work and true grit, had a heart bigger than life. He deeply loved his family and was loved and admired by them.

He heard their advice with a far away look,
And a sly little grin on his face,
Then he bid them good-bye and made up his mind,
To battle the thing by God's grace.

He vowed the thing would never win,
And went to his work with a smile;
With a will to succeed he tackled the thing,
Which threatened to cramp his style.

He slowly lost ground as the days went by,
But he went to each day with true grit;
The weakness prevailed and he posted a sign:
"Too tired to work — Too poor to quit."

He looked to Jesus for a word of advice,
As the sun sank deep in the west;
The Lord said "Quit... it's late and you're tired.
Now come home with me and rest."

So he put up his tools and cleaned up his shop,
And at the end of a long dreary day,
He looked the thing square in the eye and declared,
"You lose...for I'm leaving His way."

In spite of the pleas and advice of the crowd,
He never looked back from his plan;
With a smile on his face, his heart filled with grace,
As the Saviour held fast to his hand.

Without a whimper or a plea for help,
No grasping for life or things;
In a dignified way, he chose not to stay,
And was borne on soft angels' wings.

He's not really gone, you know;
Just out of our earthly sight.
He kept the faith and finished his course,
And won his earthly fight.

I wonder, when he slipped through the door,
And laid eyes on the Saviour's face,
If he might not have said, "I'm the Maytag man,
and I'm here by your love and your grace."

Author: Herbert L. Roush, Sr. Written October 9, 1986, in memory of George Orville Davis. Submitted by Jerry Davis, George's son.

21-001-ST-WV-001-1997

Women Doing More Than Tending Hearth And Home

hat are West Virginia women doing with their time in the 1990s? If your guess is tending only hearth and home, you had better guess again.

Judging from the fascinating personal biographies of the guests of honor at the 1995 West Virginia State Folk Festival Belle Luncheon in Glenville, they more likely are: ambulance drivers and authors; certified midwives and wives of those serving in public office; sign language interpreters and telephone operators (when the voice was that of a person, not a recording); board members and bookkeepers; quilters and quillers; line dancers and lineage recorders; painters and parents; senior citizens officials and choir/gospel singers; retired teachers and tutors of the arts; nurturers of children as well as culture; former valedictorians and community leaders; flower show judges and piano players; nutritionists in the military and dental assistants; hospice workers and the "heart of the home"; deer hunters and "dear" grandmas; keepers of history and guardians for our heritage; and organizers of youth groups and sponsors of scholarships.

All of the above were achievements and talents of West Virginia Extension Homemakers Club members who were elected to represent their home counties at the State Folk Festival. Their achievements have become so usual, even commonplace that some of the Belles say that their talents are limited or "nothing special." The humility was grossly unfounded, due to the great number of works and their impact on their home, community, and state.

Community services range all the way from youth development; care of the elderly, especially providing transportation and meals; serving in public offices such as having been a

deputy sheriff; nutrition programs; Community Action; 4-H and other youth programs; church leadership, etc. Volunteer services to individuals as well as agencies is a characteristic common to Extension members all over the state. West Virginia Belles' lifelong accomplishments have been invaluable to their state and the title of the Belle is one to desire and treasure.

Some of those honored at the festival were fulfilled by domestic activities, but certainly not limited to, or by them. One lady genuinely felt that her "very finest achievement" was "being a good mother." One "Supermom" of fourteen children still found time to mother neighborhood children as well…and without disposable diapers.

West Virginia Extension women are improving their minds for service, personal development and self satisfaction by earning bachelors and masters degrees as well as doing post graduate studies. One Belle who was present had earned three degrees and another had earned her degree at age sixty-five. Some fields of interest were nursing, clerical and bookkeeping, state government (Delegate to the Legislature) and travel. The Belles are a well-traveled group, and have visited all over the world, literally. Some places mentioned were fourteen countries of Europe, Australia, Egypt, New Zealand, and the Holy Lands. One Belle had lived in the British Crown Colony of Hong Kong. A diverse collection of spirited ladies? Absolutely! They are doing, being and experiencing life firsthand.

Several Belles and former Belles were asked what was the most rewarding aspect of their tenure. One of the former Belles, Rita Emerson, 1980 Gilmer County Belle, considered this question only briefly and then replied without hesitation, "The people, the *growing* (her emphasis) relationships and memories." As I looked into the kind, weathered face of this eighty-seven year old lady, I knew that she had just summed up quite well why we had all attended the 1995 West Virginia State Folk Festival.

AUTHOR: Ann Sams Grimm. Ann is a native of Wood County where her family has lived since West Virginia achieved statehood. Her favorite interests are travel, reading, flowers, friends, history, and MOUNTAINS! Parts of her narrative were taken from a June 30, 1995 Parkersburg News *article which she wrote, with permission.*

22-001-ST-WV-001-1997

Our Simple Freedoms

My father-in-law Fred Heim was born in Austria on November 11, 1892. The children in the "old country" were expected to learn a trade at an early age, and Fred was apprenticed to a tailor. By the time he arrived in the United States, he had become excellent at his craft.

Fred's family first settled in the New York area, later migrating to Akron, Ohio. Fred accompanied his father back to Austria while his mother and two sisters remained in Ohio. When his father passed away in Austria, Fred attempted to rejoin his family in the States. Fred couldn't just go to a port and sail. He had to have a pass and a job in another city before he was allowed to travel anywhere.

He eventually arrived back in the US by way of Ellis Island. Even though he was not a citizen, he was drafted into the Army during World War I. After the war, Fred met and married Sally Jarvis in Ohio. They had three children, Katie Ashley, Jim Heim, and Mary Heim. In 1946, Fred moved his family to the Amma area of Roane County, West Virginia. Fred worked at several different men's clothing stores around Charleston. When he retired, he had been a tailor for over sixty years.

Listening to my father-in-law taught me and my children about freedom. Freedom to him meant being able to go where and when he wanted, and being able to say what he felt without having to look over his shoulder to see who was listening. It's the simple freedoms we experience everyday in the US that my father-in-law taught the people whose lives he touched not to take for granted.

AUTHOR: Colene Heim. On November 22, 1957, Fred became a naturalized citizen. He was proud to be a citizen because, as he put it, "She's (the US) been good to me."

23-001-ST-WV-001-1997

Memories Of Grandpa Parker

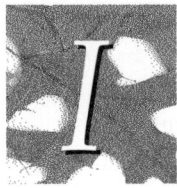

I remember watching often as Grandpa shaved his day-old gray stubble off his lean, gaunt face. It was like a graceful ballet to watch, full of rehearsed motions. First he would sharpen the yellowing ivory-handled straight razor by using a long leather strap. One end of the shiny and worn leather was sturdily fastened to the kitchen wall, and by holding the other end taut, he would methodically and melodically glide the razor back and forth, back and forth; "slap, slap, slap" it sounded.

Then, sitting next to a kitchen window as the daylight streamed upon him, he would whip up a froth of homemade shaving cream. Mixing it in an old coffee-stained mug, he stirred it briskly with a wooden-handled but soft-bristled brush. Round, round and round he churned the brush in the

Grandpa William G. Parker, August 19, 1953.

cup, "clink, clink, clink" as the handle hit the side, circle left then circle right, until he was satisfied the creamy mixture was just right.

Now he peered into a round mirror with half of its silver missing in various flecks and applied the lather to his lower face. He dabbed it on in dots and then swirled it over his cheeks and chin with small whirling circles. Always sweeping clockwise, he swirled the circles until they resembled the starry fireballs of Vincent Van Gogh. And the contrast of the snow white froth made his lips and eyes now look so deep, dark and mysterious.

The most intense part of the ballet was when he gently but steadily made first, long and deliberate down strokes, and then quick and very short upward ones. I could hear the razor blade pass over the stiff stubble with each stroke, "scrunch, scrunch, scrunch." Then "clink" as he dunked the steel blade into a pitted aluminum pan of water to rinse it off. As he scooped off waves of cream and whiskers he exposed amazingly still tender skin at the age of seventy-five. I watched in awe! "How wonderful!" I thought!

Grandpa was tall and very lanky, much like Abraham Lincoln. It seemed he was always wearing a green or blue checked flannel shirt, made oh so soft by its numerous trips through a ringer washer. His somewhat sun-faded gray pants were always assisted by striped suspenders, and if he were outside, his eyes were often shaded by an old straw hat. As I looked into his eyes searching for wisdom, I realized they were gray, truly gray, like the hull of a battleship that had set sea once too often. They appeared to be melted and lifeless, their physical beauty marred by extensive doses of silver nitrate. But I could always see the spark of spirit in them because I always looked long enough.

Because his eyes had become so sensitive to sunlight, Grandpa often sported a special pair of sunglasses. Wire rimmed with round circular lenses, they were tinted the most beautiful color of dark green I think I've ever seen — green like the rich chlorophylled canopy of a luscious forest. And the color resounded as if it were a stained glass panel with light streaming through. I thought "How neat." Later on, John Lennon wore sunglasses just like Grandpa's. I guess Grandpa was just ahead of his time.

AUTHOR: Donna Ellen Smith Davis. Donna is a wife, mother, home school teacher, and tutor. She was born and raised in Ritchie County, and currently lives in Charleston. She has one daughter, Amoret Coralee Davis.

24-001-ST-WV-001-1997

Chapter 4

Metro Valley

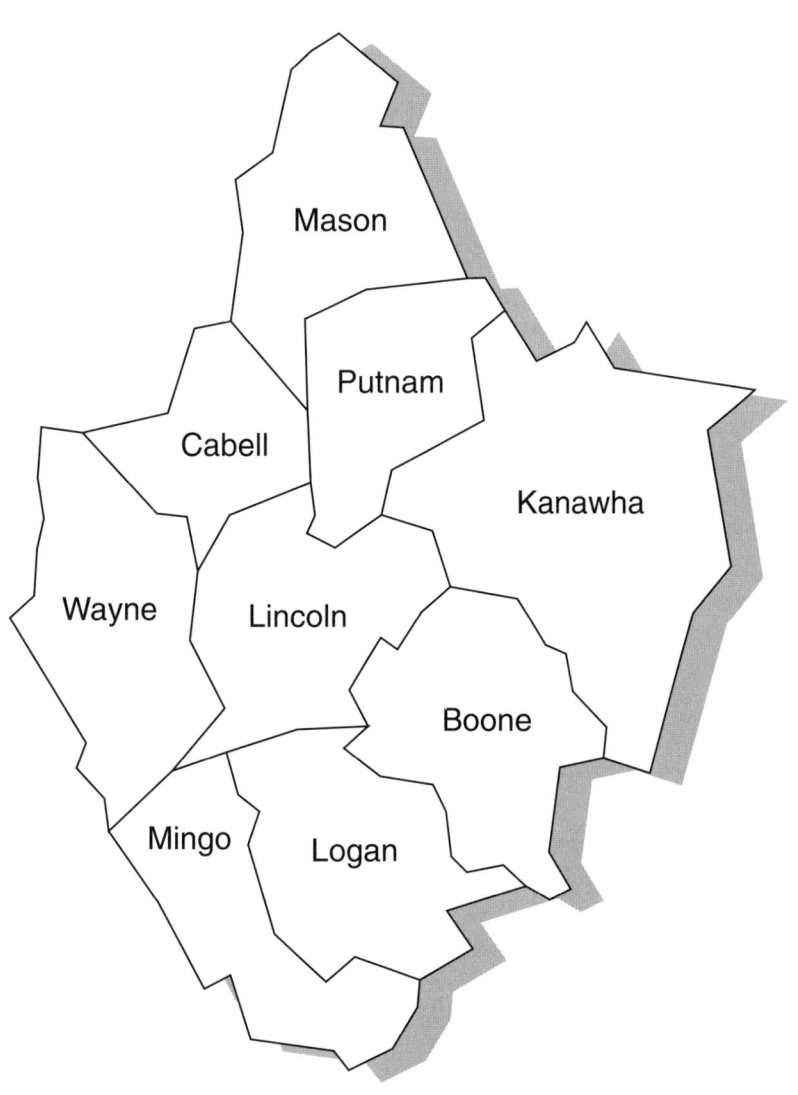

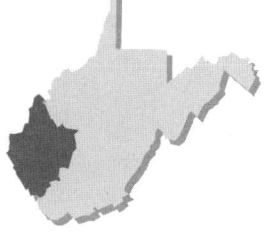

1920s Adventure

One of my memorable childhood experiences was a motor trip from Charleston to Rainelle. My family was going to visit my mother's brother "Sugar Bowl" Charlie McQuain. We traveled eastbound on old US Route 60 on a "Shoe String Road" in a Hudson Essex. The pavement was only one lane wide, so when we met oncoming traffic we had to put two wheels off the pavement. It sure was a crooked road. It wound past Hawk's Nest and Lover's Leap. Somewhere near there was a deep cut in the hill to keep the road from being so steep. This was the spot called "Wild Cat Cut." When we went past this point we kids got down on the floor of the car so the wild cats wouldn't see us. Daddy told us that we were safe that way.

When we were within five miles of Rainelle there was an old tree. I think it was a maple. Daddy pointed it out as General Lee's Tree. There was a small skirmish there and General Lee was said to have tied his horse Old Traveler to this tree while the battle took place. Much later a restaurant was built there called Lee's Tree Tavern, which was a stop on the stage coach line.

Sometime in the early 1930s, the town of Rainelle had built an earthen dam across one of the small streams and piped the water down the hill for the town's drinking water supply. The first summer, the townspeople were complaining about how muddy the running water was. Well, when a town employee went to check out the dam, he found several boys swimming in the backed up water. Yuk!

AUTHOR: *Gene Cox. Mr. Cox is a native of Charleston who now resides in Charlotte, North Carolina. He is a retired artist.*

25-001-ST-WV-001-1997

John L. Howery, owner of Brawley's Hollow.

line. Both ran parallel to the Great Kanawha River which flowed below. A culvert leading from the hollow to the river lay hidden underneath the banks. An ever-present characteristic of the hollow was the gushing sound of water flowing over rocks. This unique piece of land was purchased by John L. Howery, my grandfather, in the year 1905. Its dimensions were one and seven-tenths acres. The price: $600, cash.

At that time, only one house stood in the center of the triangle. Later, two others were built by my dad Fletcher Howery after he returned from World War I. As time passed, the houses changed occupants, but only in the family, with one exception. That exception was a widow to whom my uncle by marriage Carl Stump sold the house which had been my "babyhood" home.

In its heyday, Brawley's Hollow was a hub within its woodland borders. Grampa was a detective for the railroad, traveling quite a bit by rail. My Uncle Carl worked for Hope Gas, and another uncle by marriage, Ernest Spencer, worked for Dickenson Salt Works. My grandmother, aunts, and cousins cooked, canned, sewed, and tended gardens and children.

By the time the West Virginia Turnpike was in construction, the hollow had declined considerably. Deaths in the family had taken their toll on the spirit. Nevertheless, we who remain fondly remember the hollow now sealed over with asphalt.

AUTHOR: *Margaret Bowden. Mrs. Bowden is the mother of one, and grandmother of two. She babysits for her grandson, age two years and eleven months. She lives in Marmet.*

26-001-ST-WV-001-1997

Brawley's Hollow

Brawley's Hollow was a throbbing, thriving possession of Kanawha County. Its location was between Chelyan to the east, and Winifrede Junction to the west on Route 61. It was a triangle-shaped strip of land which lay between two mountains, with the third side of the triangle being formed by the highway which ran in front.

Below the highway on the first bank stretched the railroad tracks. Several feet below them, a second bank supported the streetcar

The Rummage Club

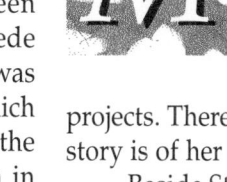

My mother was from Connecticut but made her home here in the mountains of West Virginia alongside her husband. She raised three children, the youngest adopted through friends of the Rummage Club, one of Mom's pet projects. There were many sides to my mother but this story is of her giving nature.

Beside State Highway 3 in Boone County sat the Rummage Club of Bloomingrose. People came from far and near. Everything was only a dime, and to those in real need, free. Donations were given by friends.

Dorothy M. Stone with some of her clothing assortment.

I can remember Mom making Christmas baskets and gathering toys and stockings and so much more for families. Those who needed shoes and medicine also came to Mom. There was many a time I remember sharing my bed and toys with other children who had been burned out or flooded, or just needed a place to stay. Mom often went through her belongings and groceries and gave half to someone in need. Her generosity always came back ten-fold in some way or another.

Not all things go right in this world, but it is good to look back on those people who gave a small piece of themselves to others. In her way Mom chose to give, and although she is no longer with us, she stays in the hearts of those she loved and helped, now and forever.

Author: Kathryn Campbell. Kathryn was born in Springfield, Massachusetts and raised in Bloomingrose, Boone County. She is a proud grandmother of three. She resides in Dunbar.

27-001-ST-WV-001-1997

Wild Creature

hen Dad first brought Mom to West Virginia, she was very much a city girl, not at all used to tall mountains, winding roads and, most of all, real country living. Though she is gone now, I still laugh and smile when I think about the story of the "wild creature."

One time while our family was visiting good friends, nature called and my mother headed outside to the outhouse.

Suddenly, everyone in the house heard a wild scream wailing up and down and getting closer fast! In ran my mother who all but collapsed in her best friend's kitchen. We kids came running, wondering what all the commotion was about, and most of all to see what had made my mother move that fast. She was all upset; a wild animal had attacked her — had reached out and grabbed her from behind.

Of course, we all went out looking for this horrible animal, each grabbing something with which to beat off the beast. But except for Mom's panties halfway up the path to the outhouse, there was not a sign of anything. No grizzly bear, no terrible creature of the wood or dark of night.

We did, however, find one furry critter in the outhouse, but it was long dead and preserved. I'm not sure after all these years what it was. Perhaps it was a raccoon. Our host had thought it would be most hospitable to add a softer and warmer seat for her city friend. Apparently, Mom had backed up to sit, and feeling the fur, assumed it was a wild creature. I don't believe I can ever remember Mom going to an outhouse again.

Author: Kathryn Campbell

28-001-ST-WV-001-1997

Nora Rood's Lost Legacy

ora Alice Rood (1890-1968) had little formal education but was the possessor of a wealth of knowledge acquired from generations of accumulated information and beliefs passed from a time when many survived by their own skills on marginal, self-sustaining farms with little to guide them except folklore and tradition (some might call these old wives' tales).

Among "Alice's" talents were the ability to remove goiters by the light of the full moon and warts by "secret" words; when, where and how to plant for success; and how to make medicine for most ailments from local plants and roots. Taken to an isolated environment, summer or winter, she would probably find it easy to survive off the land. Alice never claimed any special powers, she was just the "passed-down" recipient of family accumulated knowledge possessed by and believed in by many of those earlier times.

Alice met and married Hairm Jackson Carter (1879-1964) in Huntington, West Virginia. Though she had children Harry Leroy, Bertha Inez and Lillie Mae (Ruby and Carl died as infants) and many grandchildren, she was to be the last in the family to possess her unique knowledge. She talked, but few listened — the generation information transfer was to stop with her. What she had to say seemed irrelevant to a generation talking in industrial and scientific terms and where the necessities were as close

as the nearest store. As a result, when she died, her knowledge was lost, probably forever! A lesson learned too late, but a lesson to be applied to other family members.

AUTHOR: Richard Marks. Mr. Marks is Alice's grandson. He was born in Charleston, and raised in nearby Dunbar. Alice spent most of her life in Charleston, where she is buried.

29-001-ST-WV-001-1997

The Influence Of My Life

When I came home from school, my dad was there to listen to the happenings of the day. He was the greatest influence in my life. He was strong, fair, and loving. He was also strict and disciplined. He always knew what was going on with his six children.

Many of my values come directly from him. My mom and dad, Lucy and Charlie Monfradi, were truly in love; that was something I grew up taking for granted. They would hug and kiss in the kitchen, argue and make up. These are obviously strong messages that we have all lived by.

When my friends came over to visit, they didn't understand why Mom was at work and Dad was in charge of the cooking, cleaning, and us. I guess back in the 1950s that was not the norm. It seemed perfectly normal to me.

My dad knew me better than anyone knew me as a child, even though he never saw me. He never saw me with his eyes. I was born after World War II. My dad was wounded in France shortly after the war began. He lost both eyes and was told he would never use his left arm again. Of course he never regained his sight, but through sheer determination he did regain use of his arm.

This allowed him to build a house during the early 1960s. He was so happy during this time because he went to work each day. He didn't get to enjoy the fruits of his labor very long, however. We moved into the house in 1962. He had a massive heart attack in 1966, and died at the age of fifty-one. It was thirty years since his death on October 4, 1996. It is hard to believe you can still miss someone after that long, but I do.

My dad liked to bowl, play cards, and he enjoyed good food. His greatest pleasure was people. He loved people and they loved him. He helped so many people deal with their blindness. Don't feel sorry for yourself, appreciate what you have, and enjoy life was his basic philosophy.

He also liked to fool people. When people came to our house or when he went out, most people could not tell that he was blind. This truly delighted him. When my brother brought his girlfriend (now wife) to our house on a Saturday night during a card game, she became a little upset with my brother and asked him to step outside with her for a moment. She wanted an explanation of how Dad could play cards if he was blind. I guess she had never seen Braille cards.

AUTHOR: Lucille Monfradi Beck. Lucille is a middle school teacher of math and science. She is the mother of three, and grandmother of twin girls. Her hometown is Wheeling.

30-001-ST-WV-001-1997

My Mother's Stories

My mother Helen Rosella Martin Bainbridge was born on March 7, 1914, in the little coal town of Gamoca (only the name remains), located just north of Gauley Bridge in Fayette County, but she grew up in Middle Patch, now part of Gallagher, on Paint Creek in eastern Kanawha County.

Mom was the youngest of five children born to Charles Perry Martin and Grace Kelley, and she told many stories about what it was like growing up with her sisters and brothers, although she didn't remember her oldest brother Dewey very well because he died when she was seven years old. Some of these stories included running off with her sister Ruby when Mom was thirteen years old and joining the circus, and how their brother Carl brought them back home. Some thirty years later she accidentally ran into the same sister at a bus station in Bluefield. Both of them were going to see their sister Ruth who lived in Baltimore, but neither one knew the other was making the trip. They had come from different directions.

She told us about the coal camps she lived in during the early 1900s and how these camps seemed to spring up and disappear overnight. She would say, "you went where the work was, if the mines closed you moved, many times leaving only the name of the camps behind."

Coal mining was about the only major industry in many parts of southern West Virginia during the early part of this century. The miners worked under terrible conditions, not only at work but also at home: no job guarantees, they lived in company houses, and most miners were paid in "scrip," which could only be used at the company store.

Most company houses had no electric or inside water, and the only sources of heat were the fireplaces. Mom said she learned very young to prepare for simple things like getting coal for the fire or a bucket of water. She would say, "get

The children of Charles and Grace Martin: Back (L-R), Dewey, Carl, Front (L-R), Ruth, Helen, and Ruby.

those ready the night before, especially during cold weather. If it snowed overnight then you had to dig the coal out of the snow and sometimes the wells would freeze. To bring a little warmth to those bedrooms that had no fireplace we would take hot coals from the fireplace and put them in small metal boxes and then place these boxes close to our beds. It didn't provide much heat, but it made you feel warmer."

Of the stories she would tell, the ones I liked best were about her early childhood. Following are my two favorites. For one of them I was able to provide a happy ending, even after so many years.

Christmas Candy

During those years Christmas was much different, as children received few toys or gifts if any. Many times they only received a bowl of candy, nuts, and maybe some exotic fruits like oranges.

Mom and her two older sisters Ruth and Ruby all slept in the same room as children. One Christmas Eve when she was only five or six years old, Mom's sisters put her up to sneaking into the kitchen and bringing them back some candy from their bowls on the table. She said she did this four or five times before they all went back to sleep. Mom was short so she could only reach the top of the table, so she had no idea whose bowl she was taking the goodies from.

When morning came all the kids came into the kitchen and to my mother's surprise, she saw that she had been taking the goodies from her own bowl and she started crying when she saw how empty it was. She says her two sisters gave her part of their candy, but she said, "I think they did it to keep me from telling my mother what had happened the night before."

The Perfect Gift

Although it took sixty-six years to finish, the story of the China Doll has a happy ending. When my mother turned seventy years old, I wanted to do something nice for her that Christmas. But I had no idea what to get her until I remembered the story she had told me about her first real "store bought" China Doll.

One day when she was four years old, Mom's father brought her home a China Doll. She loved her new doll and took extra care of it. One day her Uncle Alford came to visit and slammed the door behind him, jarring her China Doll from its resting place. To her horror, she saw her doll fall and break into so many pieces that it couldn't be put back together. She said, "I cried and cried over my broken doll and no one could comfort me." She said she wouldn't speak to Uncle Alford for a long time because he had broken her doll. Each time she would tell me this story I could hear the tears of that little girl who was heartbroken over her broken doll.

On Christmas Day, 1984, I replaced that doll with another doll. On the accompanying card I reminded her about the story she had told us so many times and how I could hear the tears of that little girl every time she told it. The doll was an inexpensive porcelain doll, but the look on her face as she pulled it from its box was worth more than anything in this world. All she did was quietly thank me, hug the doll as a child would and cry, which started me crying. So I put my arms around my mother and held her. It was a moment I will never forget.

AUTHOR: Richard C. Bainbridge. Mr. Bainbridge is the fifth of six children. He is a lifelong resident of Montgomery, where he worked as a broadcast announcer.

31-001-ST-WV-001-1997

Reading, Writing, And Arithmetic:
Family Matters

My mother Eliza Ambler was born in Japan. Her father was a missionary who had gone to Japan in 1889. Dad, W.G. Caperton, was born outside of Beckley in Slab Fork, West Virginia.

After his education at Virginia Polytechnic Institute and the Wharton School of Finance, he went to work for Western Union in

New York. That's where he met my mother, who was working as a Medical Technician. They were married and my sister Cary, who is five years older than I, was born in New York. The family moved back to West Virginia and settled in Charleston where my dad and his brother-in-law started a small insurance business. I was born in Charleston.

A future Governor of West Virginia — Gaston Caperton.

My sister was always a star student, eventually graduating Phi Beta Kappa. She was truly great. So it must have come as a shock when, during my fourth grade year, my teacher called to tell my parents I didn't know how to read. My father took me to see a very dear friend of his who had also grown up in Slab Fork. Dr. Edwin Shepherd was a doctor, as his father had been before him. He was an eye specialist and ran the Shepherd Hospital in Charleston. My father thought there might be something wrong with my eyes and that was the reason I couldn't read. In those days we didn't know much about reading disabilities. But Dr. Shepherd, who was a very thoughtful man, a true student of medicine, had done a lot of studying and had heard about people "reversing" when they tried to read. I visited his office on a Sunday, and he started flashing numbers and letters and asking me to repeat them. When we finished, Dr. Shepherd told my father he thought I had that "reversal" problem he had read about.

There wasn't a program in the schools those days to teach children with dyslexia how to read. So every morning, my father would sit me at the foot of his bed once I was dressed for school, and as he was dressing for work he made me memorize words from a large vocabulary book he had purchased. We practiced how to read the words, how to spell the words, and what the words meant. And that's how I learned to read. I refer to that period as the "Special Education of Gaston Caperton."

I certainly never excelled at spelling bees, and school was extremely hard for me. I was tutored every summer in reading and math. I attended good schools and I always got through, but it was never easy. Some teachers were understanding about my dyslexia, some weren't. Before fourth grade, I was lucky in a way. I was good with people and I was smart enough I could fake my way through. But in fourth grade, students begin reading aloud and writing more often. I am grateful that I had a teacher who brought the problem to my parents' attention.

Being dyslexic is hard on your self-esteem; there's always a little voice in your head saying, "Why are *you* here?" It's hard to think you are smart when you have trouble reading. You are constantly reliving the embarrassment of not being able to stand up in front of a class and read aloud. Kids laugh at you. You fail spelling tests, and eventually you think you are not very smart or capable. I still don't like to read aloud, but I'm much better at it than I used to be. Early in my tenure as governor I tried to read speeches, but would sometimes skip over words or mess them up. I would be standing up at a lectern and get nervous; that little voice would come back reminding me that once upon a time I couldn't read. But when I'm alone, I love to read and I read a lot. For this, I thank my family. Without their concern and support my life might have been very different.

AUTHOR: *Gaston Caperton. Mr. Caperton served as Governor of West Virginia from 1989 to 1997.*

32-001-ST-WV-001-1997

A Brief Tribute To My Dad

Frank Meredith, born near Alderson, West Virginia, in 1909, died September 4, 1996, at the age of eighty-seven. Of those eighty-seven years, fifty-three were spent living in St. Albans, West Virginia. He and his wife Ruth raised seven children there. Ruth died in 1968, and for a couple of years Frank was alone. However, in 1970, he married Mildred Barkey and added a grown stepson and his family to the already burgeoning Meredith clan. Mildred and Frank were together twenty-six years. Between them are eight children, sixteen grandchildren, and ten great-grandchildren.

Frank Meredith worked many jobs throughout his lifetime and never truly retired. Mostly, though, Frank was a plumber.

Frank Meredith on his eighty-seventh birthday, June 28, 1996, in Montreal, Canada, on a trip with his three daughters.

Mountain State Stories Of The People

Frank Meredith, June, 1996, with his abundant hollyhocks.

Plumbing and Frank Meredith are almost synonymous throughout most of the St. Albans area. Shortly before his death, he had "plumbed" the recently restored C&O Depot in St. Albans.

He had a heart so great that it was hard for us, his family, to accept that it had reached its breaking point — his heart was simply worn out. It "broke" in the middle of the night August 24, but it didn't stop completely for ten more days. Until that night in August, Frank was an active, busy man, who attended church, worked for the city, did his own lawn work, gardened, took his wife where she needed to go, and helped his family in whatever way he could.

It is sad that our dad is no longer here. I still expect to hear his voice on my answering machine with "CALL YOUR DAD." He gave us our beginnings and we are all the better for having known him. He touched many lives and influenced many people. His faith was strong and carried him through the untimely deaths of two sons and helped him in his daily life. He truly became a pillar of the community, with daily treks to "check out the town," with an eager hand to help others, and with his trusty tools to solve most plumbing problems.

God must have needed a master plumber and took Dad to Heaven to unstop those plugged drains, to give advice, or merely to hold someone who needed a big, strong shoulder to lean on.

We miss him.

Author: Frances Meredith. Frances is a teacher in the Kanawha County Schools. She has one son, L. Richard Dorsey, II. She is a daughter of Frank and Ruth Meredith.

33-001-ST-WV-001-1997

Childhood Playhouse

On our farm in Putnam County near Hurricane, West Virginia, circa 1925, all the children had a playhouse. Without walls, roofs or wooden floors, these playhouses were very portable and were richly furnished. They were a combination of nature and imagination, located on different ridges, around different trees and easily moved to the food cellar during winter.

Our family of twelve included five boys and five girls. Daddy kept the boys busy, so I and my sisters had to build and maintain our playhouse without adult help. It was never-ending work, but our playhouse was very neat and could meet all the high standards of cleanliness and neatness demanded of our real rooms and kitchen.

We had all the things our home kitchen had. Our flour meal was dry clay, red, yellow and white. We anxiously, yet patiently, awaited the jars from the kitchen to be empty so that we could use them in our playhouse. We were full of imagination, but would have had no idea what that word meant. Soaking crepe paper in water produced blue, red and green "flavoring" to be poured into empty vanilla bottles.

The barn loft was a grocery store, where we would go to buy our basic necessities. Hickory, walnuts and even chestnuts were abundant. Walnuts, hulled dry, could be "bought" to use as decorative bowls in our playhouse. The milky glass that used to line the zinc lid of a canning jar became a plate — shhh, we had to go deep into the cellar to snitch each plate from its container.

Sometimes we really did cook eggs and oh, that potato soup! Our oldest brother built a special building on another hill where eggs, potatoes, etc., were stored. We girls would "borrow" from this storehouse then stir reality into imagination to dine on cuisine the Greenbrier could only hope for.

We had virtually no idea that we would be considered poor by modern standards. My dad owned our large farm; we were self-sufficient, had many crops in different seasons and we girls had unlimited toys and playhouse locations. Looking back, I guess we were very wealthy, in a way that money can *not* provide.

Author: Roberta Eleanor Allen Escue. Eleanor is a mother, grandmother, and great-grandmother. She resides in her hometown of St. Albans.

34-001-ST-WV-001-1997

Horse Quip

At the ripe old age of six, a fellow has to work very, very hard to show what he can do. Sometimes a "man" has to go to great lengths to conceal his hard work and daily practice in order to someday demonstrate how accomplished he is.

One dog day morning during summer

1949, my daddy, a friend, and PaPaw were out near the pasture leaning on the fence discussing farm stuff. This is my chance, I thought. I had secretly been bareback riding Red, a miscreant stallion. PaPaw had put Red out to pasture at our home place near the Kanawha, Putnam County border awaiting sale or trade because of his unruly behavior. I was therefore told not to go near Red, much less ride him. Here was the culmination of the total challenge: to teach myself to ride Red, to do it on the Q.T., and then show them what I could do.

I had practiced for days on this horse, so I could surprise this small gathering by secretly mounting, guiding, and walking Red out to the fence and beyond. As I rounded the bend and they came into view Red began to trot, so I held tightly to his mane to keep from falling off and to guide him if possible. Just as I neared this important trio I loosened my grip, and to show my mettle, I let Red gallop. PaPaw, in response to something funny in their conversation, slapped Daddy's back and yelled, "HO! HO!" sounding like Santa. Red immediately reacted by stiffening his front legs and digging all fours into the turf. As in the cartoons I flew through the air over Red's head, did a double flip end-over-end, and landed flat on my back and shoulders. Instantly the breath was knocked out of me, plus I had a very visible bloody nose. Otherwise I was fine, so they sent me on my way with no punishment; Red shared no blame.

I had a short dry spell back then of not riding any horse — from this occurrence to age seventeen. And I really didn't want Santa to visit during Christmas that year either.

This episode taught me a valuable life lesson: don't leave your parents in the dark when you really want to learn or try something new, and don't ride a fast horse around jolly old St. Nick.

AUTHOR: L.A. SQ

35-001-ST-WV-001-1997

Thank Goodness For Cans

I left West Virginia in 1946, after the end of World War II. However, West Virginia feels like home, and I come back every summer for six months and raise a garden.

In the late 1960s, I rode a Greyhound Bus from Vero Beach, Florida, to see my dad. He was in his 90s and not doing very well. When I got to the bus station in Charleston, I called my nephew and niece Jack and Martha Gregory, and had them pick me up. My father was with my sister, and she didn't have a car. When I got to Jack's house, Martha had been making bread and it was about ready to put in the oven. They had a beautiful home, and were doing well. I was so shocked when I saw her baking the bread in cans that had once contained V-8 Juice. I felt so sorry for her because I thought she couldn't afford loaf pans. When the bread came out of the oven I ate the end piece, and it was the best bread I ever tasted.

On my way back to Vero Beach on the bus, I couldn't get it off my mind that she didn't have a loaf pan. I even thought about sending her one. I didn't realize until much later that that was what she liked. Now she uses a bread maker. I think I will get her some V-8 Juice, and just maybe…

AUTHOR: Donald Williams. After reading this story, Mr. Williams's niece's daughter bought a tall can of grapefruit juice. Guess what she plans to do with the empty can.

36-001-ST-WV-001-1997

That's Just The Way It Was

My parents, Dewey Lee Roush and Hattie Pearl Short Roush, eight siblings, and I lived in a tiny three room house in Clendenin, West Virginia. My dad never had a steady job. He was paper hanger and painter for the more prosperous town people.

Our house was heated by a wood stove in one side of the livingroom/bedroom. A kerosene lamp that was lighted at dark, sat on an oak dresser. The little outhouse on the creek bank was a two-holer. Seems that little building was always occupied and a line waiting. A floor model Philco radio, powered by batteries, was our in-home entertainment.

The old swimming hole beside our house was a place of great importance in our lives. We loved that little pond of dirty water as though it was the finest pool to be had. We were nine small children, growing up playing on the hills, climbing trees and all but hanging by our tails, with never a fractured bone or anything really serious that called for immediate medical attention.

Times were hard and we were poor, but we didn't know it. We didn't have a beautiful home filled with beautiful furnishings, but we didn't miss all that, because you can't miss what you have never had. There was always water to carry in, chickens to feed, garden to tend and put up for winter, and coal and wood to bring into the house.

We kids never had money for anything,

ever. We had few store-bought pleasures. There were school lunches in brown paper bags, summers of more work than play, big Sunday dinners with mounds of dishes to wash, babies to tend to, and mudholes to play in when it rained.

AUTHOR: Lorena Mae Roush Siders. Lorena was born in 1926, in Clendenin, graduated from Clendenin High School, and married Jack T. Siders. She raised three children and still resides in Clendenin.

37-001-ST-WV-001-1997

Sisters

My mother had two sisters. I, on the other hand, grew up sisterless. Sometimes I would throw it up to Mom that she and Dad had deprived me.

"Be thankful you have Eldon and Carson," she'd say. But my brothers didn't like to have doll tea parties or play dress-up. We would never sew beautiful matching dresses for ourselves, pin-curl one another's hair, or walk arm-in-arm down the road, attracting the attention of boys in passing cars.

I loved to hear Mom tell stories about growing up in the mountains. She kept old family pictures in a big red gift box that came from the Diamond department store in Charleston. Once a year, she'd retrieve the box from its sacred place in her closet. My brothers and I would crowd around to hear the story behind each photograph.

Sisters, (L-R), Osie, Gladys, and June Carr.

I learned that my grandmother Dora Foster Carr smoked a pipe when she was four years old because the doctor said it would help with her asthma attacks. My grandfather John L Carr (whose middle name consisted of a single letter) fiddled for dances all over Boone County until arthritis locked his finger joints. Mom's brothers — Orville, Lester, Burk, and Chuck — always seemed to be playing the guitar or clowning around.

But nothing was as romantic as the picture of my mother and her sisters. Thin and beautiful as movie stars (at least in my mind), they stood in the grass in their knee-length dresses, posing for a picture to send Orville. It was May 17, 1945, and he had written from the Army that he could not remember what any of them looked like. My mother, barely sixteen years old, was sick with stomach ulcers, and had dressed just long enough for the picture to be taken before she crawled back into bed. Her sisters Osie and June stood on either side of her, lending their support, I supposed. I envied a sisterhood I could only imagine.

Years after the picture was taken, my mother was relieved of her ulcers after receiving a blessing from the Mormon elders. She married Carl Thomas and my aunts moved away — Osie to Florida with her husband Jim, and June to California with half the family in tow. "Seems like everybody scattered about the time Kennedy died," Mom says. I barely remember November 1963, but recall that I confused President Kennedy's death with my Uncle Lester's. Not long afterward, my mother stood by the kitchen window during long afternoons, listening to Hank Williams songs and watching the sky for jet trails that followed the paths her sisters had taken.

Now, when they call one another on holidays, I see in my mind an invisible triangle connecting the three of them. Their shared stories pull them to one another, root them in a way that perhaps only sisters can comprehend.

AUTHOR: Carla Thomas McClure. Carla grew up in St. Albans, and returned to her hometown after living in Utah and North Carolina. She and her husband edit a newsletter for state writers.

38-001-ST-WV-001-1997

My First Look At History

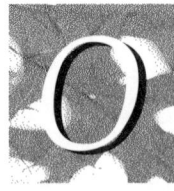

One of my fondest memories concerns my father. When I was in the fifth grade in 1935 at Midway School on Campbells Creek, West Virginia, our teacher Rose Quick asked the class if anyone could go on a train excursion to Washington, DC. I had a terrible time convincing my father to let me go. I thought it was the money that made him say no for so long. But he finally gave in.

About halfway to Washington, who did I see walking down the aisle on the train but Daddy. I was only eleven years old, but I suddenly realized he was worried about me being away from home. He had a bag of Hershey Bars for me. He had also convinced a friend, Newt Layton, to come with him.

CHAPTER 4: METRO VALLEY

I had a wonderful time on that trip. Unfortunately, I was the only fifth grader who went with Mrs. Quick; however, she had a nephew my age who went with us. She also had relatives in DC, so we stayed at their home. I was treated so well. And what a thrill it was to have my picture taken in front of the Lincoln Memorial. I had never been any farther than Charleston, and only there a couple times.

My father passed away in 1988, and I miss him. I am thankful for having had him. He was so good to me. His name was Earlie Iman Bowles, better known as Ned.

Author: Martha Gregory. Martha was born in Tad, and moved to Deltona, Florida, in 1978. She later returned to DC with her two children when they had become teenagers. She says it was still a fun journey.

39-001-ST-WV-001-1997

Picking Up Coal

As a young child, I often stayed with my grandpa and grandma in the head of a hollow in rural West Virginia. I loved to stay there because there were so many children to play with. They had ten kids, and I was older than the last of them.

My grandfather and five of my uncles worked in the coal mines up on the hill by the house. The coal bank was just a hole in the mountain that had been blasted and hand-dug by my grandpa and his sons. Inside the mine were braces made of rough lumber and a track for a coal wagon to run on. The track was often very unstable and Grandpa had to repair it by kneeling in water and mud and driving nails into the track. This was a family-owned mine — a poor family at that. There was no fancy equipment.

Sue Frye and Maw Davis, 1950.

I remember my grandmother getting the midday meal ready for Grandpa and my uncles. She would begin to prepare large pans of bread, skillets of pork, and many vegetables to go with it. She cooked on a coal stove. It was the job of the little kids to go along the coal bank road and pick up lumps of coal for Grandma to use in the stove. We would take coffee sacks and buckets to put it in. We knew that those black, shiny lumps of coal would be the main factor in the wonderful meals Grandma would cook. It was hard work but it was our job; all the family had work to do and we did it. When we picked up enough coal to fill our sacks and buckets, we felt proud pulling them down the hill to the house. Grandma would come out on the back porch and we would lay our coal piles at her feet. She would tell us what good kids we were. We always knew that the next day would bring the same reward, including another wonderful country meal from Grandma.

Author: Catherine Sue Frye. Sue is the mother of four. She is a native of and resides in Charleston.

40-001-ST-WV-001-1997

Home Sweet Home

My first wife Virginia Hardman always "had the bug" to get to Florida. So, in 1986, after I retired, we sold our home in Charleston, and rented in Ocala, Florida. From there, we explored Florida for retirement locations, on both the Gulf and Atlantic Coasts.

After a few months, Virginia and I agreed that we didn't really like Florida: too many cars, too many people, and more arriving every day. So, we built a patio home in an upscale retirement community near Myrtle Beach, South Carolina.

But, Virginia still wasn't happy. Finally, she realized that what she was missing were her friends and relatives back in West Virginia. That's one thing those retirement planning books never mention: the importance of family and friends!

So, after ten months in South Carolina, we sold our place in Myrtle Trace and moved back to West Virginia. Six months later, Virginia died. I thanked God that I was back in Charleston where I had the support of friends and relatives, instead of being alone in Florida or South Carolina.

West Virginia is a great retirement location. The cost of living is relatively low; real estate prices and the tax structure are especially attractive. Crime is not the major concern that it is in many retirement areas. And we have a nice change of seasons, with beautiful springs and falls and tolerable summers and winters.

Our state is a sportsman's paradise. For recreation, we can enjoy skiing and whitewater rafting. We're conveniently located to vacation possibilities in the East and midwest. And, in the Kanawha Valley, the cultural, social, and dining opportunities have improved a thousand-fold since I first came to Charleston in September 1942!

I continue to enjoy all that West Virginia has to offer. There's more though — an especially happy ending to my story. After my bereavement, I married my wonderful wife Sally and have been accepted by her caring family. I'm very happy to live out my remaining days in West Virginia!

AUTHOR: *Malcolm "Pat" Patterson. Pat first came to West Virginia in September, 1942, as a Georgia Tech co-op student at DuPont's Belle plant. He worked thirty-eight years for Union Carbide, twenty in West Virginia.*

41-001-ST-WV-001-1997

Be Home 'Fore Dark

How often I've heard the words, "Be home 'fore dark!" If I could sum my childhood up in one word, it would be "FEAR." I learned to feel "You should never go anywhere unless it's absolutely necessary, because: the bus might wreck, the car might wreck, or the creek may flood," and on and on.

Hill people know the true meaning of darkness. I left home before they got electricity. We had natural gas, and used gas mantles. They were fragile as they hung from the gas outlet in the ceiling of the room. They made a soft romantic light, but not bright enough for reading at times.

I'll never forget the first time I was up past midnight. Mother was working at a small restaurant, and my brother and I had gone there to wait until she got off from work. When I was still there and it was 12:30 A.M., it was such a strange, eerie feeling. I worried how we would get home, and if home would be there when we did. This same feeling occurred when I saw my first movie in Charleston. All of the children from the small country school had gone by school bus to see *Snow White and the Seven Dwarfs*. I think I was in the fifth or sixth grade. I couldn't enjoy the movie for worrying about getting home after dark, and to my astonishment it was bright and sunny when we came out of the theater!

Fear of forest fires was another of my childhood fears. I remember the time we took all the curtains down and got all our belongings together — I even had socks in my coat pockets — and waited and watched, seemingly all night, as the fire came closer and closer. We all hoped it would not come beyond the "holler" near our house, because there was broomsage all around that field near the house. Grandpa had gone to fight the fire, and we were so thankful when he came back in the morning and said the fire was out. But we had a lot of things to put back in place.

Zella Jarrett, 1996.

Have you ever heard a roof "clarping?" We had a tin roof, and with every storm the wind caught under the tin and played loud cymbals all over the roof. You couldn't sleep, and that made the storm seem a thousand times worse, and you expected the roof to go any minute. I've never been in another house that had a noisy roof like that.

Daddy and Mother separated when I was very young. I grew up with Grandpa, Grandma, Mother, and my brother and sister. Another childhood fear was caused by Mother's "smothering spells." I'd run off the high hill to get her peppermint leaves to smell when she had a bad spell. They grew in the damp earth near the sulphur spring. I was afraid Mother would die, and I couldn't bear the thought of being any more lonely. A day seemed like a week then, and a year was an eternity. Many a time we went to bed before the sun was down. Without a radio, newspaper, and only school books to read, time seemed to go so slowly. Now I wish it was so.

One of my greatest fears was my fear of my grandfather, a hard-working man, small in stature, but a giant to me. He never laid a hand on me, in affection, or anger, but he never had to; his threats were enough. He sometimes cut long, sturdy switches and set them in the corner, but never used them. When he told us something we never questioned him audibly, though often silently. Grandpa was all work and no play, and he expected us to be the same. Play was foolishness to him and we knew better than to get rowdy in his sight. He never drank, only chewed Five Brothers tobacco. If he didn't have a tool, he made one. Little did we realize that he was giving us a great example.

In later years Grandpa mellowed and started going to church again. I learned to admire the inner strength of this man I never really got to know, only in working with him, and observing his honest dealings with others.

He was one of the few people in the county who made sorghum molasses every fall. The last day of "molasses makin'" he would work until dark, and people would come from all around. One of the fun memories of my childhood was trying to stay out of the "skimmin' hole" and watching the horse go around and around, as the wheels of the cane mill squeezed the juice from the thick stalks. Then we would jump into the huge pile of the juiceless stalks thrown down a bank, or bite into the juicy cane stalks, being careful not to get our tongues or lips caught in the stalks.

Grandpa owned nothing of material wealth, but he never owed anyone. I know he loved us dearly, but people show love in different ways; his and Mother's seemed to be in worrying. I can remember when one of us would be gone to the store and a train would whistle. Grandpa would walk through the house and say, "Those kids have just had time to be on that trestle."

Grandpa would also say, "It's going to blow up something." This really scared me because it was years later before I learned he meant a change in the weather. He also had the most burglar-proof door I've ever known. He took a railroad spike and put it in its special-made hole under the door facing. A real dead-bolt lock! To fasten the two front doors he placed thick wooden sticks every night under the door knobs and braced them against the floor. They were better than any locks today, because, as one friend observed, "When you opened the door you had your weapon in your hand."

I had a special fear of one of my grade school teachers. He is dead now, but surely no one who ever had him for a teacher forgot him. He was of German descent, a great music teacher, and directed beautiful Christmas plays. But he was so strict we had to tiptoe nearly all the time we were in the school building. I'll never forget the time during warm weather when he complained about the body odor in the room. He said if we didn't come clean the next day, he would personally wash us. I scrubbed and scrubbed my feet that night. He did wash a couple of boys in a large tub and brought them clean clothes to put on. I was so embarrassed for them. Can you imagine a teacher doing that today, and not being charged with something?

Even today I still hear from my mother, "Be home 'fore dark," and I try to, but seldom make it. The expression is part of my childhood that I'll miss deeply if Mother goes before I do. I realize now it's a "love phrase" and when I hear it no more, I'm sure, to my loved ones I'll echo those same loving words: "Be home 'fore dark."

Author: Zella Jarrett. Mrs. Jarrett was born and raised in Boone County, but has lived in nine counties in the state. She writes often of its wonders and beauty.

42-001-ST-WV-001-1997

An Awkward Age

I was thirteen. An awkward age full of pain, confusion, and hard lessons to learn.

Grandma and I were sitting on the floor in front of the gas stove which was snuggled inside the old-fashioned fireplace. Several generations had been born and raised in that old farmhouse at the top of Miller Hill near Madison, West Virginia. While I stared at the blue and orange spikes of flames with other things on my mind, Grandma kept reaching for my attention as she picked up one and then another item from the well-worn paper box that held her treasures.

She was so tiny and frail. Her wispy, salt and pepper colored hair refused to stay put in the bun at the back of her head. Her round, wire-rimmed glasses kept sliding down her narrow nose. The years of hard work on the farm could be seen on her leather-like skin. Her sad, faded-blue eyes stared intently at me over the top of her spectacles as she continued with a story about her mother and how they had traveled by covered wagon to this area a very long time ago. She showed me a pair of handmade scissors that had made the trip with my great-grandmother. I don't remember all of the story now, but I remember the look in her eyes. It was as if she was trying to tell me more than just a story.

I wish I had listened more closely to everything she told me, but at that age I thought life went on forever. She was passing on her memories and my heritage. I had yet to learn that time passes all too quickly.

She was very old. An awkward age full of pain, confusion, and memories of hard lessons learned.

Author: Katie Pratt. Katie is a teacher in her hometown of Princeton.

43-001-ST-WV-001-1997

When Grandpa Was Growing Up

My grandpa Otto "Dick" Vernon Vande Linde, Jr., grew up on a hillside farm during the Depression in Boone County, West Virginia on Rock Creek, three miles from Danville. Like most people in that era, his family was very poor, although the kids didn't realize it. They thought it was normal to get up in the morning and feed the chickens, hogs, and cows and do other chores.

The kids didn't mind the work because they made a little game out of it. All of the boys got together and went to whichever farm was ready to be hoed. Everyone had their own patch to hoe. Their moms and sisters cooked for everyone. When they were done with one farm, they'd go to another. The community cooperated in cutting wood, butchering cows and hogs, and baling hay. They had as much fun doing these things as kids do today playing sports or watching television.

Grandpa loved the smells of the house on winter mornings. His mom had bacon, eggs, hot biscuits, apple butter, strawberry jam, fried apples and potatoes for every winter breakfast.

When Grandpa was fifteen, he worked twelve hours for fifty cents. Grown men would work for a dollar a day.

Every Christmas Grandpa got two pairs of long underwear, two pairs of overalls, two chambray shirts, and four tube socks. Every other year he got shoes which he would wear from frost to frost. When they were worn out, he threw them away and went barefoot until the next Christmas.

Every Christmas morning, his mama would be in the kitchen and they would call her to come see what Santa had brought, but she wouldn't come. He never knew why until he became a parent himself. The first few years he didn't have enough money to get his children toys. Just like his mom, he couldn't stand to see the disappointment on their faces.

AUTHOR: Stacey Vande Linde. Stacey is a student at Sissonville Middle School. She is the second of three girls. She likes soccer and volleyball.

Corn Cob Baseball At Millertown

A ten-quart water bucket full of broken corn cobs — red and white — and a bat of one-by-two oak, about thirty-four inches long with a handle whittled on one end. These were used in a game created by the Miller boys, Clifford, Clyde, and Lummie. There were only two participants, a pitcher and a batter. Scoring was accomplished by hitting the barn with a batted cob thrown over home plate.

The barn had a gable roof with a shed built on the right side. A batted cob hitting the front was a single, hitting the right side roof and shed roof was a double. A cob hitting the left roof was a triple, and one hit over the tin roof, not making a noise, was a homer.

The batter got three outs, which were by strikes or pop-ups caught by the pitcher. Occasionally, time had to be called to pick up a bucket of cobs.

Being younger than the Miller boys, I only played this game against Lummie, the youngest of them. Lummie was always adamant about being pitched only the white cobs. He said they were harder and wouldn't burst as often when hit by the oak bat. I believe he was correct.

Many friends of the Miller boys also played the game. The barn is gone now, but the memories will remain.

AUTHOR: Harold L. Stump. Mr. Stump is retired from Kanawha County Schools. He is the father of two, and one of ten children of Jesse and Ethel Stump. He grew up in Millertown.

The Future Is Our Children

West Virginians! God love them! And, oh, the children! Growing up in hectic and dangerous times. Flooded with information. Busy lives that may, or may not, include the languid days of summer I spent as a child reading books on the swing on my grandmother's porch, playing hide-and-seek with my brother in our grandfather's corn field, and safely walking the streets of our small town. Community! Is it gone, as the experts say? I think not.

I was talking to a large group of elementary school children on Citizenship Day, 1996. I asked them what they would do to be good citizens. Their answers included: Do not litter; care for others; vote in elections; recycle; be a good friend; go to school; help in a car pool; don't jay walk; don't be a criminal; be helpful; and don't pollute the environment.

Some of their spelling left a little to be desired; however, their hearts and minds were absolutely correct.

A friend of mine recently suggested that we lost our sense of community when we stopped building sidewalks in neighborhoods and front porches on the houses. He is right to the extent that we have traded walk-by "hellos" for drive-through everything, but to me the answers the children gave me on Citizenship Day were community of the spirit.

Friends, I suggest we need not worry about the future of this beat-up world — it will be in the good hands of our children!

AUTHOR: Sally L. Patterson. Sally is a homemaker, freelance writer, poet, advertiser, designer, and volunteer. She has three daughters, Diane, Cindy, and Elaine, one stepdaughter, Sherri, and three grandchildren, Carol, Chris, and Jenny.

CHAPTER 4: METRO VALLEY

A Nice Guy

I met Mr. Al when I worked at the Federal Building in Charleston. He operated the concession stand downstairs. His wife always brought him to work at six thirty in the morning. I had already started his automatic coffee maker at six o'clock, so he would have fresh coffee for the early morning traffic.

Sometimes he would call me and ask me to bring up a fresh case of Coke so his wife could pick it up. He never wanted anyone to open a door or push the buttons on the elevator because he knew just where they were. He knew nearly everyone by name and about what time they would be in. At Christmas time the girls from various offices would come in and decorate his place and have a party which would last all afternoon.

He always called me "Willie" and I called him "Mr. Al." After I retired I went back about every two weeks. Sometimes I would take my grandson Pat who would play the banjo for Mr. Al. He and Al became good friends and Pat was invited back many times.

Then Al's wife passed away after a long illness and there were no more parties. However, Al hung in there and worked as much as he could, given his physical problems.

Mrs. Madge Spears worked part-time for him and kept the place going. Mrs. Spears called me on New Year's morning and said they had found Mr. Al dead at his home, where he lived alone. He had no enemies, just friends. We miss him.

AUTHOR: Ralph Williams. Mr. Williams is a retired police officer. He is the father of one daughter, grandfather of five grandchildren, and great-grandfather of two. Mr. Al Hackney, who was blind from birth, lived from 1934-1990.

47-001-ST-WV-001-1997

The One-Room Schoolhouse

This one-room schoolhouse was very special. It was built on an acre of ground; however, the building itself occupied only a very small part of this land. The rest was used for playground and two outdoor toilets, one for boys and one for girls. Each desk had an ink well and a grooved place at the back of the top surface of the desk to hold a pen so it would not roll off. Underneath the top was a shelf to hold the books and paper. There were between twenty-five and thirty students, and all eight grades were taught in this one room. I am sure some of our education was obtained from the repetition of hearing the classes up front performing.

In the winter months there was a large pot-bellied stove, burning wood and coal. This stove was located in the corner of the room, and if your seat was close to the stove you felt very lucky. The teacher's desk was always up front, and to the right of her desk in a corner were a large number of fresh cut switches five or six feet long. We were told that anyone misbehaving would be brought up front and switched in front of everyone. After observing two or three switchings, everyone settled down to study and waited for recess to spend surplus energy.

Recess was thirty minutes to play drop the handkerchief and ring around the rosey, after which the teacher would ring the bell and everyone returned to their seat.

This one-room schoolhouse was used twice a year for singing lessons taught to the shaped notes of do-ra-mi-fa-sol-la-ti-do that remain in my memory today.

AUTHOR: Pearl Todd Miller. Mrs. Miller is a published poet. She was born in Raleigh County, and is the mother of five.

48-001-ST-WV-001-1997

Editors' Note: Early American itinerant singing teachers used the shape note system to teach sight reading to people who couldn't read music. The music was written in standard notation, but the notes appeared in four different shapes. Different shapes indicated different pitches, with the interval between two different shapes always the same.

The Gift Of Hope

In everyone's life there is or has been a significant other; someone who goes that extra mile to care for someone else. For me that person was Hattie Hale, my sixth grade teacher.

Mrs. Hale was new in the building that year, and of course we were afraid of her because she transferred in from high school. Besides, she had blue-frosted hair and red rouge. We just knew she was going to be hard. Surely a high school teacher from the city would not understand country kids.

Mrs. Hale quickly proved herself as a teacher, however. An excellent disciplinarian, no one got away with anything. Very prompt and strict, she jumped into science and social studies like we had never seen.

As the weeks passed by, she came to know each one of us not only academically, but personally. She knew our families as well. She knew

whose father was laid off and whose mother had run away. She picked Charlie to be the janitor's helper because he would get free lunch. Charlie came from a family of eleven. Mary Sue was chosen to go to the Salvation Army Christmas party because her family was hurting worse than anyone else's. Mrs. Hale even gave me two dresses that year.

But there is one gift Mrs. Hale gave me that I'll never forget: the gift of hope. Near the end of the year she held a textbook up high in the air and said to the class, "This is your ticket out. This can help you get out of whatever you want to get out of." I stared at the sixth grade speller in her hand.

It was not until later that I understood her words of wisdom. Education was the key. We could only break the cycle of poverty by staying in school and becoming educated.

I am a teacher now, thanks to Mrs. Hale. I try to pass on her message of hope and the importance of education to each child who passes through my classroom.

AUTHOR: Katherine P. Manley. Kathy is a writer and Language Arts/Title I teacher in her native Logan County. She is the mother of three children.

49-001-ST-WV-001-1997

Susan's Blouse

When I was a child growing up in West Virginia, life was difficult. Often it was hard for some parents in our community to properly feed and clothe all of us. Once in awhile, though, some kind soul would give us hand-me-downs or leftovers from the neighborhood ragsales. We were always grateful for any small item. Needless to say, Christmas and birthdays brought forth very little, if anything at all. That is why I'll never forget a young woman named Susan.

Susan was a secretary in an office where I worked two hours everyday after school. One day while I was working, Susan handed me a beautifully wrapped package and said, "Happy Birthday." I cried as I stared at the beautiful long-sleeved white crepe blouse that I pulled out from underneath layers of white tissue paper inside the box. This was the first new piece of clothing that anyone had ever given me and I was so happy. I felt like I had just been handed a million dollars.

Although the blouse was a present for me, I shared Susan's altruism with the other girls in my neighborhood. Whenever anyone wanted to borrow it, they asked for it by name: Susan's blouse. It came to be one of our most worn pieces of clothing because it worked well with jumpers, sweaters, or simply by itself. Susan's present not only brought joy to a poor little camp girl, but also to all those who wore it. I have always wanted to thank Susan for her act of kindness and decided this was a good way to do it.

AUTHOR: Kathy Manley

50-001-ST-WV-001-1997

A Legendary Legacy

My dad, Stan Cunningham of Charleston, and his wife Connie, are lifelong residents of West Virginia. They celebrated their fiftieth wedding anniversary in 1996. They have four daughters: Barbara, Susan (both deceased), Jane, and Becky. They also have nine grandchildren who enjoy hearing the stories that only Papaw tells so well about the good old days.

Dad is the grandson of Marshall Daniel Webster Cunningham. Marshall Cunningham captured many

Stan Cunningham holding the double-barrel shotgun carried by Marshall Daniel Webster Cunningham over his many adventures in the state of West Virginia.

moonshine stills and one of the biggest was found on Christmas Eve in 1903. It was one of the largest stills ever captured in West Virginia with 180 gallon capacity. He was also instrumental during the Hatfield-McCoy feud when the McCoys demanded that the Marshall surrender Ellison Hatfield, the murderer of their children. The Marshall held his rifle ready and took the prisoner to jail where he was later tried and hanged.

My dad is honored to have possession of the rifle that was once carried by his grandfather.

AUTHOR: Rebecca Miceli. Becky lives in Pinch with her husband Lou and their three children. Having lived as far north as Delaware and as far south as Puerto Rico, they all agree that there is no place like West Virginia and the warm, wonderful people who live there.

51-001-ST-WV-001-1997

CHAPTER 4: METRO VALLEY

Window Birth

Early one hazy summer morning in the 1950s on our St. Albans farm, there came a loud knock at our back door. I heard my mother Eleanor quickly scurry across the floor through the kitchen to answer it. There stood my paw-paw Buell B. Escue, anxiously telling Mother that he needed Daddy's help immediately to birth a calf.

My daddy Norris quickly dressed and went out to the pasture. Even though I was only eight years old, I decided to follow them. My paw-paw suggested to my father that I should go into the house, but Daddy didn't heed those instructions.

We walked closer to the mother cow in distress, and I suppose my paw-paw had not realized I was still tagging along. When he noticed my presence, he turned around said to me in a very loud and stern voice, "Get to the house!" Naturally, I immediately turned and ran into the house crying silently and went straight to my upstairs bedroom.

Lying across my bed I sobbed. With tears still flowing, I suddenly realized that my bedroom window would give me a true bird's eye view of the miracle of that baby calf being born. Both Paw-Paw and Daddy worked very hard in pulling the calf out by its hind legs. It did not take long before the new calf was standing on all fours.

It was years before I let any family member know about my secret viewing of that "Window Birth."

AUTHOR: Priscilla H. Escue Brace. Priscilla left her treasured home of St. Albans in 1964 with her husband and two daughters. She resides in Virginia, but returns home for frequent visits.

52-001-ST-WV-001-1997

The West Virginia Army National Guard Yesterday And Today

The men and women serving in the West Virginia Army National Guard (WVARNG) are carrying on the tradition of the minutemen for freedom. We are the only dual-role military organization tasked with performing both state and military missions. Through our efforts to remain a drug free, quality force, we add value to each and every community throughout our great state!

The conception of the present-day WVARNG began with the establishment of Morgan Morgan's company of militia riflemen in Berkeley County, Virginia, in what is now Bunker Hill, near Martinsburg, West Virginia. Morgan Morgan, who is reputed by some authorities to have been the first colonial settler in present-day West Virginia, was granted a commission as Captain of Militia on February 17, 1735. This group of citizen-soldiers, who frequently banded together to protect their neighbors and their country when needed, began a proud tradition that has been inherited by today's WVARNG members. Between 1735 and the present, the citizen-soldiers from West Virginia have participated in every major war and conflict in which the United States has been involved from colonial times to the Korean Conflict.

Although the first militia unit was formed in Massachusetts in 1636 and is officially recognized as the beginning of the concept of the citizen-soldier, at some point in history that unit was disbanded. The WVARNG's 201st Field Artillery Battalion, specifically, Battery B of that Battalion, can trace its lineage back to and can claim direct descent from Morgan Morgan's company of militia men. Therefore, the WVARNG has been certified as the oldest continuous commissioned military organization in the United States. The 201st is also the only remaining unit of the original eight companies that formed the US Army on June 14, 1775. The Battalion unites companies that fought for the Union and companies that fought for the Confederacy during the Civil War and is the only unit today that displays both the Confederate and Union streamers earned during the War.

During the French and Indian War (1754-1763), it was the Berkeley County Riflemen who taught the English Regulars how to adapt to the Indians' style of fighting using the terrain and camouflage to hide their movements in the forest. It was the same group of men who participated from western Virginia during the Revolutionary War with Great Britain. Although these men were called to duty during times of war, they were constantly on call to protect the settlers from Indian attacks. Up until the beginning of the 1800s, the Indians continued these attacks on a sporadic basis, trying to regain lost territory and to hold on to what was left.

These militiamen continued to function as needed, but it was not until the Virginia House of Burgesses enacted the Militia Act of 1792 that they started getting organized and preparing regulations that could bring continuity to the militia. This Act stipulated that there would be no salaries paid by the Federal Government unless the men were inducted into federal service. The state would have to pay the men for whatever service was performed under their jurisdiction. This Act is the basis for the

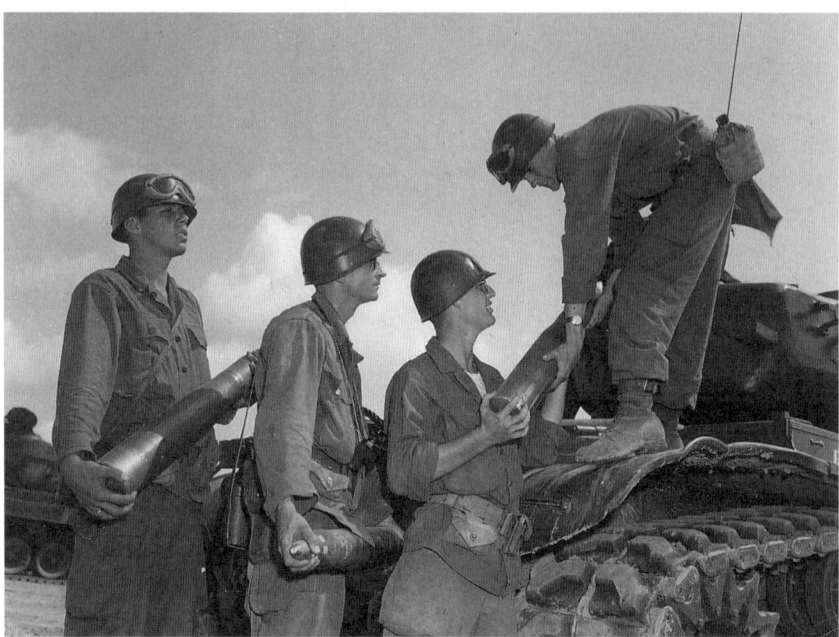

The West Virginia Army National Guard in the 1950s.

reimbursement of the National Guard today.

In the militiamen's early years, there were many problems to overcome, some of them major, and seemingly insurmountable. Two of the biggest problems were the lack of equipment and money with which to buy equipment, and the transportation problems which arose due to the distance between the units. These problems did not stop the militiamen from participating in either the War of 1812 against Great Britain or the War with Mexico in 1846. These riflemen from western Virginia were always available to serve their country when called to do so. In West Virginia, as in many other border states, the Civil War was particularly tragic because the population was torn between loyalty to the mother state of Virginia and strong feelings about the preservation of the Union.

In 1861, the year the Civil War began, western Virginia consisted of nearly 400,000 people. It is estimated that around 32,000 men enlisted to fight for the North, while 12,000 donned Confederate gray. After Virginia elected to secede from the Union, delegates from western Virginia elected to remain in the Union and also tried to keep their Virginian heritage by forming the "Restored Government of Virginia." During the course of the Civil War, there were some six hundred battles and small actions fought on West Virginia soil, and on June 20, 1863, the name of West Virginia was officially taken by the western Virginia territory. Throughout the course of the war, the state raised various groups of militiamen: seventeen regiments of volunteer infantry, two regiments of veteran infantry, seven regiments of cavalry, and two regiments of artillery.

Following the Civil War, there was the need for a military organization that could train during peaceful times to be ready for a national emergency, and that could also be depended upon for state emergencies that required action at a moment's notice. As before, money and equipment were close to nonexistent, and even more important, training was sporadic at best, and there was no incentive for men to join.

It was plain during civil unrest in Martinsburg in 1877 that militia companies were very important during peaceful times. The strike of railroad workers required a large number of troops to maintain the peace, and West Virginia could not provide the number needed. The Governor had to call upon the President to activate troops outside of West Virginia to help control the situation.

In the latter part of the 1800s West Virginia became a major coal producing state. Coal had been discovered in what is now West Virginia early in the nineteenth century, but was not produced in any great quantities until after the Civil War. With the continued development of the country and the growing need for coke to run the iron and steel furnaces, West Virginia's coal lands became very important. Before industrialization, most of West Virginia's residents were widely scattered throughout the mountains and made their living from subsistence farming, hunting, and fishing. There were not enough native workers to man the mines, so the coal companies entered upon active recruitment of immigrants from other states and countries.

The increasing development of the coal fields led to growing labor-capital conflict as the operators began to look upon labor as just another cost factor in the production of coal. When coal prices went down, miners' wages were cut. Since the wages were already low, and the work was hard and dangerous, the laborers used the only means available to fight back: they would go on strike to try to get better wages and working conditions. One of the most serious strikes began at Hawks Nest in January, 1880. The strike was enhanced by other mine operators in West Virginia wanting to cut their competition. The militia was called to intervene and keep peace, but the Governor found that there were very few militiamen available, and those individuals who were on call had no job guarantees and were reluctant to leave jobs that

CHAPTER 4: METRO VALLEY

would not be waiting when they returned home. The commanders went out and recruited enough men to cover the situation, but the incident brought to light once again the need for an organized military force to maintain order in the state.

In 1889, the West Virginia Legislature enacted a new militia law which completely revamped the state military forces and put them on a permanent basis. The new law changed the name of the military to the West Virginia Army National Guard, the name it retains today. The mid-1890s was a time of economic depression and labor conflict for the Mountain State. The National Guard struggled through these conflicts, taking them in stride as the soldiers they strive to be. It was a period of growth for the National Guard, and by the time

The West Virginia Army National Guard in the 1950s.

the Spanish-American War began in 1898, the Guard had become firmly entrenched in West Virginia, and was constantly improving its stature.

When called on federal duty during the Spanish-American War, the National Guard was ready to go. However, no West Virginia National Guardsmen were activated outside of the United States during this war. The WVARNG was activated for federal duty during World War I, World War II, and the Korean Conflict, and performed overseas duty in all three. The Guard was also activated during the Berlin Crisis in 1961.

The WVARNG has been activated numerous times during instances of natural disasters and emergencies in West Virginia. In colonial times and in today's fast-paced, constantly changing world, when there is an emergency that requires the help of the WVARNG, they are dispersed to the community in need of assistance at a moment's notice. It was the WVARNG that helped during the Buffalo Hollow, Logan County, dam burst in 1972. It took nearly a month for the residents and National Guard personnel to dig out from under the debris and devastation that left nearly every family homeless and killed more than 120 people. We performed the same service for the residents of Williamson during the flooding and resulting devastation in 1977 and during the snow emergency in 1978 when West Virginia was blanketed with more than twenty-four inches of snow overnight.

It was also the WVARNG that was activated within hours for flood disaster relief in the northeastern part of West Virginia in early November 1985. And 1996 was no easier; six times we were called upon by Governor Caperton to assist in evacuation and recovery operations. Beginning with the January snow storm and ending with repeated flooding throughout the year, the members of the West Virginia Army National Guard answered the call each and every time. We assisted with clean-up efforts, and especially worked to restore roads, build temporary bridges, and cleared out the overwhelming debris. We also cried with the residents as we watched them struggle through those awful first days; we cried for lost homes, lost memorabilia, and lost dreams. In addition to state emergency duty, members of the 152nd Military Police Detachment, from Moundsville, were federally activated in 1995-96 to support NATO peacekeeping operations in Bosnia during Operation Joint Endeavor. In 1994, members of the 2nd Battalion, 19th Special Forces Group from Ceredo and Kingwood, were federally activated to support Operation Uphold Democracy in Haiti.

People call the National Guard to help during searches for lost children, lost hunters, and others reported missing in communities in West Virginia. National Guard personnel also perform in parades, help in community projects, and live and work within the communities where they attend guard drill. The West Virginia National Guard today is a combat-ready organization that prides itself on the efficiency and effectiveness of its personnel.

At a time when we depend on a fully volunteer force, we are successful in providing the primary backup of the active Army during a national emergency or war. That our pride is not misplaced can be demonstrated by our high ratings in inspections, tests, and assigned missions.

The West Virginia Army National Guard today. An officer candidate learns to navigate at the state's military training facility at Camp Dawson, near Kingwood.

The West Virginia Army National Guard looks forward to the future with enthusiasm and a firm dedication to continued service to both our state and our country. Our members are proud to be a part of the oldest military organization with continuous service in the United States, and proud to serve their fellow West Virginians during emergencies and during our community projects.

Federal Mission of the West Virginia Army National Guard

The federal mission is to provide Reserve Components of the Army of the United States, trained and equipped, to defend critical areas of the United States against land, seaborne or airborne invasion;

To assist in the governing, mobilization and concentration of the remainder of the Reserve Forces of the Army of the United States; and to participate in all types of operations, both in the United States and overseas.

The President of the United States is our Commander-in-Chief during federal activation.

State Mission of the West Virginia Army National Guard

Our State mission is to provide organizations, trained and equipped, to function when necessary in the protection of life and property, and the preservation of peace, order and public safety, as described by competent state authorities.

The Governor of West Virginia is our Commander-in-Chief during times of state active duty.

AUTHOR: Captain Kenneth Bailey

53-001-ST-WV-001-1997

A Good Life In West Virginia

My step-grandfather John Emelene married my grandmother before I was born, and was the only grandfather I knew. He came to America — for him the land of opportunity — from Yugoslavia. When his family entered the country, they shortened and Americanized their name. They settled in the coal mining community of Cannelton, where the men in the family worked in the mines every day, and everyone enjoyed their new, good lives in America. My greatest memories of my step-grandfather are how much he loved and enjoyed his grandchildren. He would always have ice cream for me when I came to visit. He enjoyed dancing and would not forget to dance with me, a ten year old child. His favorite song was *Don't Get Around Much Anymore*. He loved jazz and the blues. He was a handsome man, not very tall, but with dark hair and eyes. He had a charisma that drew friends and family to his side.

AUTHOR: Phyllis Williams Jarvis. Mrs. Jarvis is a social worker. She resides in her hometown of Hurricane. She is the mother of three sons, and two daughters, and is the grandmother of two.

54-001-ST-WV-001-1997

The Road To West Virginia

I found my home in West Virginia more than thirty years ago after traveling to a small Kanawha County town as a VISTA volunteer. Emmons is a small coal camp town deep in the West Virginia hills, and that journey has made all the difference in my life. West Virginians have continued to remind me every day about never giving up, about the value of working hard, and about cherishing family.

When Sharon and I started our own family — when John, Charles, Valerie, and Justin were born here— West Virginia gave us something more valuable than anything a parent can hope for. In West Virginia's embrace we found

Senator Jay Rockefeller, 1996.

a place to raise good, caring children. The West Virginia roots they put down have made them humble, dignified, hard working people. I am so very proud of them — and so very grateful to West Virginia for helping them grow into the kind of children a parent can look at beaming with pride.

West Virginia is perhaps the most beautiful state in this nation. I don't say that simply because West Virginia is blessed with abundant natural beauty — the rolling hills praised by skiers, the rivers and streams used for whitewater rafting and fishing, and the extraordinary wildflowers — but because of the people who live here.

Thirty years ago in Emmons, we organized our community. We built a library. We pulled down an abandoned schoolhouse in southern West Virginia, brought the boards back one by one to Emmons, and built a community center. We won a hard fight just to get the school bus to stop at Emmons.

But in the long run, the people of Emmons gave me so much more than I will ever be able to give them. I learned that success is measured in lives changed for the better, and not by a bank account or a listing in Who's Who. I learned that true character means rising above adversity and never losing heart.

I came to West Virginia thirty years ago filled with idealism to try and help. I came here with the advice of my family ringing in my ears: Get busy and make a difference.

I am here today having learned from West Virginia so much more: That no place on earth respects hard work more than this state; that no people have a greater work ethic or sense of pride; and that having a family and friends along to help you in your work is the greatest reward.

AUTHOR: *Senator Jay Rockefeller. Senator Rockefeller was West Virginia's Governor from 1977-1985. He was elected to the US Senate in 1984, where he still serves.*

55-001-ST-WV-001-1997

Paw Paw

Paw Paw I can't begin to explain my respect for you,
The only father figure I had was definitely you.
You treated me better than I ever deserved,
You showed me a man who used actions, not words.

I know sometimes it was hard to have a grandson like me.
I was a barrel of trouble, but your love always came free.
I want you to know that it's my life test,
To be like my Paw Paw and earn his respect.

I hope that one day I'm half the man you are,
That would be a great feat, because few go so far.

I love you, and thank you, and hope deep inside,
That when I have children that I'll have the pride,
The oomph and the gumption and surely the prowess,
to be like my Paw Paw, the man of the house.

William "Trippe" and Missy Carpenter McKeny with daughter Kaylee Jane, the first great-grandchild of Bada Lee Garten and Ralph Ranson Parkins.

Ralph Ranson Parkins and all his grandsons.

AUTHOR: *William T. McKeny. This poem was written in July, 1995, for Ralph Ranson Parkins, and was read at his funeral in November, 1995. William is the oldest grandchild of Ralph and Bada Lee Garten Parkins. William's mother, Barbara Parkins Mallett, wrote the following narrative.*

56-001-ST-WV-001-1997

Triplett

estled between two rolling hillsides of Braxton County sits the tiny two-room house in which my mother was raised. We used to visit my grandmother there. I can remember my sisters and I watching Grandma pack a picnic lunch that would enable us to leave the house and go wandering into the fields. We'd find a suitable spot to eat and listen to Grandma tell us about the creatures that kept her company or stories that the mail carrier had shared about local goings-on. After Grandma passed away we continued to go to Triplett. Grandma's little house became our "camp" and we went there several times each year.

I remember such wonderful times there: picking blackberries for Mom's homemade cobblers, learning to shoot Dad's twenty-two, fishing and swimming where we took our baths, and spending family time where there was no television or radio.

The only neighbors within walking distance were Uncle Letcher and Aunt Annie who lived in the old Stonestreet homestead. We'd wander down the dirt road a couple of times a day to visit. Uncle Letcher would sing silly songs to us, chase us around the cellar, and Aunt Annie would laugh and say, "Now Letch don't be too hard on them younguns!"

Through the years the memories accumulated. Mom and Dad would ask us if we wanted to go to the beach or to camp, and we would choose the camp. Unbelievable, isn't it? The mere waves of the Atlantic Ocean were no comparison to the simple pleasures of riding horses and sliding down a waterfall in an old swimsuit until the bottom was gone.

Some grandchildren of Ralph Ranson and Bada Lee Garten Parkins. Back row, (L-R), Dustin Brock Withrow, James Ranson Cox, Benjamin Dorsey Cox, Chantil Lee McKeny, Stephen William Cox, Bada Lee Garten Parkins. Front row (L-R), Kara Beth Withrow, Krista Jean Withrow, Andrew Taylor Cox.

In junior high school I learned about the threat of Communism and about bomb shelters. I never worried about Cuba or Russia. I knew that I could hide out on Triplett and be safe from harm.

In 1967 my boyfriend spent his last week of freedom with us there before going to the Army. When he returned from Germany we spent our honeymoon on Triplett and named our first child William "Trippe" McKeny in its honor. When my husband was killed four years later I found myself driving the familiar winding road just to glimpse the old place again.

Over the years in the fall and spring a restlessness comes over me that does not quiet until I have returned there. Our extended family would try to make an annual pilgrimage to Triplett in the fall so that the grandkids could share a "piece" of Triplett with us as we roasted wieners over a campfire and told stories about our many visits there.

Dad died last year. No more jokes about him marrying the Braxton County Monster. We

Triplett Cabin, Braxton County. Home of Bada Lee Garten Parkins and Leatha Stonestreet Carroll.

skipped our annual fall family gathering, but Triplett called and each of us girls went up at least once.

We attended a reunion of Uncle Letcher and Aunt Annie's family near there this summer and drove out to sit a spell.

My sisters Beth and Bevy and I have all carried some pieces of Triplett away with us. If you look, you'll find them in Beth's flower garden (the flat rock that served as a porch step), or in Bevy's picture frame (formerly the main room windowsill), or in the boards on my dining room wall. But the real "pieces" of Triplett we carry in our hearts, and when we close our eyes and hear a whippoorwill we can be there still.

AUTHOR: Barbara Parkins Mallett. Barbara is a fifth grade teacher at Rock Branch Elementary School in Putnam County. She is the mother of two and grandmother of one. Her parents were Bada Lee Garten Parkins and Ralph Ranson Parkins of Paradise.

57-001-ST-WV-001-1997

A Rich Heritage

My children have the richest heritage in the world. From their family tree they can select any exciting character they desire. Some of their great-great-grandfathers were timbermen in Greenbrier, Nicholas, and Webster Counties. One picture published in the local newspaper was John L. Webb lying in the fork of a large hemlock tree. The lumber was used in building the Titanic. Some of Mr. Webb's relatives were Cherokees and were hidden on a mountain by a white man during the Trail of Tears march.

My children have enjoyed hearing these stories all of their lives. They have heard about small communities like Puzzle Hole, Booger Hole, and the Forks of Elk, and how their great-great-grandfather lost his farm in Crupperneck because he didn't have a proper deed. This same man raised bees and herbs, skills he learned from the Native Americans.

Their grandmother Daisy Goff told of working in a hotel dining room in Webster Springs, and riding a horse down Elk to her home on the weekends. Their grandfather Ralph Williams writes for a local newspaper, and also wrote a book about his life in West Virginia. His life revolved around the railroad, and he is now honorary conductor of the caboose museum in Hurricane.

Yes, there remain some unanswered questions about the family, such as who shot the sheriff of a nearby county. We know who served a prison term for the murder, but who was really guilty? Was another ancestor's father a Shawnee chief? What part did tobacco play in an Indian capture? My children will now pass these stories down to their children, who will know what it is to be a true West Virginia Mountaineer.

AUTHOR: Phyllis Williams Jarvis. Mrs. Jarvis is a social worker. She resides in her hometown of Hurricane. She is the mother of three sons, and two daughters, and is the grandmother of two.

58-001-ST-WV-001-1997

A Gift Of Remembrance

Tucked among the hills of southern West Virginia is a small cemetery lovingly maintained by its family. Here lie mother, father, brother, sister, aunt, and uncle, family for almost two hundred years. At this site, two sisters with all their families first set foot on their promised land. Hope, promise, fear followed each pathway until these families finally reached their western destination.

The sisters, Nancy Lillard Bryan and Elizabeth Lillard Yates of Culpepper County, first looked across Mud River from this bluff in 1826. They kept their families in the same house through the terrible winter and cradled a new child in their arms. When spring arrived, Nancy and her family trekked northwest to settle in Mason County, but sister Elizabeth remained at "Yatesmont" in Cabell County, Virginia.

The old home place and cemetery could have fallen in ruin as most of the neighboring sites did, but from this branch sprang the famous William Cullen Bryan. He remembered his history and gathered the lonely tombstones to this site where the sisters had known their first joy of a home of their own. William Cullen Bryan encouraged his family to remember and honor their ancestors by setting stones that recorded the facts of their lives. Today, this beautiful "gift of remembrance" is maintained by a loving family beside the old homestead out a little known lane in Cabell County.

AUTHOR: Carrie Eldridge

59-001-ST-WV-001-1997

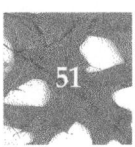

My Father, The Teacher

My family lived on Big Cabell Creek in rural Cabell County, West Virginia, the first year I attended school. I went to Upper Cabell School (one room), located about one and one-half miles from my home. My father Clyde Yoho, Sr. was the teacher. He rode horseback with me riding behind him. Ralph and Ted Caldwell lived nearby. Ralph was my age and Ted about a year older. I guess Dad had all three of us on the horse with him most of the time.

My father's teaching methods might not be approved in today's classroom. He was a strict disciplinarian and the punishment he utilized would be considered too harsh. One example occurred when a daughter of one of the school trustees was told to draw a small circle on the blackboard and stand with her nose in the circle. The next day Dad looked out the window and saw Mr. Jasper Dailey, the father of the girl, coming toward the school with a shotgun. Dad thought that real trouble lay ahead.

Mr. Dailey entered the room without knocking and Dad said, "Students, here is Mr. Dailey, our trustee. We will have him give his opinion on the subject we are discussing, current events."

Mr. Dailey sat his shotgun in a corner, removed his coat and hat, hung them on the peg on the wall, and proceeded to make a talk on the topic that the eighth grade had been studying. When he finished his talk, Mr. Dailey looked at his watch and told Dad that it was almost recess time, would he dismiss the students so they could have a private discussion?

Dad did as requested, thinking that he was going to *get it now!* To his surprise, Mr. Dailey congratulated him on his teaching, particularly the discipline he maintained in school.

At that time people hunted to supplement their larder with wild game. Mr. Dailey had brought his gun to hunt along the road on the way to visit school.

Front row (L-R), Everette Poston, Basil Poston, Haze Blake, Ivan Miller, Ferrell McCormick, Clarence Martin, Gertrude Martin, Alma Rose, Jessie McComas, and Ollie Martin. Second row (L-R), Russel Notter, Howard Martin, Jim Blake, Wilford Poston, Tom Nottingham, Lizzie McComas, Bertha Blake, and Gladys McCormick. Third row (L-R), Julia McComas, Elva Chapman, Lea Poar, Teacher Clyde Yoho, Ella Webb, Commie Dailey, Grace Poston, Lowell Nottingham, Ethel Dailey, Ruth McComas, and Anna Webb.

AUTHOR: *Denver C. Yoho. Mr. Yoho was born June 1, 1913, in Ona, Cabell County, and currently lives in Gallipolis, Ohio. His father Clyde Yoho taught school between 1911 and 1919.*

60-001-ST-WV-001-1997

Chapter 5

Mountain Lakes

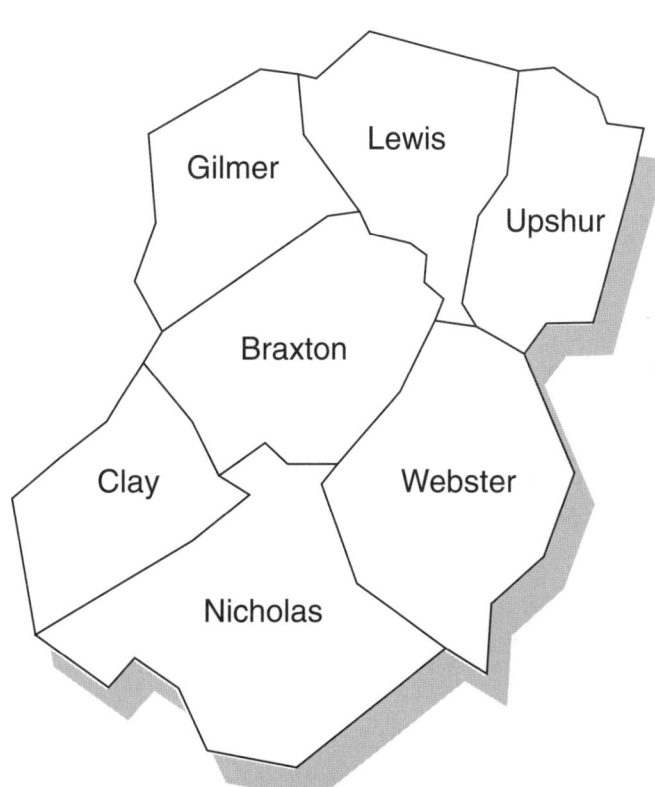

CHAPTER 5: MOUNTAIN LAKES

Job's Temple Homecoming

Growing up in West Virginia leaves a mark on your soul forever. Something special happens during those early years, described by a dear aunt of mine as "magical." Many, including myself, leave West Virginia for several reasons — economic, family, education, or military service. Maybe we are following Rudyard Kipling's advice, as he wrote:

Job's Temple, a Civil War era log church near Glenville.

Something hidden. Go and find it.
Go and look behind the Ranges —
Something lost behind the Ranges.
Lost and waiting for you…GO!
— The Explorer, Stanza 2

But, whatever the particular reason for leaving, none of us ever seems to forget our heritage and we return as often as possible.

This year during Homecoming '96, I had the pleasure of being invited as guest speaker at the fifty-eighth annual homecoming at historic Job's Temple, a Civil War era log church located at DeKalb, near Glenville. Construction on the church started shortly before the Civil War and was finished after the war ended in 1865. During this time, West Virginia had become the thirty-fifth state. The church and grounds have been maintained by the Job's Temple Association, of which I am honored to be the Secretary. The church is listed on the National Register of Historic Places.

My grandmother Ella Woofter Maxwell, and her cousin Lona Woofter, started a modest movement in 1934 to restore and save this valuable asset. Both had attended services there in their youth. The first homecoming was in 1936, which I attended as a small child. It has taken place every year since on the second Sunday in August, except for three years because of wartime gasoline rationing.

The invited speakers have been from various backgrounds and their speeches have covered many subjects. Robert C. Byrd spoke on four occasions, in 1958 as a Congressman, and as a US Senator in 1975, 1976, and 1986. Senator Jennings Randolph spoke in 1974 and came by helicopter, landing in a nearby field.

In 1996, 100 people from West Virginia and a variety of other states gathered once again to worship in this historic church as many of their friends and family had done before them. This annual gathering highlights what is so special about West Virginia — family, home and community.

As is the custom, the day was closed with a benediction and the group joining together in singing *God Be With You*. As the sounds flowed through the beautiful hills and the river valley below, it was clear that this had indeed been a very special homecoming for all of us.

AUTHOR: Charles E. Arbanas. Mr. Arbanas is a Weston native, who resides at Fairfax, Virginia. He spent many happy days at the DeKalb farm of his grandparents, the late Charles L. and Ella Woofter Maxwell.

61-001-ST-WV-001-1997

Samuel Bennett, Union Soldier, 1840-1930

The Bennett family of Ellis Fork in Tanner, was said to be one of the largest families in West Virginia. There were twenty-nine children born to Samuel and Annary Bennett, including six sets of twins. They ran out of names and called a pair Lyme and Juke, after the oxen. Other children had nicknames like Coop, Cart, Punt, Boo, Babe, Creet, Hamrocks, and Barsocks.

The Bennett farm developed into a prosperous livestock enterprise. The family worked the soil of 280 acres. The cellar was the "great

Mountain State Stories Of The People

Billy Bennett

provider," with large stone jars of kraut, pickled corn, pickled beans, kegs of molasses, cider and approximately 2,000 quarts of a variety of fruits, vegetables, jams, and jellies. They had the smokehouse for ham, mutton, and various meats. In the garden, potatoes and apples were placed in straw bins covered with mounds of dirt so as not to freeze during the winter months. Ice was cut from the streams and packed in sawdust for summer use.

The farms were self-supporting then, with all types of animals to produce the meat, eggs, and milk for food, and wool and hides for clothing. The farm also had a gristmill to make cornmeal for bread and cracked corn for animal food. There was a large flour mill in Tanner, a carding mill at the Fling place on Bull Fork, and a hat shop run by a Mr. Napier who came there from New York City.

The family traveled extensively, usually by train. The girls spent much time making dresses for the trips. The boys went to the St. Louis World's Fair in 1904. They took their fur and sold it. The total expense for three of them was forty dollars — three for train fare and fifteen to twenty-five cents per meal.

AUTHOR: Billy Bennett. Mr. Bennett is a retired Director of Transportation and Attendance for Gilmer County Schools, with thirty-five years of service. Samuel Bennett was his grandfather.

62-001-ST-WV-001-1997

Now I Am A Right-Handed Writer

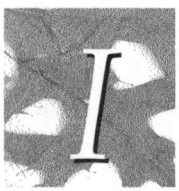

In September 1918, I was ready to attend a one-room school at DeKalb, West Virginia. Although past six years old, I was small for my age — sensitive, shy, and somewhat afraid — afraid because I had been told that the new teacher, Miss Brown, was very strict.

In my mind Miss Clara Brown met the description of a typical "school marm," with slightly gray hair worn in a bun, blue piercing eyes, narrow nose, thin willowish figure. She moved with grace and poise. The curving lines in her face seemed to be there to give her authority, dignity and purpose. But Miss Brown had a sweet understanding smile which gave me hope that she would accept me with all of my uncertainties. And even today I know where she seated me — front and on the girls' side — smallest desk just to her right. My feet did not reach the floor.

I was so proud of my new yellow pencil and my Goldenrod yellow, lined tablet. And so eager to use them. I got my chance. Writing lesson came early in the afternoon. We were to follow Miss Brown's instructions as she wrote the letters on the big slateboard — ABC. . . But soon she approached my desk and said softly, "Put your pencil in your other hand like this," showing me how to hold it. I was embarrassed. I did not know I was doing anything wrong. Suddenly I was aware that I was different from the others and had to have special help.

I tried with every muscle, nerve and will, to become a right-handed writer. With Miss Brown's help I did. She was patient with me. In every move I made, I wished to please her. I wanted to be in her favor, yet never sure of that. I so much wanted her to teach me to form my letters, as I struggled with an awkward approach.

Miss Brown taught me as she thought best and in keeping with the trend of the times. I am glad she did even though I will never know, in terms of present day thinking, what psychological damage may have been done. I accept that in whatever form.

Thank you, Miss Brown. I like being a right-handed writer.

AUTHOR: Eloise Davis Warfield. Mrs. Warfield began a teaching career in a one-room school near Parkersburg. She later became a librarian serving in Newark City Schools, Newark, Ohio, where she now resides.

63-001-ST-WV-001-1997

Have You Seen Icabod Crane Lately?

What would West Virginia be without ghost stories? Walking over those lonesome mountain trails at night listening to the mysterious sounds of nature interrupted by the fierce growl of a bobcat or even a panther might have been enough to scare some people plumb to death. But not my grandfather. He recalled walking home from his timber job in Braxton County over top of Crites Mountain.

"Sometimes it would be dark by the time I got back over the mountain from work. Crites

CHAPTER 5: MOUNTAIN LAKES

Down on the farm with Lafe and Belva Rhodes are Carla, Larry, and Terry Coffman, pictured in 1955.

Mountain got foggy, and there was nothing around for miles even in the daylight. One evening it was already dark, and foggy, too, up on top of that mountain as I was walking along back home when I heard a horse off at a distance. I looked back to see, but it was too dark. The horse was walking at a steady pace, and I wondered, who could that be? As the horse got closer I'd look back over my shoulder every once in awhile till I could see there was a man riding the horse. I could see he had a nice suit of clothes on, a white shirt and a tie. He never said anything so I kept looking till he got right up next to me, just a few feet to my side, and I saw that he didn't have any head. He looked perfectly normal, other than that. The horse walked on past me until they disappeared out of sight."

"Weren't you scared?!" I asked.

"Scared? Scared of what?" he'd say. "No, I wasn't scared. I saw him several times after that, and I was never scared. I ran like the dickens when I saw that panther, though."

"Did it catch you?" we'd ask.

"No, it didn't catch me. It chased me for a mile or more, but it never caught me."

"Then you were scared?" we'd say.

"Sure, I was scared. I ran like a *hant*."

AUTHOR: *Carla Coffman. This is a story Carla's great-uncle Lafe Rhodes used to tell. He and his wife Belva raised Carla's mother Mona, and lived in the hollow where Crites Mountain meets Carpenter's Fork.*

64-001-ST-WV-001-1997

Author's Note: "Hant" is in the dictionary under "haunt" with a separate pronunciation, meaning a regional reference to a ghost or other supernatural being. In this story, "hant" is used to mean (he ran) "supernaturally" (like a hant).

A Mother's Love

As a youngster born in the depression years, my early memories are those of my mother teaching me the ABCs, multiplication tables, and how to print my name.

Later I attended a one-room school. Students sat on seats with chair backs serving as the desk for the student seated behind them. There was a pot-bellied stove for heat, and in the winter we rotated around the room to keep warm. Water was kept in a big stone water jar with a spigot on the bottom. We made drinking cups by folding a sheet of paper. There were no inside facilities, so the teacher allowed one or two students at a time to go to the outhouse.

At recess we usually played baseball or longball. Sometimes in the winter we would go sleigh riding.

After I finished first grade, the teacher promoted me to the third. As the older students were reciting, those of us in other grades learned from them. The older students were also expected to help the younger ones with their recitations.

Of the three people in my eighth grade class, I was the only one to go to high school. I walked across the stage at Gassaway High School to get my diploma from grade school. Four years later, I walked the same stage to get my high school diploma.

Thanks to my mother, I was the first in my family to graduate from high school. She did housework for twenty-five cents a day to ensure that I was able to go. And although I only owned two dresses, she made sure that I had a clean one to wear each day.

AUTHOR: *Colene Heim. Colene is a housewife and retired Realtor. She is a Braxton County native and lives in St. Albans. She is the mother of five and grandmother of thirteen.*

65-001-ST-WV-001-1997

Blackberries And Bears

Growing up in the hills of West Virginia was quite an experience. Summers were a time when school was out, swimmin' holes were cool and full, and the blackberries were getting ripe.

Times were tough in the early 1960s. Money was scarce, very few folks had cars, fewer had televisions, and kids developed ways to earn money and entertain themselves. Exploring caves, swinging on grapevines, and getting to know the countryside were simply what youngsters did for pastimes.

Blackberries were plentiful and in ready demand by the older folks who couldn't pick them for themselves. I remember the summer of 1964 as clear as if it were yesterday. That summer I picked fifty-four gallons of juicy berries and sold them for fifty cents a gallon to buy school clothes for the next school year.

The best recollection I have, however, of berry picking is after I was married. My wife's grandpa, Pappy, and her brother and I decided to go berry picking. We searched over hill and dale for just the right patch. Finally, after a diligent search we came upon the biggest, most succulent blackberries I have ever seen.

We commenced this labor of love, filling our buckets to the brim with these luscious, wild fruits. Somehow, without knowing it, we became separated, with Pap and Terry going down the hill while I picked toward the top.

All of a sudden on the other side of this pine tree, I heard something riding down briars. "Hey Pap, got your bucket full?" I yelled. Not a sound. I picked on for a while. More thrashing came from beyond the tree. "Hey Pap, 'got your bucket full yet?" Still no reply.

I decided something must be wrong so I walked around to the other side of the tree and there stood what looked to be the biggest, meanest, and orneriest bear east of the Mississippi. She just looked at me with those big black eyes. Purple berry juice was dripping off of her chin.

Friends, let me tell you, I gave her that berry patch, bucket and all. I lit out for the house with all I had. Pap said later that when I went by him, my tennis shoes were smoking and my shirt-tail was sticking straight out behind me.

Author: James B. King
66-001-ST-WV-001-1997

Phillips Run, Nicholas County

North from Summersville, Nicholas County, via Route 119, the first road turning right, beyond the Memorial Park and the new Nicholas County High School, is a place called Phillips Run. My dad Wilbur Wade Taylor, my mother Iva Margaret (Campbell) Taylor, my sister Margaret Ann, and I moved to our farm there in 1932 — the year I was born. My family had lost their home and most of their belongings in the Fayette County, Paint Creek flood, July 10, 1932. Dad was working as a bookkeeper for a coal company there.

Nicholas County was home to both Dad and Mom. He was born in 1899 and grew up at Gad. Gad is gone now, the location under the waters of the Summersville Dam. Mom was born in 1898 and raised at Keslers Cross Lanes. She was teaching school when she met Dad and they married in 1924 at the Baptist Temple in Charleston.

I grew up at Phillips Run. We had no electricity, no telephone, no inside plumbing, and no central heat or air. What we did have were all the things we needed: oil lamps for light; a fireplace for warmth and a coal stove for cooking; vegetables to eat, can, and share; hogs for bacon, hams, and so forth; chickens for eggs and to eat; and beef also. Communication with relatives and friends was by letter or visits.

Phillips Run one room-school was one mile from our home. All the children walked to school, some farther than we did. We went first through eighth grade there, then on to four years at Nicholas County High School, now "Old Main" at Summersville.

The first family starting up Phillips Run, after you cross the "Big Bridge," was Booze and Gladys Butler and children Charles, Claude and Keith. Next was Joe and Pauline Hanna; Mark and Lora Hanna and children Mark Junior, Ruth, Jean and Roger; Bonnie and Lura Cavendish and children Charlotte and Patty; Oat and Hester Tyree and children Lee, Leslie, Lawrence, John, Lula, Lura and Leonard; Uncle Billy and Aunt Becky Fitzwater; George and Ella Chapman and children Lou, Irene, Chancy, Ruthfina and Peggy; Brantie and Hattie Carte and children Dana, Madaline, Lenora, Freida and Johnny. Our home was next. Then came Clay Wiblin's place; Frank and Artie Murphy and children Pat, Uldene, Mike, Ruth Ann, Judy and J.D.; Brent and Emma Monroe and children Marjorie, Lillian, Wilson, and twins Martha and Marie; Overbaugh; Thomas; Emmett and Marie Cottle and children Martin and Joe; Hugarts; Dennet and Rilla Cottle and children Bernard, Charles and David; Ed and Sarah Martha Tyree and children Owen, Charlie, Coleman and others; Spinks; Charlie and Pearl Brown and children Elva, Yeager, Robert, Snooky, Jimmy, and twins Eugene and Emogene; Workman; and Coulter.

I am so pleased to take this stroll down memory lane and to preserve these thoughts of my family and of our neighbors and friends at the place in Nicholas County called Phillips Run. We all lived there forty-fifty plus years ago. It was and always will be "HOME SWEET HOME."

Author: Mary Sue Taylor Cottle. Mary Sue married Bernard H. Cottle on November 12, 1953. She is the proud mother of Darlene, Brenda, Kim, and Kay, and the proud grandmother of Randy, Chad, Kimberly, Lauren, and Christopher.

67-001-ST-WV-001-1997

Our Family Strength

West Virginia was the birthplace of my seven brothers, one sister, and me. My father, a doctor in Nicholas County, provided material things, but it was my mother who provided our strength. She gave us a sense of self-esteem and encouraged our capabilities. In 1949, she was selected West Virginia Mother of the Year. At the birth of her first son Eugene, my grandmother said that my mother looked at him and said, "He's just the kind of baby I wanted," and so were the following eight babies.

Flavius Hugh Brown, Sr. College of Physicians and Surgeons, Baltimore, Maryland, 1911.

My father was away long hours; when not in his office in Summersville, he might be fording creeks in his Chevy (in earlier days, on horseback) making house calls. While he was away, it was Mama who calmed our fears and cured our ills. When her second son Dudley had Diphtheria, gasping for breath, he said, "Mama, hold me." She picked him up and carried him outside for more oxygen. He survived this dreaded disease. Flavius Jr., had Cholera Infantum. My father tearfully said, "Lizzy, I don't think he can make it." Mama replied, "Yes he will," and he did. My sister Libby had Whooping Cough when a baby. One night, with her crib rolled beside their bed, my father said, "How I wish I could do something!" Mama declared, "She will get well!" And by Mama's prayers and constant vigil, she did. I had Tonsillitis frequently when a child. The "Wonder Drug," as my father referred to Penicillin, was not yet available, so these infections left me frail with aching knees. My father brought home a bottle of thick, brown liquid he had labeled "Iron Medicine." My mother dissolved it in a glass of warm milk for me. But just sitting on her lap, with a warmed, woolen blanket tucked around my legs seemed all I needed.

Mama's gentle discipline consisted mostly of quoting old adages: "Waste not, want not"; "Don't judge a book by its cover"; and so forth. Or my father challenged us by reciting the poem "If" by Rudyard Kipling.

Four of my brothers became medical doctors and three were dentists. We were all college educated except my mother, yet her knowledge far exceeded ours. She was an avid reader, starting our family library when a bride of sixteen. Although raised in poverty, she had impeccable taste, from clothing to setting a table on fine damask. We learned much about nature from her reading to us from Gene Stratton-Porter's books and from our only card game *Authors*. I don't remember the poet, but I remember a line from a poem she often recited: "And each will make 'ere life has flown, a stumbling block or a steppingstone." She made a solid stepping stone shaped by determination, devotion, and love.

The Brown Family. Back row (L-R), Robert, William, Paul, Flavius, Jr., Morrison, Dudley, and Eugene. Front row (L-R), Alice Juergens, Elizabeth Jacobson, and Elizabeth Huff Brown.

AUTHOR: *Alice Brown Juergens. Alice Juergens lives in Morgantown and is the sole survivor of this Brown family.*

68-001-ST-WV-001-1997

Painful Lesson On Baptism

Grandmother Amick was the most disciplined Christian I have ever known; she was a staunch Presbyterian and a life-long charter member Presbyterian. My twin sister Mary and I followed behind her like little ducklings behind the Mother Duck.

As toddlers we had been baptized, a ceremony in which parents and congregation all promise optimistically to bring-up the newly enrolled infants in the "nurture and admonition of the Lord," a promise easier made than kept!

One Sunday Mary and I were invited by our neighbors, the Bostics, who were devout Baptists, to attend a church service with their children. We received parental consent and headed for the Baptist Church with our friends.

Staunch Presbyterian Grandmother Amick and friend Mrs. Tripplett. Photo taken around 1918.

The two-hour service included a baptism of several new members in the baptistery at the front of the church. Mary and I were enthralled. We had never seen an immersion baptism before, and the drama of it excited us.

The next time we took our baths together, which we did until we were five and started school, we went step-by-step through the baptismal ceremony we had observed, gravely intoning the charge: "I now baptize you in the name of the Father, Son, and Holy Ghost," and then putting each other under the water in the bathtub.

Twins Mary and Elizabeth with sister Sandy.

My grandmother, hearing this charge outside the bathroom door, burst into the room, snatched first one dripping twin, and then the other from the bath tub, and spanked each of us soundly on our bare, wet behinds. She was not shocked at our espousal of immersion, but at the thought of her grandchildren being sacrilegious by not respecting a religious ceremony of another Christian community. It did us no good to try to explain that we were fascinated by the drama — how could we at age five? We learned discretion and reverence the hard way.

AUTHOR: *Elizabeth Murray Deitz. Mrs. Deitz is a retired school teacher and principal. She lives in Richwood, where she remains a "sprinkled" Presbyterian. Mary eventually joined a church which required baptism by immersion.*

69-001-ST-WV-001-1997

Molasses Makin'

If a family planted a field of sugar cane, often during autumn, molasses would be made. But before the process could begin, the cane needed to be bladed, so stalks were cut and gathered. A cane mill crushed sugary juice from the stalks, as it drained into a bucket. A horse hitched to the mill provided the power source. The green juice was strained twice through clean cotton cloth.

Preparation of the firepit and pan took several days. The firepit was dug and lined with stones. One end was open so wood could be added; smoke exited the other end. The pan was made out of a piece of tin with wooden sides. The pan was six feet long, three feet wide, and averaged six inches deep. The pan fit over the firepit and mud was packed around the edges to ensure the heat from the fire did not escape.

The surface of the boiling liquid was skimmed constantly. Skimmings were discarded into a hole dug for this purpose. Tasting the skimmings while greenish definitely made you

Chapter 5: Mountain Lakes

sick. When the skimmings were warm golden brown, the molasses was ready. Just before the molasses was taken off and placed in bottles, everyone tasted the delicious finished product.

This process usually started about dawn and lasted late into the night. With the hot fire, the juice boiled, and slowly the liquid began to evaporate. It eventually became molasses. It was quite a time consuming process.

It usually took a family several days to work up the molasses from the field of cane they had planted. At times, several families would combine their efforts, and then everyone would share the delicious rewards. In the blustery cold of winter, molasses always tasted mighty fine on hot biscuits.

Author: Patricia Samples Workman. Although born in California, Patricia's family members are all native West Virginians. She has lived in the state for thirty years. Her husband's family has made molasses since he was a young child in the 1920s. They choose to continue to use the older method, as opposed to using the new aluminum pans with compartments.

70-001-ST-WV-001-1997

Phyllis Hinkle, Steve Bryant, Emma Bryant, and Ken Bryant.

Birthday Home

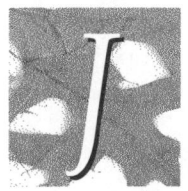January 31, 1996, was a special time for Emma Wiseman Bryant of Canvas, West Virginia, celebrating her eighty-sixth birthday in the log home where she was born. Emma is the daughter of the late Bowling and Anna Wiseman. They were living with Mr. Wiseman's father at the time Emma was born. The log cabin had housed thirteen children.

Log home of John Wiseman. Birthplace of Emma Bryant, Canvas, West Virginia.

Taking time off from his contractor work and farming, Steven restored the log house on the H.A. Huffman farm, Wady Feiran, in Mt. Nebo, where he resides. Memorabilia now fills the cabin, bringing back recollections of the Wiseman, Bryant, Champe, and Huffman families of the area.

Several friends and family were present for the celebration including three of Emma's six children, Ken, Steve, and Phyllis Hinkle. Also attending was Emma's sister Frances Morris. The cabin was filled with happiness by those present sharing stories, photographs, and memories of the past.

Author: Nancy A. Huffman Bryant. Nancy is a Nicholas County teacher of thirty years. She is the daughter of the late Carrie Jo (Champe) and Henry A. Huffman. She is married to Steven Bryant, and they have one daughter, Suzanne, who is a registered nurse.

71-001-ST-WV-001-1997

Emma Bryant and Frances Morris.

Emma's son Steven discovered that the log home was being used as a barn on the Wiseman farm. He bought it, tore it down, and moved it.

Old Treasure Trunk

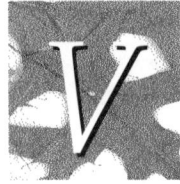

Visitors to my home often comment on the small trunk sitting in the hall. It's similar to many I've seen, but in better repair than most. The hammered metal vines twining around the top and sides are still in good relief, bright red against a gold background. It belonged to my mother's paternal grandmother, Kate Kirtley Harbour, whose family has lived in Cabell and Putnam Counties of West Virginia since the 1680s.

When my mother and I first removed the trunk from an aunt's attic, we found some remnants of her grandmother's time — several handfuls of Confederate money. Whether these were an indication of the woman's sympathies could only be surmised. In West Virginia you can never be sure!

Clarice "Kate" Kirtley Harbour (b. July 28, 1851, d. May 1, 1919).

The trunk, itself a thread of my history, now contains objects that have become personal totems for me. They evoke connections, rootedness. There is a delicate ebony-wood rosary which belonged to my great-great-grandmother Frances Huber Kiefer. I can only guess the details of her life, but perhaps the rosary comforted her during her trans-Atlantic voyage when she left Bavaria in the mid-1800s. The almost glassy slickness of the beads tells me she was a woman of prayer.

A shiny silver dollar is there, one of a dozen my grandfather J.T. Warren gave me. Interested in my progress at Kanawha City Elementary, he offered the silver dollars as a bribe: one for every "A" on my report card. During my teen years when I was likely to spend any money I had, I never parted with those silver dollars. I knew somehow the contest had been devised because "Scoop" wanted me to have them.

And then there's a pair of white ladies' gloves — the kind I used to hate wearing to church. They belonged to my grandmother, Isabelle Hanna "Izzy" Warren. One day in 1960, the democratic presidential candidate John F. Kennedy was meeting folks in a restaurant parking lot in Charleston. Izzy and my Aunt Dot joined the crowd, but Scoop, who suffered from emphysema, had to wait in the car. Izzy expressed her support, and told Kennedy my grandfather regretted his inability to greet him personally. The candidate then made his way through the crowd to their car to shake Scoop's hand, and Izzy's gloved one. She was so favorably impressed by this kindness, she put the gloves away and never wore them again.

AUTHOR: Carol Warren. Carol is a religious educator and writer living in Webster County with her husband Todd Garland, and daughter Joy. She is a native of Charleston.

72-001-ST-WV-001-1997

Rich In History — Rich In People — Richwood

The City of Richwood has many nicknames, all of them very appropriate. Richwood was first dubbed "The City Merry on the Banks of the Cherry." This referred to the fact that the Cherry River cuts a path through the city. In fact, the city itself was incorporated in 1901, after the establishment of the "Big Mill," the Cherry River Boom and Lumber Company, built where the north and south forks of the Cherry join. That mill, now owned by Georgia-Pacific Corporation, continues to operate and is the longest continuously operating sawmill in the entire state of West Virginia.

Mill owners saw that houses were built for the workers who poured into this virtual wilderness that would soon become a thriving metropolis due to the vast supply of virgin timber that grew on the mountains that surrounded the valley. True, there had long been a small settlement on Hinkle Mountain, some eight miles north of this fertile valley, but with the opening of the Big Mill came progress that included, in addition to this lumber mill that was one of the largest east of the Mississippi, the world's largest clothespin factory, one of the largest paper mills and tanneries in the nation, and other smaller, wood-related businesses. Soon the former settlement of "Cherry Tree Bottoms" became "Richwood."

Richwood is also known as the "Eastern Gateway to the Monongahela." The entrance to this National Forest is literally at Richwood's doorstep. The scenic beauty offered here is beyond compare and recreational opportunities abound. One of the best trout streams in the East, the Cranberry River, alone attracts thousands of anglers annually. Mountain trails accommodate bikers, hikers, hunters, Nordic skiers, along with many naturalists and

CHAPTER 5: MOUNTAIN LAKES

Richwood's fun-loving Cherry River Navy Admirals don their stripes, side bar giant clothespins, and sleeve epaulettes before climbing aboard their flagship, Mopswab, on Navy Day Maneuvers at the annual Cherry River Festival. True to every sailor's motto, there is a pretty girl in this port of call! This time around it is Miss USA who happens to be in town for the festivities.

botanists, attracted to such spots as the fabled Cranberry Glades.

With tongue firmly in cheek, Richwood touts itself to be "The Ramp Capital of the World." For those unfamiliar with the lowly ramp, a wild onion-like delicacy that grows in profusion in the area, one whiff is all that is needed to educate the curious drawn to the "Feast of the Ramson." After dining, that distinct, though unbelievable odor that is the ramp's claim to fame, remains on the breath of the partaker for days. It is this mystique of the ramp that makes Richwood a bustling community for one day in April. This "Feast" is just one of many special annual events staged with an eye towards tourism.

The moniker "Home Port of the Cherry River Navy" also has special significance and dates to 1937, when a group of men formed a dry-land Navy, composed of a fleet of Admirals, hoping to draw attention to the need for a paved road over Kennison Mountain. The Richwood of that day found itself in danger of becoming a ghost town as the virgin timber had been cut, and all except the Big Mill had abandoned the local work force. There was no paved road east of Richwood on the twenty-three miles that connected the city with points east. To stimulate business, this "missing link" had to be paved and so the Navy was formed.

Indeed, the road was paved, the Navy still holds maneuvers at the week-long Cherry River Festival, and the city has survived in spite of a steady decline in population that continues today. However, the people who have remained are a loyal, hardworking class of Mountaineers. Such distinguished gentlemen as the late Ed Buck, an authority on wildcats and a volunteer fireman known throughout the land, a hunter and trapper, and a friend of rattlesnakes; Sterling Spencer, a naturalist and woodcarver supreme; and Jim Comstock, founder of the *West Virginia Hillbilly* and the foremost authority on the history of the Mountain State; have all made outstanding contributions to the survival of Richwood. Modern-day, community-minded citizens such as Bruce Donaldson who almost single-handedly worked to achieve a Rails-to-Trails project for Richwood; Maria Dooley who works diligently on every special event and project in the community; and Mike Hewitt and Bronson McClung who continue to work on bringing jobs to Richwood, casting off disappointment after disappointment; have accepted the reigns passed-on by these pioneers.

Richwood will survive. Perhaps a new nickname should be "The Little City That Tries," for certainly the hearty Mountaineers who live in Richwood can never be accused of giving-up on any project that is proposed. The residents saved their hospital from bankruptcy through community cooperation. They support their library, fire department and schools. Richwood is indeed a community of volunteers, working together to assure the City of Richwood never vanishes. That is as it should be, for ultimately it is the people who ARE the heart and soul of any community.

AUTHOR: Maxine Corbett. A native of Pennsylvania, Maxine found a paradise in Richwood at age twelve and never left. She works as a news reporter and secretary for the local Chamber of Commerce.

73-001-ST-WV-001-1997

A Lasting Paradise

Many West Virginia communities have an "ol' swimming hole" but few, if any, are as memorable as "The Falls" located on Cherry River on the outskirts of Richwood. With few houses located to the east, the water here is as pure as it gets in modern-day times.

The intake for the municipal water supply is located just above the swimming hole. Water rushes over the dam there, causing twin cascading rapids on either side of a rock formation that appears to have been created by God for the express purpose of sunbathing.

The Falls is sheltered from noise but not totally isolated. It is indeed a place to dream. Birds serenade the visitor in the lazy summer sun. Often hawks fly overhead, their wings dipping in hasty recognition. A rabbit nibbles on a blade of grass and a groundhog scampers at the approach of a human. Butterflies frolic around a stray, tiny, isolated water hole.

A log becomes a Loch Ness monster to an imaginative swimmer enjoying a dip at the Falls of Cherry River.

The water itself hums a soothing lullaby. There is no problem that cannot be solved, no irritation that cannot be forgotten on a sunny afternoon in this isolated paradise. The water is never warm no matter how hot the day. It seems made by God to refresh those weary of everyday living. Those who swim are rewarded with a refreshing new outlook on life.

It is the children who reap the most benefit here. The idle days of summer pass all too quickly. A child gains new confidence because he learned to swim. Another child delights in finding a fish, albeit a mud sucker, on the end of his pole. A roller coaster ride down the far rapids on a make-shift innertube raft, delights but also frightens those brave enough to try, while the family dog races the rocks and barks furiously at the danger sensed.

On one idle summer day, yet another child discovers a mystery of Mother Nature as he spies a water dog for the first time. This creature is crawl-swimming in shallow water, the sun's reflection making the mermaid tail seem flecked with gold, and for a moment, this ugly creature with the tiny feet and face so like a pug-dog's features, become almost beautiful.

On the last day of summer, that same child uses a paper cup to explore, and finds a tiny creature that is not the usual minnow but instead a tiny, baby water dog. The cycle of nature is complete when the boy lovingly places the baby back in the stream, hoping it will survive a harsh winter and await his first visit next May as yet another summer at The Falls begins.

My sons and grandson, their cousins, and other assorted friends and relatives, have been afforded the privilege of growing-up on the banks of the Cherry River. This spot in West Virginia hides a paradise of treasures that will be discovered and enjoyed for the ages, preserved in pristine splendor, waiting to be discovered by yet another child of nature long after those who love The Falls "best" have passed on.

Author: Maxine Corbett

74-001-ST-WV-001-1997

CHAPTER 5: MOUNTAIN LAKES

The Schoolteacher

It was hard to believe that death had come to this kind, considerate, intelligent man who had been so many things to me throughout my life. He was one of a particular kind, a teacher in a one-room rural school.

Don Lowe believed English grammar to be the most important subject he taught, as the following excerpt from a 1915 report written by Supervisor B. White of the Lewis County schools states.

The Schoolteacher Don Lowe.

"...Another trolley ride left us at a station about half a mile from the Butchersville school taught by Don Lowe. Like the Jordansville property at the beginning of school, this house was in bad condition, but both houses have been repaired and painted. Mr. Lowe, in his interesting school, is teaching good old-fashioned English grammar, a task difficult of performance with the textbook in use. The people down there are much pleased with improvements already made, and with the progress of the school. In some schools much time is lost by interruption while the teacher is conducting recitations. This is not true at Butchersville this year..."

I stood looking at him as he lay in his casket. Instead of this beautiful suit, he should be wearing an old one, worn shiny. His pipe, if not in his mouth, should at least be visibly sticking out of his breast pocket. I thought of how he would sometimes blow warm smoke from his pipe into the ear of a child crying with an earache. It always eased the pain.

He fostered in his students discipline, a competitive spirit, and an interest in politics and government. Reading was his favorite activity. He was ahead of his time, possessing a strong belief in the separation of religion and state and a desire for year-round schooling. He'd personally known characters like Jack Dempsey's father, and "Devil" Anse Hatfield, and he shared stories with us each week during "entertainment" period.

I only heard him speak of death once. And now it had happened to him. Smiling through tears, I could imagine this beloved teacher lining up the little angels in his new classroom.

I knew I'd have to leave soon. He wouldn't want me to cry, for any display of emotion tended to embarrass him. Saying softly, "Good-bye, Dad," I went outside to my waiting husband and sons.

AUTHOR: Mildred Marshall. Mrs. Marshall is a native West Virginian. She has received many creative writing awards, and in 1995 was honored with the West Virginia Celebrate Women award in the category of Labor.

75-001-ST-WV-001-1997

Love Created This Community

West Virginia is a unique and unusual place. I believe this status exists because it took struggle to create, mold, and build our state. Struggle builds character and character begets love.

This is our heritage — struggle, character, and love. We do not have a need to struggle as we once did, but hopefully we still have character and love. Perhaps, remembering how it was, the struggle, and how it built character, will give us more strength of character, and more insight into the decisions we make and help us to better project love into these decisions. Therefore, I would like to retell a story that I wrote in March of 1994 about Tanner life. Tanner is a community in the DeKalb District of Gilmer County. The DeKalb District created a high school at Tanner in 1925 which at first met in a church, then in an old store building, the Barnes Building, and in 1929, a building was built to house the school. In 1962, this school closed as a high school, and it closed as an elementary in 1988. I attended school there from 1940 to 1952, and I taught there from 1979 to 1988.

This story is simply a retelling of the great love that created this community and this school, and I believe that this story can be projected into every community in West Virginia by just changing the names, because our state was founded on love and freedom — real freedom for mankind.

Memories of Tanner Life

The flow of the years takes on the taste of the ages and only the good remains, because love outlasts every other feeling there ever was. When we close our eyes and sit really quietly, we can feel all this goodness that was Tanner School and Tanner life, and we know that it is not gone and

it will never be gone as long as one memory remains of what was.

How does one explain the loving and the caring that was life in this school community and make others feel it as we felt it or live it as we lived it?

When did the deep caring start? It started when our ancestors came to America and moved into these backwoods and had to really depend on each other for survival. All people seemed to become equal — the wealthy and the poor — for survival was the name of the game. In the Tanner community this closeness lasted much longer than elsewhere, perhaps, because we always seemed to be the last to get so many things. We were the last first-class high school in the state to get paved roads (*Gilco*, March 1935), the last high school in Gilmer County to get a school bus (*Gilco*, Fall 1936), the last high school in the county to get typewriters (Betty Wright, first Business teacher 1953-1960), etc. We were often thought of as the step-child. But if we were without many material objects, there was one precious commodity we were not without and that was love.

As a student in the 1940s and early 1950s, I saw how love decorated our stage at each junior and senior play as Mrs. Asa V. Cooper (Reta) loaned us her living room furniture. Reta Cooper also played the piano for the musical Christmas programs. Love sewed the costumes for the *many* elementary stage productions; names that come to mind are: Rugie Fling McGee; Mrs. Clarence Cunningham (Marie); Mrs. Roscoe Webster (Olive); Mrs. Harry Robinson (Anne); Mrs. Earl Hardman (Elizabeth); Mrs. George B. Riddle (Aunt Ada); and Hallie Wilson. Community love cooked the food for the Junior and Senior Banquets each year. Love called our softball and baseball games (Hall Wilson and Gail Wilt) on a field donated to the school system by the love of Lyde and George B. Riddle. Love gave kids a place to stay before home basketball games, and love fed these kids. (Here one could name any family living close to the school.) I remember soup at 4:00 in the lunch room served by the cooks before away basketball games. The love of the coach and principal saw that the players and cheerleaders got home after away basketball games. Love gave kids a place to sleep when they needed to stay over. I immediately think of Doc and Gertrude Bush and the corn bread they had every evening for supper, and the open doors of Tom and Joe Loudin, Gail and Mable Wilt, and Bill and Mable Mahaney. Mable Wilt and Mable Mahaney never knew for how many they were cooking supper or breakfast.

Love fed the basketball teams and cheerleaders after away basketball games. I was fed after *every* away basketball game for five years. Among those who fed us were: Carl (Doc) Bush, Avon Ellyson, Grant Greynolds, and principals placing money made on sports back into building young people. As well-fed children, we felt very loved, and love perpetuates love. (In 1983, Gilmer County High School Girls' Track Team won the State Championship. I took these girls and their

"Memories of Tanner Life." Tanner High School

coach Janet James to dinner in Clarksburg. After dinner they asked me, "Mrs. Radabaugh, why did you do this?" I said, "Because someone did this for me.")

Love also made our cheerleading uniforms: Elma Jean Woofter, our Home-Economics teacher and Janis Maxwell (Martin), my sister. And love, in the name of Lyde Riddle, supplied vehicles for transportation to sports events before the days of the school bus. Love kept a quiet hall, as Asa Hardman, our janitor, donated a box of candy each month to the classroom of students who walked the quietest in the halls.

How many boys could say, "Billy Bennett bought my basketball shoes," or how many girls could say, "Mrs. Zillah Hare, my Home-Economics teacher, bought my first glasses," or "she made it possible for me to attend high school," or how

CHAPTER 5: MOUNTAIN LAKES

many boys could say they graduated in a suit furnished by J. Therin Rogers, Principal, and how many students could say Bill and Audrey Cunningham gave them articles of clothing from their store? How many sick kids were bedded down under Reta Cooper's loving care in her home? How many remember the sports banquet of 1952 given by Gladys Frymier at her home on Bull Fork? How many remember the recesses at Tanner School where the teachers seemed to have built-in springs that never ran down. Mrs. J. Leo Riddle (Lucille) had one of the most durable springs, leading her students in ring games or playing basketball or softball with them at *every* recess. It's her laugh as she raised her arms and attempted to make the basket that I remember most. (I am sure angels look and laugh like this after a visit to earth when they lift their arms and fly away to Heaven again.)

Here I must insert a paragraph by Marge Waggy Lewellen, for it explains Tanner people and West Virginia people in general better than I ever could.

"Asa Cooper was a favorite teacher and was principal when I graduated. Our class of ten was the smallest one up to that time (1954). I was Valedictorian and got a scholarship to Glenville State. However, due to the combined efforts of Asa Cooper, Joe Gluck (who was commencement speaker), and Dr. Patrick Gainer of the Tanner community and instructor at West Virginia University, I ended up going to WVU. Joe helped me get a scholarship and Pat found a place for me to live in Morgantown with the Brawners. Dr. Brawner was head of the English Department. The Brawners became my second parents, since they had no children of their own, and when I married Steve Lewellen, they gave me my wedding. Our sons, Kevin and David, became their grandchildren. There is an interesting afterthought to all this. Dr. Brawner died 1984 and the English Department at the University has just published (1986) a memorial book to him using some of his writings and tributes written by several of his many friends. It was rather strange for me to read the one written by Dr. Harry B. Heflin. He tells of his first contact with Dr. Brawner when he (Dr. Heflin) was president of Glenville State College and an honor student had been awarded a scholarship to the college. Then he was notified a few weeks later that she could not accept it because she had been awarded a scholarship to WVU. He was concerned that she was being led to enroll where a complete lack of home support would surely cause her to drop out of school because of so many extra expenses. It was not until years later when Dr. Heflin became president of WVU that he learned she had been taken into the home of the Brawners to become the daughter they never had." (Tanner High School Alumni Association Newsletter, No. 47, Spring 1987, with permission.)

Our family of "parents" extended far beyond ourselves in time and personality, and they too loved us, fed us, and cheered us on. Back in 1928, Nate Rohrbough, Coach of Glenville Normal School (high school and college-level students) gave Tanner School the Normal School's old football equipment and football uniforms to help Tanner start a football team; however, although Nate's Normal School team played J. Therin Roger's Tanner team five times that season, those football jerseys worn by the Tanner Bulldogs remained undefeated. Nate Rohrbough loved this! This was a game in which he could not lose, for Nate was now the God-father of two football teams in Gilmer County. The Rohrboughs were among Gilmer County's great givers. Every Gilmer Countian for years and years has attended football games at Rohrbough Field in Glenville.

One should also mention here that Glenville Normal School is the present Glenville State College, and at the time of its beginning in 1872 as a Normal School, it was the means in this area of obtaining a high school degree, known as the Short Normal Course, as well as a college degree known as the Standard Normal Course. The possibility of obtaining a high school degree at Glenville Normal School continued until the fall of 1929 when Glenville High School was built.

Tanner High School was called DeKalb District High School until the fall of 1933. School was held in the Barnes Store Building in Tanner from September 1926, to March of 1929, when it was moved into the new Tanner High School Building. The Barnes Building was provided for use as a school by the love of several persons: Dewey and Denver Barnes; Emma and Albert Springston; Clara Snider; and Bill and Audrey Cunningham. What a gift of love! Prior to being held in the Barnes Building, the high school had been held for one year, 1925-26, in the Baptist Church in Tanner which stood on the hill beside the two-room Tanner Elementary. This Tanner Elementary stood on land which had been donated by Earl, Karl, and Lona Hardman in 1915, and had been built by Frank Stalnaker.

Another special type of caretaker deserves mention, those who delivered the babies. How many students who attended DeKalb District one-room schools and Tanner High School were delivered into this world by Mrs. Charlie Maxwell (Ella), mid-wife, just for the sheer love of delivering God's creations and giving them her blessing? Her records showed 385. The last baby my grandmother delivered in this community, about 1947, was a baby who the doctors would not deliver because the mother did not have the money for an examination before delivery. As I watched from my fence post, I recall that grandmother made daily trips up the road to care for this household for two weeks after the birth of the baby. It was I who ran to Grandmother with a chair, as she held on feebly to her cane when her legs would not hold her up any longer, as she came within sight of our house. She died in 1949, at age seventy-five. Ada Riddle and Anne Robinson provided mid-wife services, also. Anne was Dr. Bartrum's right hand. As they drove and walked up the many dirt roads that are drained by Tanner Creek, Anne would hold the flashlight so that they might see to arrive at their destination. April 2, 1957, was quite a night and morning for Dr. Bartrum and his helpers as they delivered two babies in the early morning hours of April 3. Teresa Jo Woodford (Maxwell) was delivered to Robert and Lorena Woodford above Tanner, and Diane Lynn VanCamp was delivered to Harlen and DesDemona VanCamp on Kanawha Drive below Glenville. Mrs. Ted Ellyson (Ruth) launched her baby birthing career that night on Kanawha Drive, delivering Diane just at the moment Dr. Bartrum stepped in the door as he was arriving from delivering Teresa. This was before the days of telephones in this area, and doctors' helpers were most welcome. Anne Robinson contributed to life in the Tanner area in yet another way. Should someone pass-away, she was in great demand to lay-out the corpse.

This was life from the 1920s through the 1950s in this small village where an end-of-school field trip was often a picnic-hike back over the hills to the homestead of Henry Everett Engle (1849-1933) where in 1885 he composed the melody for *The West Virginia Hills*. Did this lifestyle continue into the 1960s and 1970s after the school closed as a high school but remained as an elementary? My son Bob Radabaugh spent one year at Tanner School, his eighth grade year (1968-69). One of his classmates who was transferred from the Glenville Elementary School with him, Kim Ellyson (Norman), said of Tanner life, "Here we are just one big, happy family."

And let's not forget the marvelous 1980s! One Friday during the 1980s while I was teaching at Tanner School, a child accidentally broke a front tooth. I called her mother, then I took this child to the dentist, Tom Lilly, after school at Grantsville eighteen miles away. Tom repaired the tooth and as I took the child home, way up Trace Fork, over a dirt road for about three miles, with room for only one car, I realized I must travel back out again over this same road by myself, and what if I met a car and got in the ditch or my car broke down? But as I traveled back out of Trace Fork, a house came into view, and although I did not know who lived there now, the light of the house where Tracy Lydick had once lived permeated the darkness with a warm glow of love which filled my heart, and I knew that only friendly people could possibly live there now or elsewhere in Tanner — and I might add in Gilmer or Calhoun Counties, as Tom Lilly would not let me pay for the cap that he placed on Sharon Bush's tooth.

Love has a way of sifting down and hiding in the cracks; it's in the very air that we breathe and the ground that we walk on and appears to us in the most unusual ways. But it is always there warming our hearts and our lives. The tragedy is that dust has these same qualities, and many mistake love for dust and brush it away.

In 1993, our Tanner Alumni Organization published a year book/history called *The DeTannera*. As I wrote letters and called graduates and former teachers, who were now spread out all over the United States, to get pictures and information, the quote that I heard most often coming from those who had taught at Tanner School was, "There's something special about that place. Of all the places that I have taught, I enjoyed teaching there the most." And, although, I was attempting to repay some old debts by donating two years of my life writing *The DeTannera*, it turned into the greatest blessing of my life, as old debts cannot really be repaid. Can we really repay God because he loves us?

As spring comes into being, I get excited as I know that I will once again attend our Tanner Alumni Reunion (and I realize now, not even death will keep me away), and I will see Tanner High School students from 1925 to 1962, as well as many associate members who come to visit and partake of our day. And as part of our gathering we will also bask in the warm memory of the members of our Tanner family who have passed away.

This poem which I wrote in 1990, on Monday after our alumni reunion on Saturday, explains the magnitude of my feelings for my Tanner family.

Tanner Homecoming 1990

The day was, oh, so very special,
So many memories now freely flow;
They stand like "time's tin soldiers,"
Very neatly in a row.

Tanner life was, oh, so special,
And these people made it so.
They had come back to recapture memories,
Of a life-time long ago.

I stood there breathing in the goodness;
I could not sit down in my seat;
Their vibrations — I must catch them;
This family of friends, I must meet
    and greet.

    Their faces all were smiling brightly;

The woes of yesterday had flown away;
They were gathering strength for tomorrow,
Which would be another day.

But today all things were happy;
We went back and lived again,
All those good, ol' Tanner memories,
That had meant so much back then.

Certainly, it might be said of Tanner life, "To everything there is a season, but love endureth forever." Our Tanner High School Alumni Association gives one and sometimes two scholarships each year to graduating seniors from Gilmer County High School who live in our DeKalb District.

Author: Mary Ann Radabaugh. Mary Ann is a retired teacher. Her students called her "The Story Teller." But to quote Mary Ann, "How can one keep from telling the beautiful West Virginia story?"

76-001-ST-WV-001-1997

Addie Dawson:
Clay County Storyteller

Addie Dawson was born June 21, 1910, the eighth child in a family of eleven children. Her parents were Laura "Alice" Dodd Samples and Abner Jehu "Hooge" Samples.

The family lived out on the end of the Twistabout Ridge down on Big Laurel Creek. They were poor and had no water or electric in their home, a plight quite common in those days. The children never had a chance to obtain much education. Addie's mother passed away when Addie was sixteen years old.

Addie had platinum blonde hair and grew to only four feet, ten inches in height. Her ma Alice was just sure that Addie had been witched because as a youngster at one point she hadn't grown an inch for about four or five years. A local woman had taken a liking to little Addie and was always bringing her small gifts. Well, Alice decided that this woman must be "a-witchin'" Addie. The common belief was that if someone gave you something, you were then under their spell, a witch's spell. And with the little gifts and Addie's small size, her ma always thought this was true.

Addie always loved to tell stories. She could do funny voices and characters as well as sing. She loved to recite poetry, recount folklore, tales, and childhood memories. She collected ghost stories and tales from older relatives and friends. Some of her stories were inspired by the Bible. Addie was a devout Christian from an early age.

Addie had five children, but the eldest child, daughter Carol Ann, died in a tragic accident while still a toddler. When her children were small, Addie always shared her wonderful stories and tales with them.

Addie Dawson passed away on June 22, 1993.

Author: Evelyn Eagle McLaughlin. Mrs. McLaughlin is a retired teacher. She is the mother of three children, Bradley, Ellyn, and Rodney. Addie was Evelyn's mother. She resides in her hometown of Procious.

77-001-ST-WV-001-1997

Grandad And Old Sam

Okey E. Mullins, my grandad, lived on a farm near Craigsville, West Virginia with his family and lots of animals. One day in the early 1950s, Grandad went to Richwood. While there, a man came into town with two bears which

Grandad Mullins with Old Sam.

Grandad bought for $200.00. Grandma Emma was "madder than an old wet setting hen."

Money was scarce, and every penny was accounted for in those days. But Grandad had an idea about how he could earn money with Sam, the male bear — train dogs to bear hunt. Grandad charged $2.00 per dog per two minutes of training with Sam. Grandad always rewarded Sam at the end of each session with a tub of water to sit in, as dogs always nipped his backside.

My most memorable event with "Old Sam" was the family reunion in July 1951, held on Uncle Frank's farm which bordered Creasy Road, only a hop, skip and a jump from Grandad's house. Late in the afternoon someone suggested Grandad go get Old Sam. He agreed! People gathered around to watch. Grandad placed Sam's chain around an iron pipe, holding it tight. Using a rock as a hammer he pounded the pipe into the ground, then stepped back, his job done. He thought! Old Sam stood up on hind legs sniffing the air where the food aroma was coming from. When he came down on all fours and got loose, you would have thought an "ol' egg sucking hound dog" had run in the middle of a flock of chickens. People ran in every direction, climbing over fences, up cattle racks on trucks, trying to grab their children as they were running. Martha had not walked in years, but she ran and jumped on the back of a truck. It was a sight I will never forget.

Before he was caught, Sam devoured apple pie and sat in the tub of ice water left from the watermelons.

AUTHOR: Barbara Mullins Parsons. Barbara is retired from General Tire in Akron, Ohio, and currently resides in Bolivia, North Carolina. As a child, she spent her summers in Nicholas County with her grandad and grandma. She enjoys returning to visit friends and family.

78-001-ST-WV-001-1997

The Barn

The barn on my grandparent's farm in Clay County, West Virginia, where I spent as much of my summer vacations as my parents would allow, was a place of discovery and adventure. It was a tall building with a peaked roof that sprawled wide to enclose sheds that ran parallel to the main structure on each side. It was built around the turn of the century from poplar logs roughly hewn to about twelve by twenty-four inches. The gray logs were worn smooth and shiny from years of wind and weather.

Near the center of the barn was the vault. A room approximately twenty feet by twenty feet, it was the only part of the barn that was ever locked. As you stepped over the high, log threshold, on the left was a potato bin that stretched the length of the room. In one corner were numerous hand tools: hoes, shovels, mattocks, crow bars, post hole diggers, and much more.

On the wall to the right of the door hung horse collars, harnesses, chains, a cross-cut saw, ropes, singletrees and various other implements and tools which had become obsolete long before my time. In another corner stood an old potato grader with its many wheels, handles and trays, covered with layers of dust and dirt from years of disuse.

Feed grain, used to supplement winter feeding for the horses and cattle, was also kept in the vault. To me, the grain had a wonderful aroma. I was often tempted to sample the grain myself it smelled so good, and the methodical, satisfied crunching of the animals as they ate made it seem all the more appetizing.

I rode my first — and last — calf in the barn. I had accompanied my Uncle Glen, the youngest of my Mom's six brothers who is five years older than I, to do the evening chores. In the lower shed, a few young calves were penned up, so Uncle Glen decided it would be a fine opportunity to indoctrinate me in the art of calf riding. To demonstrate, he deftly mounted one of the animals for a ride any Old West cowboy would be proud of, dismounting on his own before being thrown.

He dared me to do the same. Of course I could not let my honor be stripped from me. With the full knowledge that I would in a short time regret it, I climbed on what I thought looked to be the friendliest and most docile of the calves. My posterior had no sooner touched the calf's back when he seemed to jump three feet straight up, bucking and running toward the board fence of the shed in an attempt to brush off his unsolicited burden.

In my mind I knew that the intelligent thing to do was to let go, to bail off. And I had a sincere desire to do that, only my hands would not follow the orders my brain was giving them. I had a death grip that I could not release on the ears of the poor beast that was trying to thrash the life from me.

Throughout my ride of poorly disguised terror, I heard a strange sound. It was Uncle Glen, cackling in delight with what was happening to me. After what seemed to be an hour — and was probably only ten seconds — the calf made a turn-hop-twist maneuver that the laws of physics prevented my body from accommodating. My death grip broken, I sailed free of the beast, and made a perfect belly-flop landing in a pile of fresh, green cow manure. Once my uncle had recovered from nearly being

incapacitated with laughter, he helped me up to devise a story of explanation for Mom.

My favorite part of the barn was the hay loft, the second story of the main section. In my earliest memories, the hay stored there was loose, not baled. The loft would be filled with hay from the fields, cut and raked by horse-drawn equipment, hauled in a pick-up truck and horse-drawn wagon, and unloaded by pitch-fork to the loft. In later years, the hay was baled in seventy pound bales and stacked neatly in the loft — more efficient, but not nearly as much fun to romp in.

Some of the most peaceful moments of my life were spent alone in the north loft. From the window on the north side, looking straight away, I could see the knobbed hay fields of the King farm, two miles distant as the crow flies. Looking down, about eighty yards from the barn's back gate, I could see the gray, weathered remains of the original farm house, long abandoned, sitting forlorn in a quiet, sloping meadow, the once stately, two story house slowly succumbing to nature's patient march.

The roof of the barn, always in some state of disrepair, was covered with tin, man's inadvertent collaboration with nature to make a wonderfully soothing instrument. How I loved the summer rains that would begin, slowly at first, as the clouds would release a few drops against the roof, "tink, tink-tonk, tink-tonk-tink," as if warming up for the concerto to follow, gradually increasing to an intoxicating crescendo as the clouds expelled their moist contents. Then, the lightning would crack, illuminating the sky like an elaborate marquee, as if to draw all creation's attention to the splendid performance. And the thunder would answer with a great roar, a heavenly timpani roll, extending an ovation on behalf of the silent, thirsty earth below.

I would lie in the hay breathing in its sweet aroma, gazing up toward the roof or out through the window. Listening to the powerful, enchanting symphony that only God could create, I would be captured by the sights, sounds and scents that enveloped me, and drift away to a sleep of exquisite, restful surrender.

I have not been inside the old barn now for nearly twenty-three years. Today my Uncle Chilton owns and works the farm, and the old barn is proudly serving its third generation, receiving the animals in its sheds like a mother hen gathers her chicks under her wings, storing the winter feed in its bosom. I think I shall soon visit the old barn. I hope it rains.

Author: Preston Fitzwater. Mr. Fitzwater, a chemical operator and part-time technical writer, was raised in Clay County, spent seven years in the Navy and returned to West Virginia. He has lived in Clendenin with his wife Teresa and their daughters Amanda and Amelia for eleven years.

79-001-ST-WV-001-1997

Making Music

usic was always a part of my life as I was growing up in West Virginia. In the late 1930s, my dad had a country western band called The Cherry River Ramblers. We lived in Richwood, but the band made personal appearances throughout the state. I can remember my mother dressing me up in clothing that matched the band members' outfits and sending me out on stage. I can't remember what I did after I got out there, but I can remember getting a lot of attention.

Music was played by everyone in the family. A trip to my grandfather's house on the weekend consisted of singing and playing on the front porch. My grandfather's family sang mostly hymns. Two of my aunts were on the Beckley radio station where they were known as the Bluebirds. I'm sure my dad recalls these memories when he sees his grandson pick up a banjo and cut loose on "Cripple Creek" or "John Henry."

Author: Phyllis Jarvis

80-001-ST-WV-001-1997

The Blizzard Of 1993 Brings Life

arge, beautiful, star-like snow flakes were floating from the sky in the beginning, but within an hour these beautiful, soft flakes had turned into a wet, heavy blanket that covered the earth and everything around. Three hours and three feet of snow later, we began to panic. Usually my family enjoyed snow, but today was an exception. The Blizzard of 1993 had arrived, and my pregnant wife was expecting to give birth on Monday.

By night-fall on Saturday we were facing four feet of snow, closed highways, and an anxious mother-to-be. The white covering had blanketed everything in sight by Sunday, and I knew I had to start shoveling our way out of the house to the car. I couldn't even see the car; snowdrifts were six to seven feet high. After toiling for a couple hours I made my way to the driveway where our Bonneville was buried. I started digging for the driver's door. After several attempts I thought I found it. But to my dismay, I had found the rear fender. After uncovering the car, I started the task of removing mountains of snow from our driveway. Walls of snow fenced me in as I scooped shovel after shovel of wet snow overhead. The final embankment that I had to burst through had been made by the State Department of Highways on Saturday by the snowplow.

At seven o'clock Monday morning we left our cozy, warm home to face the blizzard-handicapped state. We were the only vehicle on the closed highways as we pushed our way through the desert of snow. It felt strange and scary driving through a maze of white. Everything everywhere was white. All the whiteness never stopped us as we trudged through the ruts in our frontwheel drive. The one hour trip to the hospital turned into a six hour struggle. On March fifteenth at 1:59 P.M. on Blizzard Monday, during the worst storm of the century, our beautiful daughter Whitney was born in a warm, safe hospital.

Author: Damon Hanshaw. Damon is married to Sandra Duskey Hanshaw and they also have a son, Zachary. Damon teaches English 12 at Nicholas High School in Summersville, and is a contributing writer to The Nicholas Chronicle, *a weekly newspaper of Nicholas County.*

81-001-ST-WV-001-1997

The Making Of The Mill

Few places in West Virginia evoke more pleasant memories in the minds of so many as does Jackson's Mill. No single phrase or group of words can be used to describe it and thousands upon thousands of pages would be needed to tell all that has happened there since a man named Petro first built a fishpot in the West Fork River near where the old Jackson mill now stands in the days when Indians were still roaming the West Virginia hills. But that is not our purpose here. Instead, we're here to share the essence of Jackson's Mill and touch on the charisma and lore that has built around it during the two centuries since eleven-year-old Edward Jackson crossed the Alleghenies in 1769 and cast his eyes on the broad valleys and tall hills of today's Central West Virginia.

Jackson's Mill is named for Edward Jackson. He was a young man of twenty-seven when he petitioned the Harrison County Court in 1786 to build a mill "at Peadros Fish Pot." From that day forth, his name was inexorably tied to the land there. Around the turn of that century, he finally built his mill across the river from the present mill.

A couple of years later, Edward, now called Colonel Edward for his leadership in the local militia, brought his family from Buckhannon to Jackson's Mill to live. His first wife, Mary Haddan, had died leaving him with six children. In 1799 he remarried to Elizabeth Weatherholt Brake. At least seven of their nine children were born at Jackson's Mill. These fifteen children resulted in a "passel" of grandchildren, the most famous of whom is undoubtedly Confederate General Thomas J. "Stonewall" Jackson.

The orphaned Tom Jackson came to Jackson's Mill to live when he was seven and remained for ten years, leaving in 1842 to attend West Point. He never returned except for an occasional visit. Most everyone knows the rest of his story: hero of the Mexican War, teacher at Virginia Military Institute for ten years, nicknamed "Stonewall" for his stalwart courage at Bull Run in 1861, wounded by his own men during the Battle of Chancellorsville, and death after the amputation of his left arm in May 1863. His final words were, "Let us cross over the river and rest in the shade of the trees." Some say they referred to his boyhood home, Jackson's Mill.

It is a certainty that had "Stonewall" not passed his boyhood years at Jackson's Mill, it would have passed into obscurity as did most of the mills that bounded in every county until midway through the twentieth century. Instead the mill became a West Virginia treasure.

In 1915 the Monongahela Valley Traction Company (MVTC) acquired title to the property. The site had long been favored as a place for picnics and outings; and, for a time, there was talk of turning it into a memorial park honoring the famous general. In 1919, a marker was placed on the site in his memory.

In 1920 West Virginia 4-H leaders felt a need for a central meeting place where boys and girls from all over the state could gather. Jackson's Mill was suggested. William "Teepi" Kendrick and Charles Hartley of the State 4-H staff visited the Mill and were impressed with the potential of the property. They convinced the MVTC to donate five acres (which included the mill) to the state as a 4-H campsite. The next year an act of the West Virginia Legislature named Jackson's Mill as the state 4-H camp, the first such camp in the nation. It was placed under the care of West Virginia University.

The first camp was held the same year with tents and the old mill providing shelter. Boys and girls brought fresh eggs, slabs of bacon and other farm produce as part of their tuition. They were instructed in life-skills, went swimming in the West Fork, and gathered around the campfire on starry summer nights in ceremonies that honored both their youth and some of West Virginia's first citizens — the Seneca, the Delaware, the Mingo, and the Cherokee.

Dedicated to providing educational and leadership opportunities for boys and girls of the Mountain State, the camp soon became one of the best known spots in the state as youth from every county traveled to the Mill for the camps.

Gradually, under the leadership of "Teepi"

CHAPTER 5: MOUNTAIN LAKES

Friends of photographer W.E. Carpenter pose for a photo in front of the mill in 1904. (Photo courtesy of Hacker's Creek Pioneers Descendants Library, Creed Shutts Collection.)

Recently, a dream inspired by "Teepi" Kendrick and kept alive by his successors and thousands of others came true — a grist mill is grinding again at Jackson's Mill. A ten-year project that involved moving the two hundred year old Blaker-Hockman Mill from Greenbrier County to the Jackson's Mill Historic Area came to fruition. In 1995 the historic Mary Conrad Cabin was also moved into the area and placed near the McWhorter Cabin which was relocated to the Mill from Jane Lew in 1924. A new building, Mountain State Building, houses a meeting area and comfort facilities.

Many of the buildings and facilities are a tribute to the 4-H'ers and other interested citizens and groups who made them possible. With funds raised or donated from various sources and work completed by thousands of volunteers hands, they stand as a representation of the deep-seated affection most West Virginians and former West Virginians have for this state treasure.

Today, Jackson's Mill is more than a shrine to Stonewall Jackson and to 4-H in West Virginia. It is much more than a museum. It is a living institution which is continually expanding and changing, meeting the needs of the present, preparing for the future, and preserving the past.

Where once the programs at the Mill were primarily devoted to providing state 4-H'ers with education in agricultural and home economics skills combined with leadership training, today's programs are much broader and more comprehensive. It still retains its designation as the official state 4-H camp, but approximately one hundred other diverse organizations use the facilities annually.

and his successors, residents from all over West Virginia went to work and converted the old farmstead into a fine camp.

Today, amid a backdrop of open fields bordered by quiet woods, winding roads, and sidewalks flanked by stately trees and the bright colors of an occasional garden, Jackson's Mill has 523 acres and numerous buildings including fourteen cottages, the Jackson Lodge, the Mount Vernon Dining Hall, the West Virginia Building, the All Faiths Prayer Chapel, a large livestock complex, and the original five-acre historic site. Also featured are an outdoor theater, numerous gardens and shrines, recreational facilities and travel-trailer sites.

The premier event at Jackson's Mill for the past twenty-some years has been the Stonewall Jackson Heritage Arts and Crafts Jubilee. Conceived by a group of Lewis Countians in 1974 to showcase West Virginia arts and crafts and named in honor of the Jubilee festivals held at the Mill in the 1920s and 1930s, the present-day Jubilee draws approximately 75,000 visitors to the Mill each Labor Day weekend.

AUTHOR: Joy Gilchrist. Joy is a noted storyteller and author. She serves as the chairman of the board of directors of the Jackson's Mill Heritage Foundation. She was born in Harrison County, and reared in Doddridge, Harrison, and Lewis Counties. She and her husband Charles have five children and fifteen grandchildren.

82-001-ST-WV-001-1997

Chapter 6
New River / Greenbrier Valley

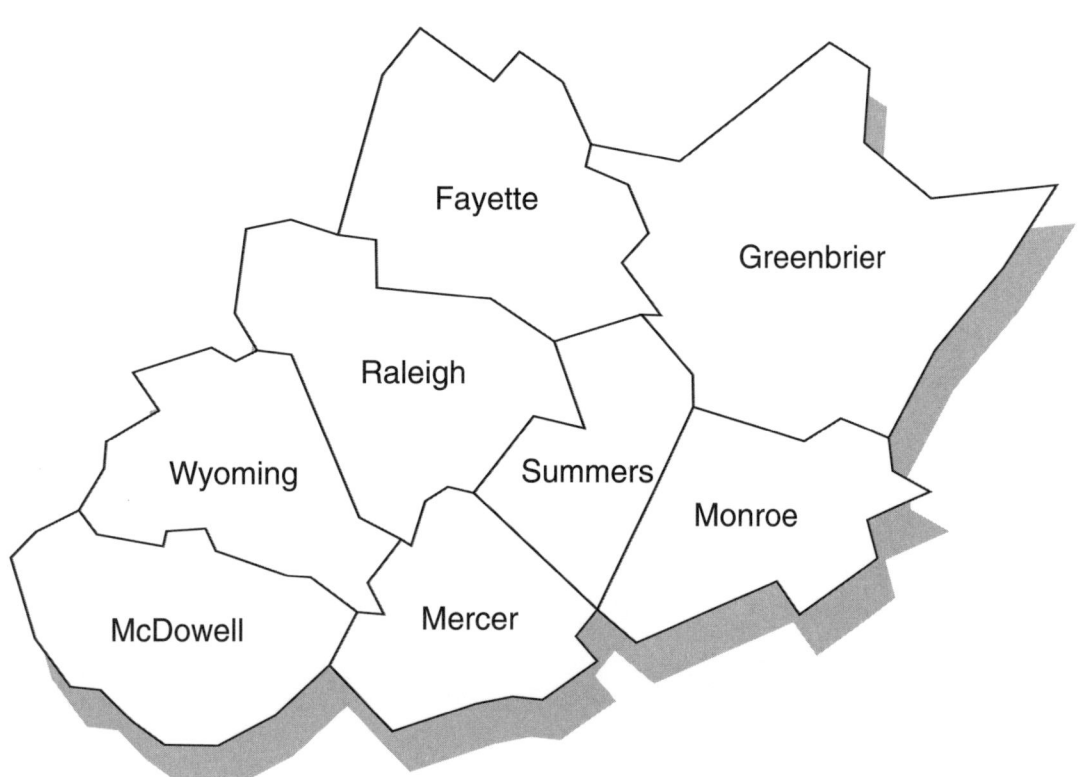

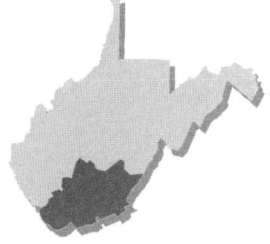

Granny

My grandmother's name is Juanita Basham. Granny is an eighty year-old mother of six, grandmother of twelve, and great-grandmother of three. She's quite short, about five feet four inches, with small feet and quaint, little hands. She has a beautiful face, although wrinkled by time, and perfect, loving, deep blue eyes. Her hair is long and flowing, but she insists on keeping it twisted up in a bun on the top of her head. I guess this fits her image, though, because she is a retired school teacher of thirty-two years.

Granny Basham, 1996.

Granny has always been a major influence in everything I do. She's always pushed me to do my best and to never give up on anything until it's right. Whenever I make bad grades on papers or tests, she always says, "We both know you can do better than that," or "You'll just have to try harder and get it right next time!" That's pretty much all she has to do, because I love to make her proud of me almost as much as she loves for me to make her proud.

Besides being proud of me, there are two things in this world that Granny truly loves: cooking and flowers. I remember the whole time I was growing up, my granny would always bake cookies and candy or something sweet to spoil all of us kids with. In addition to that, she would always cook a pretty large supper. I can't remember too many evenings when Granny hasn't had something hot on the table, except the times when she's been sick or in the hospital.

As for her love for flowers, there isn't a window in her house that isn't full of flowers. She also has them sitting on the floor, the porch, and even hanging from the ceiling. Sometimes, when she's watering them, she'll start to talk to them, saying things like, "Well, aren't we thirsty today," and even, "How are you feeling today?" This used to really scare me, but after a while, I got used to it.

All of the people in my family, and even a lot of people outside my family, care as much about Granny as I do. I imagine she has had some influence on everyone's life who knows her very well. She also has this unique quality about her that keeps me wondering. She's always right! Whether it's matters of the heart or just the weather, she hardly ever misses. I sure hope this quality is inheritable.

Overall, I think my grandmother is a cool person, definitely one of the best in the world. She has done a lot of good things for me and numerous others in her life. She once told me, "You can do anything if you just set your goals and keep reaching for them." I truly believe this advice, and I owe her more for it than I can ever give to her.

AUTHOR: David Austin Rodes. David is the son of Wilma and David Rodes of Brooks. He wrote this essay when he was in the seventh grade, while attending Summers County High School.

83-001-ST-WV-001-1997

Homecoming For Mrs. Basham

How does one put to paper a story of a truly remarkable woman — one who has touched the lives of so many just by being? Mrs. Basham is just such a woman. She is a wonderful spirit who has graced us with her guiding, loving, and strict hand all our lives.

Juanita Austin Dove Shepard Eades Eads Lilly Basham's eyes have mirrored it all. She has experienced the depth of despair, the height of joy, the tears of sadness without so much as one complaint.

This small, gray-haired teacher could write a book which could move even the hardest of heart, but that is not her way. Juanita has

Mrs. Basham's Homecoming, her children. Back row (L-R), Billy Earl Shepard; Wilma Jean Lilly Rodes; Kenneth Theadore Lilly. Middle row seated (L-R), Margaret Louise Eads Temple; Juanita Austin Dove Basham; Elizabeth Ann "Annie" Eades Crook. Front row kneeling, Monroe Darrow Eads.

inspired many a pupil to reach for the unreachable, and asked only that they give the best they have back to society. With this woman, there was never a word known as "can't." "Can't was taken out and buried under a rock," never to present itself to her pupils in that one room schoolhouse of not so long ago.

For sixty years, Mrs. Basham had a wish hidden deep within her heart. It was known to only a few of her dearest friends. Then in May 1996, what had been prayed for became a reality, and Mrs. Basham had a homecoming. This was no ordinary homecoming, because for the first time since rearing six children, they were all traveling home to see her. Never before had they all been able to come home to Little Bluestone, West Virginia. Never before was she able to have a picture of herself with the six precious jewels she had struggled over great odds to love, guide, protect, and allow to grow into adulthood.

Yes, Mrs. Basham, somehow you knew that even though life has its broken dreams, broken promises, broken lives, if your faith was strong and if God let you live long enough, there would be a way to triumph over the greatest of odds. And with your homecoming, your wish — a prayer — that your family, no matter how distant, how long separated, remain forever connected came true by and through the prayers of others, some of whom you may not ever know existed.

AUTHOR: Wilma Lilly Rodes. Mrs. Rodes is Mrs. Basham's daughter. She has two children, Shannon and David. She says her family is "forever bonded through ties of love, honor, and our heritage of being West Virginian."

84-001-ST-WV-001-1997

Thinking Of Appalachia

Embrace me, Respect me, Love me,
For I have given you the roots,
On which to become
All that you are
All that you might be and
All that you hope to be.

I am not to be shunned
As you have so often been told
Instead, I am to be heralded
With the loudest of voices
Because you see...
I am You, Your Heritage
Your Appalachia.

AUTHOR: Wilma Lilly Rodes

85-001-ST-WV-001-1997

The Story Of Alta, Fayette County

T'here was a Post Office which was located in the small town of Gamoca, in the northwest corner of Fayette County just north of Gauley Bridge. In 1950, this Post Office was being closed and this meant that the local residents would have to travel to either Belva or Gauley Bridge to get their mail.

At that time we ran a small store right across the river from Gamoca and we were asked by the residents living in the area if the Post Office could be moved into our store, which we agreed to. My husband George would run the store and I would handle the postal duties. When all the paperwork had been completed we had everything but a name for the new Post Office. My husband told them to name it after me since I would be the one running it.

In the meantime we had decided that it would be too much trouble to try and run both the business and the Post Office at the same time. But all the paperwork had already been printed with the name Alta, West Virginia. This Post Office officially closed in 1977, but the small community is still known as Alta, although the Post Office was never located in our store.

AUTHOR: Richard C. Bainbridge. Mr. Bainbridge wrote this story as recently told by Alta Allen. This story was first told to Mr. Bainbridge by the late George Allen in 1984.

86-001-ST-WV-001-1997

Sweet Kiss Of Blackdamp

"Call the Springton Company Store. Get somebody to go tell his wife. He's a goner," the coal-covered foreman muttered as he pronounced Clyde Boyles dead.

"Well, there's another one we won't be workin' anymore," a miner humphed as he came over and nudged the cot. "The Dead Wagon's on its way."

When asked, Clyde's helper explained, "He was just operatin' the Joy machine as usual. He seemed fine. I went back up the line a ways and as I was a comin' back I saw him just reach down real slow like and turn off the machine and then he just fell right off real slow

Clyde Boyles was a near victim of blackdamp in 1961 at Tralee Mines in Wyoming County. Photo taken in 1947.

like. The last thing he said to me was if I smelled that sweet smell like flowers. I didn' smell nothing."

Clyde, when carried out of the mines, had been given oxygen, but to no avail. He was laid off to the side to "rest" and wait for the wagon. The sweet kiss of blackdamp had claimed another life.

The ambulance trudgingly ambled out of Tralee Holler. The driver diligently avoided each bump in the road, respectful of the last rites he was performing. But as he turned onto the main road heading for Foglesong Mortuary, he heard a low, dull moan. As the moans and groans became more evident, curiosity prompted him to pull off the road at Mullens Hospital. When he flung open the back doors, he was met with a full blown case of reality. The dead man was alive!

They, Clyde and the driver, were both white as chalk. Clyde, however, spent some time throwing up in the emergency room. The doctors wanted him to remain in the hospital, but after much argument he went home — barefoot.

Once he'd had several days of rest he was ready to return to work. His wife Velva began to fix another set of mining clothes for him. She couldn't, however, find his dinner bucket, belt, or shoes. Where were they?

Well, once they were located, Clyde said, "You know, it sure makes a feller consider his way of life when he has to go to the morgue to pick up his shoes."

Author: Glenna Carroll. Glenna is the daughter of Clyde Boyles who worked in the mines in Wyoming County from 1946 to 1985. He passed on in 1991. This story was written as told by Glenna's mother, Velva Boyles.

87-001-ST-WV-001-1997

Editors' Note: Blackdamp is a poisonous gas found in mines after fires and explosions of combustible gases. It is a mixture of carbon dioxide and nitrogen.

The Simple Pleasure Of Being A West Virginian

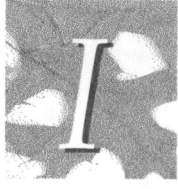

I must say that growing up in West Virginia was a delightful and most enjoyable way to grow up. I spent most of my youth, all of my youth I should say, in a southern West Virginia small town not far from Bluefield called War. I played in the mountains; I played cowboys. I think at one time I even played dolls with the girls. But I remember that what I loved most was roaming the hills of my hometown.

My dad worked for a lumber company; mom kept house. They saw to it that my youth was well-spent. My parents watched over me and took care of me, as most families do, and ensured that I had what I needed in order to be happy throughout my childhood. We had friends, a large family and all the happiness that goes with family life. Our days were filled with joy. And, of course, we had the gifts of West Virginia. I'll always love the peaceful nights and the pleasures galore provided by the scenery.

After I grew up, I moved away from West Virginia and stayed in Tennessee for about thirty years. But when my father passed away the time came to move back home. Now I live close to my brother and he takes care of my needs, although he stays busy all of the time and has a family of his own. And I still, in spite of all the trials, troubles, and tribulations of life, enjoy being a West Virginian and being called, from time to time, a hillbilly. Some people would consider it an insult, but I consider it an honor and a privilege.

Author: Robert Overbey. Beginning in his teens, Mr. Overbey underwent a series of brain surgeries to relieve pressure due to a spinal abnormality. Although his doctors offered little hope of survival, he went on to become a newspaper columnist. He still continues to write, despite retirement.

88-001-ST-WV-001-1997

How I Conned Movie Fare

In April of 1934, when the West Virginia sales tax went into effect, I was thirteen years old and could easily pass for under twelve. The cost of a movie ticket for kids under twelve was ten cents, and I never told the people at the ticket window that I was over twelve.

The sales tax was one cent on anything above a nickel to fifty cents. Every Saturday was a movie day for kids: News Reels, Little Rascals, and other short subjects, then the main film. I always managed to pick up a dime somewhere during the week. But with the sales tax, I found that I could get movie fare much easier by walking up to a railroader or a miner and giving him a sob story on how I needed a penny for the sales tax to go along with my dime to go to the movies.

The approach wasn't any problem, because most of the men would pull out a penny or even three or four and give them to me as they expressed their opinion about Governor Kump's administration for putting the sales tax on the people of West Virginia. After going to eleven railroaders or miners I found that it was no problem to con enough money for a movie, and sometimes I would get enough for a five-cent bottle of pop or ice cream cone, and a hot dog for ten cents. Sometimes I could con enough to build a little nest egg of pennies for other things. I tried to always make a mental note so I wouldn't con the same man out of a penny the next week.

I never told my parents until years later how I got movie money. For awhile I was doing quite well at my con trade and having fun, but it finally faded away.

Author: William C. McGhee. Mr. McGhee is a retired professional soldier and locomotive engineer. He is now a community volunteer, muralist, and member of the EcoTheater of West Virginia.

89-001-ST-WV-001-1997

The Phantom Cat:
A True Story

In the early 1930s my parents owned a little general store on Dry Creek Road in White Sulphur Springs. We don't know where Bobbie, "Bob," came from. She looked like a he. She just appeared in the doorway of the store one evening about closing time. She was raggedy, gaunt and vicious! And with paunches on each side denoting kittens inside. Daddy very gingerly picked her up, took her to the back of the store and poured milk in an old saucer. She lapped it all up and settled in. Daddy thought she'd be at the door wanting to leave when he opened the store the next morning, but she was still there. A box was set in place, but she refused it. So Daddy laid down an old shirt of his and she was in possession of it and us from then on.

She fattened up with our feeding tid-bits, and soon, very soon, there were four fuzzy yellow, blue and calico kittens. I forgot to tell you — Bobbie was a yellow striped Manx cat. Manx cats have only stub tails. (She looked like a bobcat — hence Bobbie.) A Manx cat was a rarity in those days and a subject of conversation and viewing.

We thought she was a rare prize and coddled her. But she would not have anything to do with me, my brother or mother. She would only eat what Daddy provided and only permitted his petting. She would growl, spit, snap and strike out with her claws unsheathed. But she loved Daddy and would sit on his lap and snooze along with him in the early afternoon when customers were scarce. He would sit on a straight chair and rear it back against the supporting post with a newspaper over his face.

Bobbie was not the maternal type — being part bobcat (we thought). After about two weeks or less she would abandon the kittens and go off hunting or exploring. So I had to feed them milk and bread and little scraps of meat or anything I could scrounge from the icebox or kitchen. They grew and developed into playful kittens. Being in the public where customers could see them, it was easy to give them away. Except it was hard for me to part with them. I felt they were my babies. This happened over and over. We always had kittens in the store. I always had to rear them. Bobbie still had only purrs and eyes for Daddy.

Suddenly, Bobbie disappeared; we searched everywhere. We asked everyone — no reports, no sightings. So we gradually almost forgot her. But not Daddy. He never gave up inquiring of her. Two years went by, and in the fall of '31 Daddy became very ill. Had an operation but didn't improve. It was near Christmas and Daddy was failing each day. On Christmas morning I opened the door to see how much snow had fallen and feel just how cold it was. In walked Bobbie as though she had never been away! It made Christmas for us, for we knew it would make Daddy happy having her back, and it did. He perked up right away and felt it was the best Christmas ever!

Bobbie stayed around and kept Daddy company. But he was failing fast. In March he died. Bobbie left too. We never saw her again.

AUTHOR: Nell C. Corkrean. Mrs. Corkrean is a native of White Sulphur Springs, where she has lived for seventy-nine years. She never left home! Her parents John and Mary Cary owned "The Wee Store."

90-001-ST-WV-001-1997

The Risen Dead

My grandparents were Betty Walkup and Richard Benjamin Neal of Fayette County. My grandmother died before I was born and I knew my grandfather only a short while before he died in 1928. But my mother told so many stories about them that I feel as if I knew them both well.

One of the stories occurred in the 1870s when my grandmother was a young woman. One of the neighbors had died and she and some friends were "sitting up" with the corpse. The night was long, and toward morning they decided to sing some hymns to help keep them awake. My grandmother held the lamp so they could all see the one hymn book. At some point during the singing, the corpse sat up with a "snap." The singers moved as one through the door. They ran for about three-fourths of a mile before stopping. Although their path had crossed a foot bridge, they were all wet to the knees. Not one of them had used the bridge to cross the creek. My grandmother also realized she was still holding the lamp above her head.

When daylight came, the group got up enough nerve to return to the house. As they eased back into the room they discovered that the "risen dead" was still risen, and still dead.

The explanation for the incident was that the man had died in a sitting position and his body had stiffened before the neighbors had "laid him out" for burial. They had forced the body to lie flat by tying it down. During the night the ropes had stretched and loosened and allowed him to return to his sitting position.

AUTHOR: Virginia Forren Hudson. Virginia is a native of White Sulphur Springs, who now lives in Inman, South Carolina.

91-001-ST-WV-001-1997

The Little Pump Organ

In the 1870s, in Fayette County, the little church which my grandfather Richard Neal attended, acquired a small pump organ. It created great dissension among the members of the church; some believed it was an asset to the services, while others felt it was the work of the devil and against their beliefs. The arguments were tearing the church apart.

My grandfather and a friend went to the church late one night, picked up the little organ and carried it away. They threw it over a cliff into the Gauley River. It was never found. The young men did not tell of their deed until years and years later. However, it served its purpose. The membership became a united group while trying to solve the mystery of the organ that disappeared.

AUTHOR: Virginia Forren Hudson

92-001-ST-WV-001-1997

Richard and Betty Neal of Fayette County with grandchildren Troy, Everette, and Ester Neal.

Barefoot Mountaineers

This little incident occurred during the 1948-49 West Virginia University basketball season. Jack Fleming, "The Voice of the Mountaineers," will probably recall. We were on a road trip to Washington and Jefferson in Washington, Pennsylvania. There was a freshman game and a varsity game. I was student manager for the freshmen and Nicki Cavallero was the varsity manager. Well, when we got to the gym and started laying out the uniforms, we noticed we had loaded a bag of dirty laundry instead of the varsity shoes. Mark Workman's "gun boats" were of no use to anyone. Ha! Luckily we were able to contact one of the assistant Athletic Directors, and he made the sixty or so mile trip in record time. The bag of shoes was on the sidewalk right where we had left it at the old field house. Needless to say, the wire picked up on the story and sent it nationwide.

AUTHOR: J.D. Moore. Mr. Moore, formerly of Welch, is now Mayor of Lapwai, Idaho. His story lends credibility to comments heard during the January 1, 1997, Gator Bowl about "barefoot Mountaineers."

93-001-ST-WV-001-1997

Liver For Thanksgiving

That fall evening in November, 1996, Lee, my husband of thirty years, drove the one-lane road for forty-five minutes to get to McComas, an abandoned coal camp that left more memories of an era forever gone than people and buildings. When we arrived, he parked the truck where the post office once stood, got out and glanced at the tall mountain in front of us, seeing what I could only imagine. "I lived at the end of Church Hollow," he said to me as he looked at its dirt road no longer littered with coal, slate dumps, and garbage.

He told me about his childhood spring trips to Browning Lambert Mountain with his dad to purchase pigs. Lee explained how the two of them would walk hours carrying sacks to a black farmer's place. He laughed, "The farmer was old. Of course, then, anyone bigger than me was old. Although everyone else called the aged farmer by his first name, Dad made me call him 'Mister' as a sign of respect. The hog farmer's house looked like ours and the other camp houses dotting that mountain with their white lapsiding of wooden strips and tarpaper roofs."

As Lee and I walked up the road, he bragged, "I wore bibs just like his." He explained that while the old man and his dad did their four dollar transaction, he was in the pen chasing pigs with their momma sow on his heels. His dad would always pick two black pigs with white striped bellies and stuff them into the sacks. "You'd think carrying those pigs home in a burlap sack would have been easy, but mine squealed and kicked my butt into a blister."

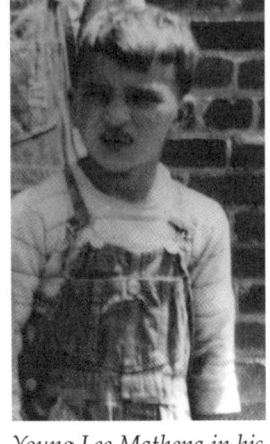

Young Lee Mathena in his bibs, circa 1946.

It was hard to imagine him dumping the pigs into the pen and know that at age six, suffering from rheumatic fever and medicated with lamp oil and turpentine, he was obligated to feed them twice daily.

"Like clockwork on Thanksgiving Day," he said, heading back to the truck to go home, "that old farmer would come to our house carrying buckets for blood and chitlins. That evening for dinner, he would have blood pudding and fried chitlins; we had fresh hog liver and onions."

AUTHOR: Carolyn Mathena. Carolyn lives in Princeton and has worked in various educational levels promoting literacy, adult education, and college support services. She writes stories about West Virginia and has recently been published.

94-001-ST-WV-001-1997

The Christmas Tree

"Oh, Christmas tree, how lovely are your branches." How exceedingly lovely to a four year old who accompanied her father, older brother, and her sisters to cut the tree and participate in the joys of decorating its branches.

Our family lived on a farm on Bluestone River at Spanishburg, Mercer County, West Virginia. My father Clyde Maxey, a teacher/principal, was on Christmas break when the longed-for day finally arrived. The year was 1938. We planned to go to the lower part of the farm, made up of hillside pastures and forest, to find our Christmas tree.

Sweaters, coats, caps, mittens, and overshoes piled on the kitchen floor were sorted out as kids dressed warmly against December's cold. Soon everyone was ready. Dad shouldered the ax and we were off.

Excitedly, we talked about the tree we

would find. "Where shall we look for the tree?" Dad asked.

"We'll just walk until we find it," I replied, not knowing exactly where, but certain the tree was waiting.

"Let's go this way," Dad suggested. "I'll bet we can find a pretty tree this way." Several paces more and there it was — a splendid white pine. Following a few vigorous blows of Dad's ax the tree lay on the ground. Going home, Dad and John took turns carrying the ax and tree. Also, a tired four-year-old coaxed Dad into carrying her part way home.

Upon reaching the house, Dad assembled a stand by cutting board lengths into sections then nailing them together cross-arms fashion. I was permitted to help string the single strand of electric lights and garlands as well as my homemade paper chains and to position glass balls and tinsel icicles. "Santa Claus can tell who decorated the tree," Dad declared.

"How?" I queried.

"Well, he can tell by the smell."

I wanted Santa to know that I helped trim the tree, that my small fingers lovingly placed those icicles one by one, retrieving any that fell to the floor, carefully on the tips of those shiny green branches. I knew Santa Claus would be pleased that I had helped create what I saw as a shimmering beauty for him.

For a few years until about 1943, near the time of the winter solstice, the expedition for the Christmas tree repeated itself. Each year Dad always knew just where to find the best tree — knew so assuredly that we walked directly to it.

AUTHOR: Lois Maxey Rosenow. Years later Mrs. Rosenow learned that her dad had selected the Christmas tree with its lovely branches months beforehand. Mrs. Rosenow resides in Sedona, Arizona.

95-001-ST-WV-001-1997

"Flimflam"

I remember my father telling me that when he was young all the children living in the Dry Creek area of Marsh Fork District of Raleigh County, West Virginia, spent hours hunting for buried treasure. Although no treasure was found, my mother has Indian arrowheads and other artifacts Dad found while searching for the elusive treasure.

My father, listening to the old timers spin tales, had a favorite story about Wilson Abbott. In 1850, he became the first Raleigh County assessor. He collected the local taxes and was also the Sheriff of Fayette County, Virginia, now Raleigh County, West Virginia, from 1853-1855. Wilson had just collected the taxes when the Civil War broke out, and he was afraid to deliver them to Richmond, Virginia. He placed the money in a strong box and hid it while waiting for more favorable conditions.

At this point, *fiction* overcomes fact. My father, a descendant of Wilson's brother St. Clair, believed the old folk's tale. It was said that Wilson buried the money where he could see its location from his porch. He died one night without revealing its location. Thus, some forty years after hiding the box, many people, including my dad, still searched for the treasure of gold and silver coins.

However, the *fact* is that some time after the box was buried, an official-looking man came to Wilson's home with three Confederate soldiers as his personal guards. After producing papers, he announced that he was sent by the state to collect the taxes that the local assessors had collected and were unable to deliver to Richmond. Believing this to be true, Wilson gave the tax money to him in exchange for a receipt.

Wilson had been flimflammed. The state of Virginia sold Wilson's home to recoup the stolen tax money. Wilson and his wife Mary then lived with their son William until Wilson died in 1874. Wilson, Mary, and William are buried in the Cooper Cemetery at Dry Creek.

AUTHOR: James R. Pettry. Mr. Pettry is a retired electronics engineer. His hobbies are southern West Virginia history and genealogy. His hometown is Packsville.

96-001-ST-WV-001-1997

Aunt Pheobe And Uncle Ike

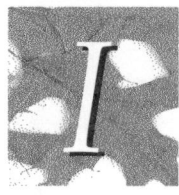

Isaac and Pheobe Tetter Sizemore lived on a forty-eight acre farm located on Burke Mountain at a place known as Mitchem Ridge in McDowell County, West Virginia. Uncle Ike was my dad's uncle. To visit him and Aunt Pheobe was always a special event in my life.

I knew, as we traveled through the forest lane that we were going to see two very special people. Uncle Ike's farm was immaculate, as was Aunt Pheobe's house. Nothing was ever out of place and the atmosphere was always one of welcome.

Uncle Ike and Dad would always go outside and walk the familiar paths to the garden, the barn, and the fields. There was always something new to see and experience: newborn animals, how the garden was growing, feeding the work horses, chasing the pigs, and tasting yellow tomatoes.

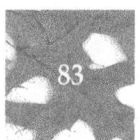

Aunt Pheobe and Mom would go to the kitchen and start to cook. Aunt Pheobe kept her flour in the lower drawer of her kitchen cabinet. I never saw her measure the flour with a measuring cup — she just went to the drawer and used her hand. I knew biscuits and the best cake I have ever tasted were on the way, as was homemade butter and a cold glass of "straight from the cow" milk.

Uncle Ike was always dressed in bibbed overalls and Aunt Pheobe always wore her hair in a bun. I remember being at Uncle Ike's wake when he died. I can still see his coffin in the parlor. Sometimes, to escape the frustration of this jet set computer age, I take a trip in my mind back to see Uncle Ike and Aunt Pheobe and my heart still flutters with happiness when I reach the farm gate.

Author: Cathy A. Sizemore Helms. Cathy is an Office Manager for West Virginia University's Monroe County Extension Service.

97-001-ST-WV-001-1997

The Year Was 1937; The Month Was September

I had finished high school with plans already made for me to go to college. It was following the Depression, and my father had been back to work only a short time. One income was the usual for a family then. My aunt was running a drugstore, following her husband's death, in the college town. Arrangements had been made for me to live with her and work some in the drugstore. My room and board was fifteen dollars a month.

I went to Concord College in Athens, Mercer County. College was different then. My tuition was fifteen dollars a semester. I took extra classes because I felt that I must be ready for any work available. I had twenty-five cents a week for spending money on personal needs and pleasure. Another niece was there under the same arrangements. We occasionally split a five-cent popsicle as a treat.

My clothes were minimal. I had one navy blue skirt, one brown skirt, and a tan button-up sweater that I could wear with each skirt. Also, I had five white boys' shirts that were cheaper than girls', a pair of saddle shoes, white socks, and underwear. In addition, I had one Sunday dress, and a pair of good shoes. All of this packed in a weekend suitcase. I carried my lightweight coat.

As the four years passed, I was able to get an evening dress and a warm winter coat. This was the way life was. No one had much more. My new best friend's coat was darned. Nobody seemed to notice, realize, or care. Everyone had so little.

At that time some students began teaching on a one-year certificate, some on a two-year certificate, but I stayed four years with about forty in my graduating class. I began a long teaching career with a beginning salary of ninety dollars a month and no benefits. The state and nation have profited from those attending the college at that time. I have always been thankful for this opportunity.

Author: Lucille Litz Walthall. Lucille is a retired teacher. She is the mother of three, grandmother of four, and great-grandmother of one. She grew up in Bluefield, but has lived in Princeton since 1944.

98-001-ST-WV-001-1997

My First Mallet Steam Engine

In 1954, I moved from Kansas to Montgomery, West Virginia, to accept a teaching position at West Virginia Tech. When I first arrived I was housed at Maclin Hall which was one of the dormitories on the campus. The C&O Railroad main lines literally run right down the middle of Montgomery, and Maclin Hall sits across the street from the tracks.

Not very long after I had moved into my room I heard this awful racket which I recognized as a steam engine coming through town. I didn't know it at the time, but just west of Montgomery is the town of Handley, where the C&O Railroad had a rail yard. What I was hearing was a heavy coal train pulling out of this yard and making its way through Montgomery.

Maclin Hall is U-shaped and my windows were located in the deep corner of the U-shape so I couldn't see the oncoming train until it got right in front of the building. When I first saw the train I just stood with my mouth open, and I think my eyes may have fallen out of my head. I didn't know what to think. Pulling this train was not one, but two of the biggest steam engines I had ever seen, "double-heading" they called it.

Where I had lived in Kansas, it wasn't anything to see trains go by at fifty or sixty miles an hour. Even the small steam engines could do good speeds on that flat land, so you can imagine my shock at seeing my first Mallet steam engines, the local people just referred to them as "Big Mallies."

I later found out that this type of engine was specifically designed to pull heavy coal

trains across the mountains of West Virginia and Virginia. With a 2-6-6-6 wheel alignment they were among the largest and most powerful steam engines ever built. They were named after the mountains they worked in and were officially known as the "Allegheny Class H-8" by the C&O Railroad. Big doesn't begin to describe them; they were huge monsters of steel, smoke, and steam.

AUTHOR: *Richard C. Bainbridge. This story was told by the late Wendell Silvius. His wife Carole submitted this version written by Mr. Bainbridge, a longtime family friend.*

99-001-ST-WV-001-1997

Papa Jim

West Virginians are proud, independent, and self-sufficient people. No handouts for these hardworking people. My grandfather James L. Mullins of Princeton, West Virginia, epitomized this ideal.

With little education, Papa Jim became a carpenter. His common sense enabled him to figure in his head the amount of lumber needed to build a house and its cost faster than the estimates my mother could provide on paper.

Papa Jim became well known in the Princeton area in the 1920s and 1930s for building quality homes. Many of his contracts were negotiated with a handshake. His sole income came from building houses and selling them every two to three years.

In the Depression years not many homes were being built and sold. To help the unemployed, President Roosevelt introduced the Department of Public Works to pay the unemployed to work and beautify the community. The Princeton Post Office on Mercer Street was built under this program, and Papa Jim signed on to feed his family.

Soon Social Security was introduced, and all workers were expected to join. Periodically,

"Papa Jim," James L. Mullins (1880-1963).

government agents would arrive to ensure that all employees were participating. Not trusting the government, and not wanting to give up a portion of his much needed income, Papa Jim hid in the basement of the Post Office until the agents left.

Did Papa Jim ever regret his decision? No one knows for sure, but later as an old man, sick and fragile, Papa Jim and Mama had no income. Again, there were no handouts for them!

To survive, they used their own ingenuity. Papa Jim continued to buy and sell homes. He grew a vegetable garden with harvests sold or canned for winter's food. Another source of income was from raising chickens for food and barter. In the late fall, chickens were killed and taken to the cannery at Glenwood Park and canned for food for another year.

Work was continuous; survival was dependent upon one's own hard work. Papa Jim continued to trade, sell, and barter as long as his health endured — well into his mid-eighties. Stubborn, determined, and self-reliant describe Papa Jim and many West Virginians who learned to survive the many hardships they encountered.

AUTHOR: *Gayle Walthall Wise. Gayle is a native of Princeton. She is a former teacher and teacher educator, and is currently a fashion consultant for Doncaster clothing.*

100-001-ST-WV-001-1997

The War On Two Fronts

The Civil War was fought by people like Robert and Christina Hughes, my great-grandparents. In the fall of 1862, Robert left home to join the Union army. His father Francis Tincher Hughes told the boy never to return — there was no family left for him in Fayette County on Bell Creek in western Virginia, a state that had already left the Union.

Robert sneaked past neighbors and through Confederate lines to reach Gauley Bridge where he signed up for the North against family. His records show enlistment September 30, 1862, discharge June 28, 1865. He experienced soul-shattering fights at Antietam and Cedar Creek. He was left for dead on the field at Lynchburg, only to be found unconscious with malaria by the cavalry. He received no physical wounds from the war.

In 1863 he deserted while on picket duty, going back to Fayette County to marry Christina O'Dell. I imagine the wedding was bittersweet, in a divided family in a southern community. When he returned he was reinstated and fined

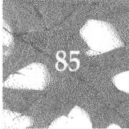

twenty-four dollars for taking a rifle belonging to the government.

Nine months later Christina delivered a baby girl. Soon she and the baby moved in with Francis Hughes. Robert received a letter saying if he wanted to see his wife and daughter, he would have to come home to do it. In 1865, he did.

Christina, who permitted no one to speak ill of her husband, probably played a major role on the family front. I imagine she let ol' Francis know that if he wanted to see his grandchildren ever, he'd make up with his son. With that understanding, they quickly worked out the details. The Civil War was healed by people like Christina and Robert Hughes, in just such a way.

Author: Michael Hughes, a poet of strong West Virginia lineage, lives in Romney with his wife Janet Gould.

101-001-ST-WV-001-1997

Pearl Buck Of West Virginia

"Had I been given the choice of place for my birth, I would have chosen exactly where I was born." Pearl Buck's birth house – her mother's home — overlooked a beautiful landscape of green plains set against the Allegheny Mountains. She maintained that she remembers her birth. The intimate knowledge she retained of the large white house where she seldom visited, and never lived for more than a few weeks at a time, seems to support her claim.

"The first time I walked into it on my own two feet I was already nine years old. Yet already I knew every room I was to see. Up the stairs with the hand-carved balustrade is the room where I was born... I remembered being born there... I see the wide old-fashioned bedstead... there was a dressing table, although it has not been there in my lifetime since I was taken by my parents to China... But it was there, I maintain, when I was born because I remember it.... There were white ruffled curtains at the windows... From the visit when I was nine years old, I remember the dew shining on the grass in the morning sun." (Harris, Theodore, F., *Pearl S. Buck, A Biography*)

With this statement Pearl Buck lays claim to West Virginia. Unfortunately, West Virginia would not lay claim to Pearl Buck for many years after she had made that statement. As an English teacher, I wondered why this native author, the only woman to receive both the Pulitzer and Nobel Prize for Literature did not command more attention in her native state. Like most, I dismissed the thought until around the middle of the nineteen sixties when I began to hear of a program promoted by Jim Comstock who was encouraging West Virginia schoolchildren to bring their pennies to school for the Pearl Buck Fund.

What, I wondered, is the Pearl Buck Fund? A little research revealed that Pearl Buck had wanted to offer the governor of West Virginia its first great enterprise as a tourist attraction — the house where she was born complete with her memorabilia. That governor refused to see her, although she tried several times to contact him. He would not even acknowledge her request for an appointment. She left the state feeling very much rejected, to establish her home in Bucks County, Pennsylvania, where, today, we can visit and see what West Virginia lost.

Mr. Comstock, believing Buck deserved such an honor, and realizing the possibilities of such an attraction, began the campaign to buy the house and present it as Pearl Buck's birthplace. That would give her some recognition in her native state and provide that state with a tourist attraction. Along with educating the children through the "donation campaign," he approached the West Virginia Federation of Women's Clubs asking them to assume the challenge of the purchase and restoration of the house. They agreed in 1966, establishing the Pearl S. Buck Foundation, Inc.

Someday, perhaps, Buck's deep involvement in humanitarian projects will be recognized by her birth state. Through her humanitarian outreach she established an orphanage for abandoned children of color, all colors, who without such a champion had little chance of survival. Her book, *The New Year*, tells the story of such a child. She personally adopted ethnic children providing a home with mothering and educational opportunities for many who would not have had those opportunities.

Her great statement, delivered in a speech presented at Randolph-Macon College, her alma mater, challenges all West Virginians. "I believe only in life, tragic, gay, glorious, incomprehensible, life. I believe in Human Beings and in the good and evil mingled in us all. I believe in art, that is to be kept to its one holy use, which is to portray faithfully, as only the purest art can, life itself and life only." What better model can an aspiring writer have?

Author: Geneva Anderson Wynne. Mrs. Wynne is a teacher and writer who, although retired, still teaches and still writes. She is married to James B. Wynne, and is the mother of two sons, Stephen Lee and Joseph Anderson Wynne. Pearl S. Buck was born in 1892, died 1973.

102-001-ST-WV-001-1997

Chapter 7

Potomac Highlands

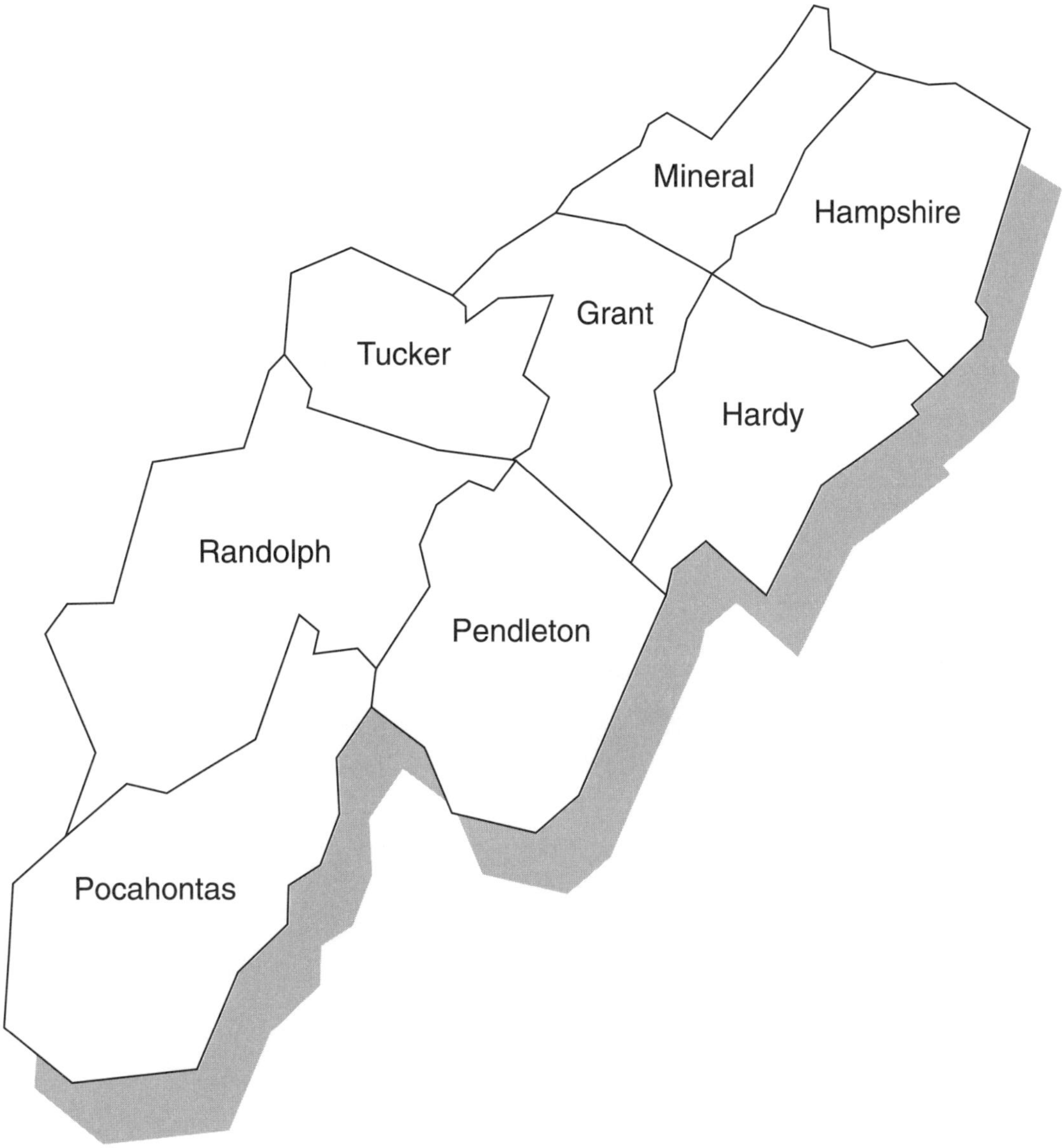

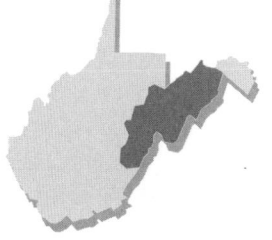

The Vegetable Vendor

Born and raised in West Virginia, I have never felt the need to live elsewhere. I love the mountains, the changing seasons, the simple way of living that's possible here, and the people who are the state's essence.

One such person was my grandmother Grace Ferguson. Hard working and uncomplaining, she never had much in the way of material things, yet she left me an inheritance of priceless memories. I spent all my summers with grandma in Wheeling, and have a trunk full of stories I could tell. But one of my favorites comes from the late 1940s, when a unique way of shopping was to make purchases from the Vegetable Vendor.

Grandma lived in a third floor apartment. No elevators there! On Saturdays a rickety old truck would stop in the alley below, a large cast iron bell ringing. Grandma would precariously lean out the window, one hand firmly keeping me safely at her side. A shouting conversation followed about fruits, vegetables, price, and purchase desired. With this accomplished, grandma opened her small black change purse, placed the required amount of money in a big basket tied to a rope and carefully lowered it to the waiting vendor below.

Shopping from an apartment window was such an odd thing to a six year old "country" girl. I watched in eager anticipation for the basket to be pulled back up full of vegetables, melons, big yellow bananas, bright red apples, and sometimes even a bag of candy!

I know now that it was often a sacrifice to pay for the contents of that basket, but doing things for others was important to grandma. She was a tiny lady with a big heart and I believe she was the epitome of West Virginia and its people.

AUTHOR: *Barbra Borror. Barbra is a native of Morgantown but has resided in Mineral County for most of her life. She says, "Anyplace is home — as long as it's West Virginia."*

103-001-ST-WV-001-1997

The Outhouse

It was May, that magical month of spring that raises havoc in schools everywhere. In Sandy Hollow School, nestled in a small valley three miles from Purgetsville, West Virginia, that magic brought out the mischievous nature of every boy in that little log schoolhouse. A frog in the drinking water bucket, a crab in the dipper, a lizard on Mary Lou's desk, and a grass snake in Miss Pancake's desk drawer.

I, of course, had nothing to do with any of it. After all I was just a third-grader and scared to death of our switch-wielding schoolmarm. But that did not stop me from appreciating the ingenuity of the older boys. And I always felt sorry for them when they were caught and switched.

On this beautiful May afternoon, just before we went back inside from lunch hour, Teacher went to the outhouse. While she was inside, Mary Lou rang the bell to call us back to class. As we filed in, two of the older boys slipped out to the outhouse and turned the button to lock the door. They forced a stick behind it so Teacher could not wriggle it loose. Then they came in and told us that Miss Pancake had gotten sick and gone home and that school was dismissed. Kids scattered in every direction.

The next morning, when we returned to school, two of the older girls went to the outhouse. They were quite surprised to find Miss Pancake still locked in the privy. In all my life, I can never remember seeing anyone in a greater fit of rage than Miss Pancake. She went to the woods, broke off an armful of switches, which looked like clubs to me, and stormed into the schoolhouse. She lined up every boy from the fourth grade up and whaled the fire out of them. For the first time, I was glad to be only a third-grader.

AUTHOR: *Edward Hartman. Mr. Hartman is a Korean War and Desert Storm veteran. He has taught at West Virginia University, Frostburg State, Purdue, and in Mercer County public schools. He is retired and lives near Athens.*

104-001-ST-WV-001-1997

Pure West Virginian

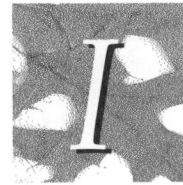

I am a pure West Virginian. I was born July 25, 1935. I come from a big family of twelve siblings. There were seven girls and five boys. I have two brothers deceased: one died at age thirteen from polio, and the other one was killed in Vietnam in 1967. One sister was stillborn. Both of my parents are now deceased.

Our family was poor but we had plenty to eat and clean clothes to wear. We helped each other. There was love and closeness, too. We had chickens, hogs, cows, sheep, and goats, so we all had chores to do. We milked the cows for our own milk, butter, and cottage cheese, and we produced our own meat.

The girls helped as well as the boys, inside the house and out. My sister and I helped Dad cut pulpwood and mine props. I remember one

time I mixed up homemade bread when I was only ten years old.

My brothers and sisters and I went to a one-room schoolhouse, nothing like today's schools. We walked three miles to attend grades first through eighth. We also had several good teachers.

I graduated from Romney High School in 1954, and got married in 1955. My husband and I have five daughters. I lost a son at birth. My daughters are all grown and married. I have three grandchildren: two grandsons and one granddaughter. They live in Woodstock, Virginia. My husband Robert worked for Potomac Edison Company for thirty-two years and is now retired. We are both in fair health and we enjoy our life. We have been married forty-two years.

AUTHOR: *Freeda Davy. Mrs. Davy is a native of Hampshire County. She is a mother, grandmother, and homemaker. She enjoys sewing, especially pillows and quilts.*

105-001-ST-WV-001-1997

The Markus cabin.

The Meaning Of A Photograph

Above my bookcase hangs a small frame. It holds my favorite photo of me and my best friend Michelle Markus. Oversize styrofoam fishing hats protect our sunburned cheeks and ears as we lean against the wooden railing outside her family's cabin in Elkins, during summer 1994. We had set the timer on her little

Hanging out and bonding in Elkins, Amy and Michelle.

thirty-five millimeter, scrunched together, and hoped for the best; the result is crooked, the background somewhat fuzzy. A picture is worth a thousand words, they say, but that photo — amateurish as it is — is worth much more to me.

From self-consciousness at Morgantown High, through college exams and their associated headaches, to post-graduation "I have my bachelor's, now what?" quandaries, Michelle and I have faced trials and tribulations together. Throughout it all, she has remained my confidante, my cheerleader, my best friend. But it was on our trips to the cabin in Elkins that we learned to laugh at life and ourselves and to face misfortune with a sense of perspective.

The cool waters of Shaver's Fork, which flows gently behind the cabin, helped soothe the burn of the disintegration of my relationship with my college love — my first serious, albeit flawed attempt at lifelong bliss. And Michelle's presence, always supportive, never faltering, reminded me that happiness comes from inside, not from someone else. When she suffered the pangs of heartache, we ventured to the cabin to lose ourselves in afternoons spent catching crawdads and drifting lazily in the shallows on innertubes. The combination of water, the warm sun on our shoulders and the love of a true friend formed a curative, almost magical barrier against sorrow.

Later, huddled around a campfire at dusk, covered with goosebumps because we'd just left the river, and the young fire still demanded our attention, our conversations centered around mundane events. But when our hair was dry, and our bodies warm from a combination of fire and a drink of something "homemade" left on the inside table from the last trip, we spoke of hopes, dreams, love, life and death. We cried over sentimental stories and laughed until we cried some more. Eventually we even came to the realization that, yes, our mothers were right, we would both love again.

We never worried about the hour; there was no one to disturb. The little, three-room red wood cabin next door sat empty and overgrown. It had belonged to Michelle's late grandparents, and her father Joe was raised there. Her grandfather always took his baths in the river. I heard often about her buxom grandmother. "She'd laugh and shake like jelly. And, oh, the songs she would sing." Michelle's face lit up when she talked about her. She misses her, I know. The sole purpose of that cabin now is to keep firewood dry under its dilapidated back porch.

The cabin we used had been the family store, conveniently located alongside the road. Cinder blocks painted white, it has two rooms, one crowded with two bunk beds and two doubles. The other room has a table, wood-burning stove, and the recently added refrigerator, sink, and gas stove. There's no indoor bathroom. The decor consists mainly of fishing paraphernalia: poles, nets, bait, hats, and dusty wooden plaques extolling the virtues of the ancient pastime. On the shelves lay my personal favorite: the tangled strands of white, owl-shaped outdoor lights.

We never spent much time inside unless it was raining. The morning after a storm was glorious. Enhanced by the sun reflecting in the raindrops, the grass looked the brightest green, like that in a child's crayon rendition of a summer day. The woods smelled of fresh, fragrant pine. Shaver's Fork ran clearer, faster, deeper. Colder. Michelle and I yelped simultaneously at the sting of the water on our toes, then we laughed and dove in head first. Life's possibilities were limitless.

Michelle and her fiancé Bryan Wood are getting married August 16, 1997. I have the distinction of being her Maid of Honor. Although she currently lives in New York, the wedding will take place in Morgantown. I'm sure we will need a marathon planning session. Call it a hunch, but I think it will take place in that little cabin just inside the Monongahela National Forest in Elkins, West Virginia.

AUTHOR: Amy Stevenson. Amy is a Morgantown native and graduate of West Virginia University.

106-001-ST-WV-001-1997

The Smoking Smokehouse

Living in a rural area of Randolph County, West Virginia, afforded my family a certain amount of entertainment, especially when "city folk" would move into the area. Such was the case during the 1960s when a young wildlife biologist, fresh out of graduate school, and his family moved into the house behind us.

My parents took a liking to the newcomers and shared a lot of knowledge with them about "country ways." Mom taught them how to plant their garden according to the "sign" and Dad taught the man a lot about raising "yearlings."

Although my family had several cattle and sheep on a nearby farm, we only had chickens where we lived, and an occasional pig. About every other year we rotated raising a beef or a pig for butchering. This particular year we had raised what would be our last pig, so we decided to convert the hog house into a smokehouse and smoke our own hams and bacon.

After converting the hog house and making a trip to Middle Ridge for cutting a load of hickory, we set everything up. We were pleased with our smokehouse.

On one cold Saturday morning, the young biologist came to our front door. Our neighbor was dead serious with concern when he asked if we should call the fire department. My dad asked why, and the neighbor explained that our building was on fire.

Dad got that twinkle in his eye, patted the neighbor on the back and said, "Son, let me show you something." They left to check out the smoking smokehouse and upon return we all had a big laugh — especially my dad!

I'm told that over the years that wildlife biologist, Jim Rawson, has become a bit of an expert smoking his own quarry.

AUTHOR: Sally A. Phares. Sally is a computer center administrator from Beverly. She currently resides in Las Vegas, Nevada.

107-001-ST-WV-001-1997

Early Stitches

Many young girls have a grandmother to teach them the "old ways." That was not the case for me. Instead, I had a great aunt Effie who lived in the last house of the city limits of Beverly. When I was little I couldn't say her name, so I just called her "E" — a name that stuck for the rest of her life.

I remember E quilting every winter. She would set up the quilting frame in her living room. There would barely be room to walk around and get to the chairs. She would quilt every evening, sometimes finishing several quilts during a winter.

I received a bride doll for Christmas in 1959, and soon decided it would be nice for her to have clothes other than her gown to wear. I asked E to help me make some. E sewed without using patterns. She made the doll a couple of dresses, and decided that it was time for me to learn to sew.

She started by teaching me stitches in fabric. Then she taught me to use the old treadle Singer sewing machine. After that, she declared that I was ready to work on my very first quilt. I couldn't have been more than seven or eight years old.

E's favorite piecing pattern was "nine patch." She helped me cut out the pieces and showed me how to piece them together. Then she helped me put the back, the batting, and the top together for my first nine patch doll quilt. I was so proud of it. It fit my dolls in their carriage perfectly.

Thank you, E, for your patience that led to many years of sewing pleasure, both in clothing and many more quilts!

Author: Sally A. Phares

108-001-ST-WV-001-1997

Surprised By Joelle

It all started with that smelly hitchhiker I picked up on the way to Seneca Rocks, West Virginia. Of course, I regretted it instantly. I fought back the gag reflex as he followed a wave of noxious body odor into the front seat of my car. Before completing the two hour journey, I had overcome my elitist bathing prejudice sufficiently to discover that he was actually a wonderful guy — I stood better informed of local environmental issues, and in the bargain, learned a shortcut via Flatrock Road and State Route 92 that shaved valuable seconds off the trip. I suspected there might be a lesson for me there somewhere but didn't give it another thought until after the events of the next two days forced me to reconsider my outlook on climbing, living, and other chores.

Ron (my climbin' pal of old) and I met in the parking lot, and plotted out our course for the day. In consideration of the threatening weather forecast, we opted for a classic Seneca moderate aptly named Ecstasy (Climbing Gallery #138) that would stay relatively dry in the rain. I'd done this particular climb a few times already and found myself feeling almost indifferent when he mentioned it. A terrible feeling that is — a bit like falling out of love, I guess. I mechanically made my way through the moves. Hand, foot, pro, hand, foot …too intent on maintaining a fast pace to relish the exposure and scenery. We finished on a more difficult variation called Muscle Beach, a 5.8 with a truly imposing roof finish. It felt too much like work; hands on wet slopey holds, my small pack smacking me in the head and pulling me downward like Jacque Cousteau's lead diving sled. Just when all was lost, my frantic groping uncovered a horn so perfectly shaped for the human hand, Stalone could have used it for his one-arm hang poser shots.

No sooner had we finished with the obligatory handshakes and backslaps that a yodeling, fear-drenched scream cut the humid air not far from us. It seemed to last an eternity, and then we heard (and felt?) some muffled sound like a watermelon smacking into ground 200 feet below us. Even the locusts were silent for a few seconds, then a woman screamed "Oh my God, somebody help me!" Ron leaned out over the edge to find the voice while I set up a top-rope anchor. "He must have fallen off the last Ecstasy belay," he said. It was maybe forty feet below and to the right of us. As Ron rappelled down to the girl left at the belay, I scurried down the long down-hike, fearful of finding what there was to find of the man, and hoping I would know what to do if I did. He was lying in the fetal position, head pointing down hill. A big lump protruded from his lower spine, twisted at some weird angle. Blood spilled from his ears and rectum. Unbelievably, miraculously, incredibly, he was breathing and talking after taking a 180 foot fall. "I know my back is broken, probably my ankle, and some ribs," he said through loose teeth, as calmly as if he were talking about someone else's cold symptoms. A small assortment of hikers and climbers were already assembled there with a ranger, but progress on the rescue was excruciatingly slow, and my presence did nothing to accelerate it. I went back to join Ron at the pigeon-dung encrusted belay, trying to lower the fallen man's partner the last fifteen feet to the ground. She had lost the use of her hands owing to severe rope burn. Ron said, "It could be worse," and I thought he meant that at least it wasn't raining. "It could be raining," he finished. We were both too wigged-out to notice the down-pour.

That night, we didn't feel like setting up our tents in the rain, so we joined a party of cavers/climbers under the camp's pavilion. I put my sleeping bag on the stage, feeling a little homesick, and wondering how much money I could get for my climbing gear. I was confident that from now on lawn darts would replace climbing as my idle passion. I was less than thrilled about spending the night with a bunch of screaming high-school kids, but then I remembered the smelly hitchhiker and decided to engage myself. What a gift those kids turned out to be! I was talking to one of them about the age we would like to be stuck at. I suggested twenty-seven, since that was such a personally historic time (I met my wife, and quit a boring job). Joelle looked at me, her eyes full of hope, innocence, and youthful vitality. "Twenty-seven is too close to thirty, which is definitely over the hill," she said. I laughed, reveling in my over-the-hillness, and grateful for the mortality that made Joelle possible. Without death, there is no renewal. For a moment, I saw our future in these young people and all seemed grand and just. No, I wasn't drinking.

Very late, I burrow my way to a restless

sleep, but nightmares haunt me. I am alone at an airy belay. Sorting gear and lines, I stop myself three times before releasing anything, too keenly aware of Gravity's "no return" policy. Some voice in my head tries to reassure me; "This thing really is clipped there, so you can let it go now without dropping it." For some reason, the time has come to release a rope, which I do. I watch as the end whistles wildly into the void, all the while vaguely aware of having made a dreadful, irremediable mistake.

Somehow, the next day finds Ron and me back at the rock. The pace is slower and sadder, but everything is so beautiful. I find myself full of hope for tomorrow's humans, thankful for mortality, thankful for that wonderful horn on the roof of Muscle Beach, thankful for the wind swirling in my helmet as I stand on this 900 foot quartzite fin rising out of Allegheny foothills choked with green. I wonder how I could have stopped noticing the tendrils of mist hiding distant ridges, the gray clouds pregnant with rain, the sun, the splendid sun, giver of life.

On the way home up the newly discovered shortcut, everything conspires against me. Route 92 is the heaven of John Denver's song. Faure's Requiem blaring from the tape deck is making me think about that far off Northern feeling that C. S. Lewis says is God. Cresting a hill into a glorious evening-sun-filled valley, I am so overwhelmed by it all I have to pull off the road. I'm not sure if I'm laughing or crying, or why I would do either. Maybe it's for that man whose blood was mixed with the rain in the rocks and mud at Seneca; maybe for his partner, who must wish the black trenches cut in her arms and hands leave the most lasting scars; maybe for my mother-in-law whose life was just ruthlessly cut short by a freak illness. Beyond reason, I feel exuberantly alive, surprised by Joy.

Author: Renaud Stauber. Renaud is a Morgantown native studying physics in Boulder, Colorado. He is an avid outdoorsman. According to newspaper reports, the man injured in the story recovered from his fall.

109-001-ST-WV-001-1997

Gramma's Day Out

My Gramma Ressie lives alone in a holler in West Virginia and seldom gets out much. Last summer I decided Gramma needed more excitement in her life, so I gathered her up and off we headed to the Apple Harvest Festival at the Children's Home in Burlington. They have crafts, yardsale items, homemade apple butter, and the best tasting apple dumplins you have ever set your teeth into. The festival proceeds go to the Home.

On the way down you could hear the excitement in Gramma's voice. As we neared Burlington, she went crazy when she saw the flea markets. I had never seen so many people in one spot at one time. Gramma and I had to park nearly a mile away, and I thought Gramma was "a-going to keel over" from the walk. At last we made it to the festival and Gramma found herself a seat. Well since Gramma was pooped, I felt it my duty to have enough fun for the both of us. I brought her so much food I think she felt sick, but she just kept smiling. Then I'd buy something at the yardsale tables and show it to Gramma. If she wanted, I'd run back and get her one just like it. The singers came on stage and sang about the prettiest singing we had ever heard. They sang country, gospel, bluegrass, and rock 'n' roll. Gramma was smiling from ear to ear, and tappin' her toes. The day was drawing to a close, and Gramma and I figured we had better get our tails out of there. I wished I had thought to get Gramma some more food on the way out, for a walk like that takes a lot of energy. As we made it to the car and headed home, I listened to Gramma chirping about what a day she'd had. I realized this was a day well spent, for Gramma had never been to a festival before.

Author: Beverly Sue Ketterman. Bev is a freelance writer and author of short stories. She is the mother of one. She resides in her hometown of Maysville.

110-001-ST-WV-001-1997

What Grandma Said

The speech patterns of the natives of our Appalachian mountains and valleys have changed considerably in the last few years. Modern communication and transportation have altered the way we talk, but occasionally, I hear the early speech patterns, and to me, it is a beautiful language, full of history and expression.

Our language has been termed a dialect, which is the particular language pattern of a certain region, or a language having the characteristics of a more primitive time surviving chiefly in specialized areas. The way we speak has been called "pure Chaucerian," and also, called "debased and ignorant," and the more critical the term, the more likely it comes from someone outside the area who knows considerably less about the English language than he or she thinks he or she knows. Instead of ignorant and corrupt, our language should be labeled "archaic," or surviving from the past.

Our first settlers were the Scotch-Irish (so-called), along with Germans and Pennsylvania Dutch. Remnants of the language brought by the Scotch-Irish can be found in our English. Linguists place the general historical period of our language in the days of the First Queen Elizabeth whose reign was from 1558 to 1603. Our speech is actually a sort of Scottish flavored Elizabethan English.

During that time, James I united Scotland and England. During his rule he decided to settle Northern Ireland with Protestants from Scotland and England. Through the years the Scots multiplied and grew tired of the unreasonable trade and religious restrictions imposed by England. Beginning in the 1700s great numbers began migrating to the English Colonies in the New World. Now they called themselves Scotch Irish.

These immigrants landed on the East Coast and found all the good land taken. Many traveled through Pennsylvania, down the Ohio and settled in the South and West, part of which is now West Virginia. They virtually isolated themselves from the mainstream of American life because of the mountains. They kept the old speech patterns and forms that had long since fallen out of fashion elsewhere. These patterns are found in Chaucer, Shakespeare, the Wycliffe Bible, and English writers of the period.

Some of our dialect's words and phrases that I've heard through the years and that have fascinated me are: *brenth* of cloth — the amount of material that you can measure from the end of your nose to the tip of your outstretched thumb and finger; *fernenth* — near to, "set the box fernenth the table;" *briggity* — acting naughty; *warp* — to hit (Chaucer); *redd up* — to clean up (Old English); *whelks* — what you get from a bee sting (Chaucer); *slue of fish* — a lot of fish (Old English); *wampus* — coat (Old English); *her'n, your'n, his'n* — her, your, his (evolved from *mine* and *thine* from Wycliffe Bible of 1380); *back-jawed* — argued; *fritter away time* — wasted; *chimley* — chimney; *pert-nigh* — nearly; *pavish* — walk around doing nothing; *bat-brained* — foolish; *sight of folks* — a crowd (Old English); *et* — eat or have eaten; and *"acka-fortis"* (really, aqua-fortis) — strong water, nitric acid.

My mother had a fourth grade education, but the wisdom of a Solomon. A book could be written about this little mountain woman. She had axioms (self evident truths) for everything. It's easy to wonder how much of them is "dialect" with roots in our Scottish flavored Elizabethan English. Here's some of what I remember hearing her say: "Right's right and right don't wrong nobody," "What goes over the devil's back, comes around under his belly," "She's too iffy to suit me," "They ain't a bit of difference between tellin' a lie that hurts someone, and tellin' a truth that hurts just as much." "Hit's about time they learned the hand-writin' on the wall," "The onliest things we really keep are the things we give away," "They ain't no rewards a gonna' be offered for findin' fault," and "Ya' jest as well eat a piece of the devil as to drink his broth."

AUTHOR: *Macel G. Gear. Mrs. Gear (b. Pickens, 1918) grew up in the Sugar Creek area of Webster County. She resides in Elkins and is a retired teacher. Of her interest in the speech patterns of our mountain folk, she says "I grew up in these mountains, and by the time I reached high school, I was cognizant of the fact that my mother and our relatives and friends used words that weren't printed in the English texts to which I had been introduced... in about 1975 I enrolled in a summer class at Davis and Elkins College entitled Appalachian Dialect, and I become 'hooked' on the whys and wherefores of these new words (new, to me) and the history behind them. Mrs. Wylene Dial taught the class and she was the first real authority I had met who also loved the subject."*

111-001-ST-WV-001-1997

Tales And Mountain Philosophy

Never try to match wits with a mountaineer when it comes to tall tales or having the last word. The following two stories illustrate this admonition:

Cheat Mountain

During the winter of 1855, the Trotter brothers had a contract with the US Government to carry mail between Huttonsville in Randolph County, West Virginia, and Staunton, Virginia. The brothers had made the trip to Staunton and a severe storm came up while they were in Staunton. On their return trip they could not cross Cheat Mountain, and as a result of the delayed trip, the people of the Tygart's Valley complained to the postal authorities about the delay in the delivery of their mail. The postal authorities wrote to the brothers for an explanation, and the following is an exact worded copy of their answer:

Mr. Postmaster General
Washington, DC

Sir:

If you knock the gable end out of hell and back it up against Cheat Mountain and rain fire and brimstone on it for forty days an forty nights, it won't melt the snow enough to get your d____ mail through on time.

Yours truly,
Trotter Brothers
By: (s) James Trotter

Back Roads

The city slicker had been driving the back roads and lost his way. He noticed a farmer standing by the road, so he stopped and said, "Mister, can you please tell me how I can get back to Interstate 79 so I can return to Charleston?" The farmer said, "No, I can't tell you which road to take." The driver said, "Well, you don't know too much do you?"

"*I* ain't lost," replied the farmer.

If philosophy is a search for truth through logical reasoning, then mountaineers are philosophers:

"Most men don't understand the value of knittin' to us women...it gives us something to think about while we're talkin'," "Some folks with little minds are like a gallon jug...the less they have in them, the more noise they makes when they starts pourin' out," "My cousin says you can't pay no 'tention to that old sayin' that worry don't do any good. She knows it did, cause everything she worried bout never happened," "Hit sure does look like some politicians would learn that nothin' ain't right that's morally wrong," "Aunt Caroline used to say that worry is like a rockin' chair. Hit allus' gives you sumpin' to do, but hit never gets you anywhere," and "My Pa said Aunt Susie was the one who could always smile when sumpin' went wrong cause she had already thought of somebody to blame it on."

AUTHOR: *Macel G. Gear*

112-001-ST-WV-001-1997

Papaw's Bike

Back in the 1930s, when Papaw was thirteen years old, he wanted a twenty-six-inch bicycle. In the Montgomery Ward catalog was a black bicycle priced at twenty-nine ninety-five. In order to earn the money to purchase the bike, Papaw went to work in the hayfields on a dairy farm near his home in Mineral County, West Virginia.

Carpenter's Dairy paid him ten cents an hour. The hours were hot and long in the summer. Late in the summer, he had earned enough to order the bike from Wards. Several weeks later he received a postcard that the package had arrived. He hitch-hiked to Cumberland, Maryland, with several dollars in his pocket to pay the freight house in Cumberland for the freight and shipping costs. With the hand tools that he had brought from home, Papaw opened the wooden box. Inside was the bike, but it was in several pieces. Carefully he laid out all the pieces and looked them over. It was the bike he wanted, now all he had to do was assemble it.

Luckily, his friend Jack had come with him. It took an hour for the two boys to fit it all together. Then both of them pushed the bike across the street to a gas station and put air in the tires. Papaw rode the bike home with Jack on the handle bars. It was three miles.

He rode the bike to school for many years. In the summer it was loaded with camping gear and carried him along the path by the river to his favorite camping spot. Papaw sold the bike when was sixteen and used the money to help pay for a Harley Davidson motorcycle.

AUTHOR: *Erica L. Stratton. This story is about Erica's grandfather Robert L. Spriggs of Carpendale. Erica is ten years old and resides in Morgantown.*

113-001-ST-WV-001-1997

General Lee In Slatyfork And Linwood

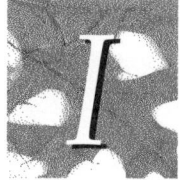

In about 1862, General Lee was in Pocahontas County to lead his men and to dislodge the Yanks in Randolph County when and if orders came from Richmond, Virginia.

On one occasion, General Lee was invited to eat supper with William and Rachael Dilley Sharp. He accepted and shared in the supper prepared by Rachael. The meal presumably consisted of corn bread, baked potatoes, cooked dried beans, dried berries, maple syrup and blackberry pie for dessert. Two of General Lee's soldiers stood guard outside the front door while he ate. The Sharp's log house still stands.

At the time the Confederate soldiers occupied the Linwood area, a thousand or so soldiers camped one night in the meadow in front of the present Sharp's Store at Slatyfork. The captain ordered every man to get a rail from the meadow fence to keep the fires going all night. They burned every chestnut rail, which had taken many years of labor to cut and split. Several soldiers discovered an apple hole covered with leaves and filled their pockets.

The Confederates moved out of the Linwood campground on their way to Virginia. One wagon was loaded with minnie balls. When it crossed the creek at Linwood, a wheel collapsed and the load was left in the creek. William went there and brought back all he could carry to mold bullets for his guns.

There were reports that hundreds died one winter at Linwood, but no graves were ever found. One theory was that the dead may have been dropped down a vertical cave called "The Devil's Dining Room," a name derived from a sound like dishes being broken when rocks were dropped down the cave, banging the walls on the way down.

AUTHOR: Luther David Sharp, Jr. Mr. Sharp, of Slatyfork, contributed these stories which were told to his father L.D. Sharp (1872-1963) by L.D.'s father Silas Sharp (1842-1899). Silas Sharp was a civilian captured and taken as a prisoner to Libby Prison in Richmond, and Salisbury, North Carolina, for twenty-three months and twenty-four days.

114-001-ST-WV-001-1997

Chapter 8

Eastern Panhandle

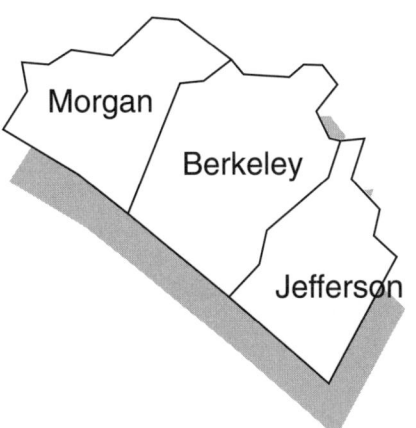

The Face Of America:
From Tyler, Texas, 1936, To Martinsburg, West Virginia, 1996

It was a Dorothea Lange Tableau:
Two women in thin cotton dresses
Surrounded by four hungry-looking kids dressed in
Worn, but clean, clothes

The Face of America, Martinsburg, West Virginia. (Photo by Paul Grussendorf, with permission.)

The kids' mom, in her early thirties,
But with a face much older
(Like her clothes, worn but clean)
Stands there chatting with the other woman
While the kids fidget restlessly in a loose circle
Around the two adults

(No one, in fact, is closer than a couple of feet
from the next nearest person)

The other woman finally speaks to one of the kids,
A girl of nine or ten,
"What's your name, honey?"
The girl just stands there, staring at the woman,
And says nothing...

The mom, with a stern look on her face,
Reaches over and shakes the girl's arm...
"Hey! Somebody's talking to you!" she says

I hear her thoughts as I pass by
"Even if we are poor, we do have our pride."
"We won't wear dirty clothes, and we will
mind our manners."

The picture dissolves as I enter
The pawn shop
They have just come out of

AUTHOR: Riccardo Accurso. Having traveled extensively throughout the world, Riccardo gained an affinity and respect for the type of experience which inspired this poem. Although the event described in the poem is specifically West Virginian, the conditions are universal. Riccardo recently settled in Shepherdstown following travels in Mexico and three years in Spain.

115-001-ST-WV-001-1997

Come Home To West Virginia

Through years of sweat and lone despair
And seasons made of toil,
The skirmishes of tender boys,
Their blood upon the soil,

The West Virginia soul of grit
Was toughened hard with years.
The West Virginia heart's encased
In weariness and tears.

But from the pain and dreary days
And broken dreams abounds
A hearty West Virginia soul
Whose joyous voice resounds

In endless praise and worship for
A land whose beauty fills
The richness of the wilderness —
A pageant in the hills.

Cathedral spires no church can match,
No bells can sing her praise.
No voices raised in joyous song
Can e'er reflect her ways,

Nor mark her footsteps on the sod,
Nor sculpt in bas relief
The living tableau as her sons
And daughters in belief

Devote their days and dignity
To worship, hope and prayer,
To laughter, love and thankful praise
For ever living here.

The lives of West Virginians
Are bless'd with wealth sublime.

The beauty and the golden days
Bedim the march of time.

Forever in a unity
Of past and future goals
We're one in solidarity
With hearts and minds and souls.

Come home to West Virginia!
Come home again today!
Return to her outstretching arms
Forevermore to stay.

AUTHOR: N.J. Lewis. Ms. Lewis now lives again in Charles Town. After an adult lifetime away, she has finally "Come Home to West Virginia."

116-001-ST-WV-001-1997

Chapter 9

Mountaineer Country

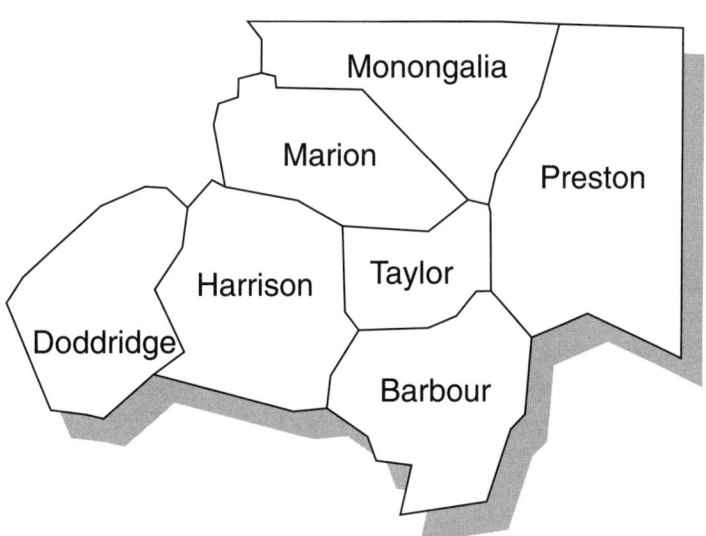

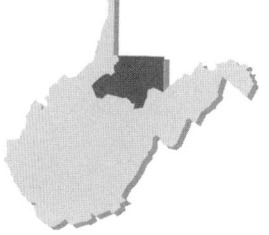

CHAPTER 9: MOUNTAINEER COUNTRY

Of Memories, Magic, And Mulberries

Today the massive mulberry tree reaches for the heavens only in my memory. But during the 1950s, it graced a quiet country road near Gladesville in Preston County, not far from Fortney's Mill. Each summer during the weeks I spent on Okey and Grace Brewer's farm, the old Rogers

Visiting the mulberry tree in the late 1950s. (L-R), Danny, JoAnn, Faye, and Bill (in the tree).

place, that tree was as much a part of daily life as evening Bible lessons, snap beans and corn-on-the-cob fresh from the garden, and poison ivy blisters. Most likely the rash came from contact with the mulberry tree where the creeping ivy encircled its trunk. Despite the risk, however, the tree was a favorite afternoon retreat during those hot July days.

After morning chores and lunch were finished, all six of us kids, and any other visitors who dared, gathered at the upper gate to make the journey through the hilly field without attracting the attention of the ram and his ewes who lived there. Despite his bell which always gave us ample warning of his approach, our bodies pumped adrenaline as we raced along the sheep path to the beckoning tree.

Entrance to the tree's safety meant grabbing an overhead limb and swinging our bodies upward. Once astride the wide branches, we moved effortlessly from spot to spot, sharing the fruit with one another and the many birds who found mulberries as tasty as we did. We gorged ourselves on mulberries — first cousins once removed from blackberries — until our tongues, lips, and clothes were stained purple. When we could hold no more, we remained in the tree's shade, speaking of dreams and dares and childhood tales as the afternoons wore on.

When we needed pennies for the occasional trip to Trickett's Store, we left a few baskets of mulberries by the road with a "For Sale" sign. Sometimes John Forman, the mail carrier, or an infrequent traveler left a dime or a quarter behind. We added that to our booty from capturing beetles on the corn and headed down the dusty road to the store three miles away. Returning from work in Arthurdale, Uncle Okey was always willing to give us a lift home in his pickup. We bounced along in the back, grinning broadly at one another, eating dust, and savoring the bliss of penny candy, already planning our next adventure at the mulberry tree.

Author: JoAnn Danks Dadisman. JoAnn is an Adjunct Professor in the English Department at West Virginia University. She lives with her husband and son in her native Independence.

117-001-ST-WV-001-1997

A Country Serenade

Being raised outside of town in Marion County, and schooled in Fairmont, I knew little about country living and customs, but I was about to learn. In the fall of 1944, back in the back country of Marquess in Preston County, where I had recently moved, there was no electricity or indoor plumbing, and many old customs were still popular.

One common custom was to be serenaded when you got married. Being young, only seventeen, and very naive, I only half knew what was going on. My husband Harold, just home on leave from the Navy, brought many relatives out to see him and the new bride. Another couple was going to be serenaded, too, and being quite popular, invited their friends also. Quite a large crowd had gathered.

Things started to happen all at once. I thought it was a big party. Guns began to go off.

Big saws began to whine, and cow bells to ring out. I was a little taken aback to say the least. Next thing I knew, the women had me blindfolded in a washtub, and were carrying me up the road. We got up the road quite a ways and they let me out of the tub, took my shoes and blindfold off, and all took off running back to the house, leaving me to walk back down through a swampy field alone. Because I was a stranger, one of my husband's sisters stayed and walked back with me.

My husband, meanwhile, was ridden all over the place on a rail and heaven knows what else. After all the excitement was over, refreshments were served and great fellowship followed. Many lasting friendships were made at that time.

AUTHOR: Mary Lee Shriver Matlick. Mrs. Matlick is the mother of two, grandmother of three, and great-grandmother of one. She and her husband Harold reside in Parsons and have been married for fifty-two years.

118-001-ST-WV-001-1997

Shaw's Run

With the taste of the first snowflakes on our tongues, my sister and I hike up the road on Shaw's Run off Little Bingamon Creek in Marion County. The leaves wear their autumn color, and their rustling sounds almost like laughter… How many times Mom and Dad had hiked these hills to Charlie and Minnie Criss's home to play, laugh and eat.

At the bend of the road stands the ghost of a barn and ahead are the remains of the homestead. The woods are silent and filled with earthy smells of autumn and the approaching snow.

Further up the stony road appears a knoll called "the flat." Only mountain people could name this terrain THE FLAT. It is steep and rough to climb. Near the top sits the Nay-Hess Cemetery, overgrown and covered with myrtle. The old wise ones claimed that myrtle keeps away demons. Three generations of our grandparents sleep beneath this myrtle. We freeze as we photograph their tombstones.

Over the hill lies the Holbert Cemetery, where Charlie and Minnie Criss rest. Their only child preceded them many years ago. Minnie's parents and other kin lie buried there.

The descent from the knoll is hurried, as the snowflakes sting the skin. Huge grapevines creak and groan overhead as the wind cradles them. The sky is grey. We are quieter now.

Passing the old house and barn, we stop our downward climb to listen to the wind laugh among the ruins of the farm. A spirit of youth and fun still lingers. We walk again on the stones Mom and Dad once danced over. We know a little of their energy, and we feel stronger as we approach the Run. The water picks up a ray of sunshine and sparkles for our pleasure. Life and death are so connected; how can we separate the water from the sun?

We pass down the winding road, across the little creek, and life goes on, and on, and on…

AUTHOR: Phyllis J. Carpenter, SAC. Phyllis is a retired teacher. She was born in Monongah and currently resides in Morgantown. She is the daughter of William H. and Vivian (Tichner) Carpenter.

119-001-ST-WV-001-1997

Teaching In The High Lonesome

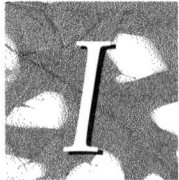

I started teaching in 1924. My first assigned school was located on what is now Highway 50 in Preston County, West Virginia. It was a school high in the mountains between Rowlesburg and Fellowsville called Fairview. Mr. Willis Fortney and my father Albert Bickford took me out to the Ridenour home where I was to live during the school year. It was so lonesome when Dad left me that I felt like crying. Mr. and Mrs. Ridenour were a young couple with a little girl about two years old named Wilda. Mr. Ridenour, "Red," was always singing hymns while he worked.

At school I had no more than ten or twelve students: a couple of girls ages sixteen and seventeen who were "no grade" but who fit about the fifth grade; a boy and two girls in the fourth grade; three girls in the first grade. It was an easy assignment, but I felt lone-

The new school teacher Alice Bickford.

some a lot. Each Friday in the fall I dismissed early and walked the six miles to Tunnelton, and two more out home. It was so wonderful to be back home.

I remember one pretty day in February when there was no snow on the ground and I decided to quit early on a Friday and take off for home. Coming up through the woods I could smell meat smoking. It was the most delightful smell to my nose. As I got nearer to home I could see the smoke from the smokehouse and I thought I was in Heaven sure. Home sweet home.

I was so happy when the last day of school rolled around sometime in April. I can't remember how I got home, but I think Dad must have picked up me and my belongings. I never wanted to go back to Fairview school. Happily, the next term I was assigned to the Tunnelton grade school.

Author: Alice Bickford Farley. Alice is a housewife and mother of four. This story was submitted by her son Donald Farley of Kansas City, Kansas.

Rose Bud

The first time I saw her, she was beautiful! Her fur glistened in the sun like fine black and white metallic jewelry. That long tail of hers was magnificent. She could spray up to eight feet away when aggravated or just plain scared.

Rose Bud, a fun-loving back woods skunk.

Two young women brought her to me because they knew I had a way with animals, especially this particular breed. She had been mauled by a large dog, very badly hurt, and was in need of surgery. One of the young ladies worked for a veterinarian and saw to it that she received what was needed. She had regained her health pretty well when I received her.

When I looked into her eyes, I saw a gentleness and wisdom in this creature and called her Rose Bud. Rose Bud was a West Virginia skunk from the back woods. Her nature was fun-loving, inquisitive, and very shy. As time went on she ruled the house and usually got her own way. If she didn't, she would stomp her feet, stand on her nose and growl until she did. Skunks are not usually verbal unless aggravated, hurt, or startled.

Rose Bud was always into trouble by stealing rugs, rags, toilet paper, anything to build her nest. She would also get into handbags if they were left on the floor and steal something, especially if it was edible.

I remember one time when we gathered at my house for a meeting. One fellow named Jim always sat in the rocking chair. Now Rose Bud had been left with many problems after being mauled by that dog, and she came through the living room after using the litter box, rubbed up against Jim's shoe, then went her merry way. After a while, Jim looked down and saw the little gift Rose Bud left on his shoe, and we all had a good laugh.

When Rose Bud was three years old she became lame and sick. After a short period of time she passed on. She left a lot of friends behind, including friends from a nursing home she used to visit, but will be remembered for her antics, good nature, and fun-loving ways. She was just one of God's small creatures that was loaned to us to enjoy for a little while.

Author: Sandra Bunner. Sandra has three children, all graduates of Wilmington High School. Originally from Philadelphia, Sandra has lived in West Virginia for thirty-six years and loves the state.

Kohl Lined With Coal Dust

This newborn heart and his beat as one
Like Porgy, he sings
"Summertime"
His little honeybunch am I
And the livin' is easy
My first true love
Kohl lined from coal dust
I see his green eyes
His fabulous face I smell
Old Spicey, pinchy, smoke scented
Crisp, raw smell of just mowed grass
Mild misty rains of early spring
Sudden bursts of apple blossoms
 Icing covered conifers of winter
 Vanilla ice cream in sugar cones, he is
 And hand-packed gallons
 Hand-picked berries in pies

Coconut birthdays, essence of orange cakes
Cosmic colorbursts, thunderbooms, Fourths of Julys
Old Glory, Ole Saint Nick, Glory, Glory Hallelujah
Sandlot baseball, Sunday Mass, Saturday Night boxing
Segovia's chords, the Fighting Irish,
Crayola colored mountain memories of autumn
The pride, heritage, grand child legacies
Style, sparkle, splendor, savoir-faire
Soft snowfalls of Christmases past
Memories become memories
Cognizance ceases, senses desensitize
The heartbeat of summertime gone
Kohl lined with coal dust
The explosion...I died

To my dad, David Mainella, Sr., who loved and lived his life to its fullest. He, along with seventy-eight other magnificent miners, was killed in the Farmington, West Virginia, Consolidated Coal #9 Mine Explosion, November 20, 1968.

AUTHOR: Aida J. Mainella Everhart. Mrs. Everhart is a teacher and writer of poems, eulogies, and stories of local color. She was raised in Fairmont. She currently resides in Morgantown with her husband Ron.

122-001-ST-WV-001-1997

A Tribute

My mother Jeanette (Concetta E.) Stingo Mainella taught me, my three sisters and brother, and all of our children how to pick a good book and a ripe tomato from the vine; how to plant a flower and love; how to wear a hat and a smile; how to make a salad and friends; how to respect our heritage and ourselves; how to spell and rhyme a word and to reason. She instilled in us her exquisite taste and gave us her European class; she taught us the value of an education and how to share and care for others and to love life. My mother never knew a stranger. She loved doing for others as she shared her Italian gourmet dishes, her famous biscotti (ciambalites), her home-grown herbs, vegetables, and flowers. My mother lovingly baked and gave hundreds of her cookies, pies, and cakes to family, friends, and strangers. Anyone so fortunate to have been touched by this small, precious piece of perfection will forever cherish her sweet love and all those sugar-coated memories.

It's Yesterday
(For my Mother and all Alzheimer's patients)

I miss your face, your little nose
I miss the way your garden grows
I miss the trips to Gabes, Big Lots
I miss your lentils by the pots
I miss our house on Warren Street
I'd love to have a ciambalite
I miss your tulips, jonquils, pussy willows
I miss sleeping on your feather pillows
If these memories start fading and falling apart
A bright colored spare set lives on in my heart
So kiss me, and love me, don't go away
I know you, I love you. It's yesterday

I wish we could go back in time
To dance and sing a nursery rhyme
At Christmastime together we'd be
Music, fun and food and family
The Fourth of July, remember that day
Of family, tradition, patriotic display
Seasons come and go with celebrations
And with each new one, new generations
If these memories start fading and falling apart
A bright colored spare set lives on in my heart
So kiss me, and love me, don't go away
I know you, I love you. It's yesterday

I wish we could go back and do
The things we did at twenty-two
We'd giggle when we'd kneel in prayer
You gave, gave, gave, with all, you'd share
Cobblers, cakes, cookies, sweet memories
You'd knead, dip, roll, frost; took eternities
To give your sweet love; they devoured nonetheless
How soon they forget you; they're ageless, I guess
If these memories start fading and falling apart
A bright colored spare set lives on in my heart
So kiss me, and love me, don't go away
I know you, I love you. It's yesterday

If we could just go back in time
We'd do then what now we know is prime
We'd talk and laugh and hug more often
And take more time to heal and soften
We'd shop Hartley's, Jones', Vogue's again
Spend all that money; What a sin!
I'd be your little honeybunch
We'd fry green tomatoes for our lunch
If these memories start fading and falling apart
A bright colored spare set lives on in my heart
So kiss me, and love me, don't go away
I know you, I love you. It's yesterday

AUTHOR: Aida J. Mainella Everhart

123-001-ST-WV-001-1997

Memories

The year was 1939, the movie "Gone with the Wind" made its debut, and I was born the third of four daughters to wonderful parents who were decent, honest, hard-working people. Having come from large, poor families, both had to quit school after the eighth grade, but they were wise in ways not found in any book. They taught us that life wasn't a free ride to success; to reach our goals in life, we must work hard and make sacrifices to get there and to experience the joy of accomplishment.

We lived on a small rented farm in Reynoldsville, a rural community on the outskirts of Clarksburg, West Virginia. We had a couple of cows, some chickens and turkeys, and we raised pigs which Dad would butcher on Thanksgiving Day. Although Dad worked in the glass factory, money was tight and didn't stretch very far. In spite of this, we always had plenty to eat. We had our own eggs, milk products, and meat. Dad always cured and smoked his own hams, bacon, and sausage. On those cold winter mornings nothing tasted better than sausage and gravy over homemade bread before we started our mile-long walk to school. Mom canned all she could from the two large vegetable gardens we grew. She also made jam and jelly from the berries we picked. I remember how my dad would dig large, deep holes under our back porch and line them with straw so he could bury the potatoes, cabbage, and apples from our orchard. Mom baked seven loaves of bread twice a week and made cottage cheese while we kids churned the milk into golden, creamy butter. On Saturdays, I would peddle my buttermilk in order to have the money for a trip to the movies on Sunday afternoon. This was my one big thrill back then, to see Roy Rogers, my idol. Mom also made our clothes from the flowered feed sacks that the livestock's grain came in. Our dresses and petticoats were quite pretty after they were washed, starched, and ironed.

We had an old black 1936 Ford that we named "Black Beauty." Dad had gotten a good deal on her because she had no windows except the windshield. The original owner, in a fit of drunken craziness, had taken a hammer to the windows. In spite of this, and the rusted-out holes in her floor, she had, as Dad said, a really good motor and, boy, could she go! My eldest sister always wanted to sit in the middle because you got less windblown there. (She was beginning to notice the boys and had become quite prissy. She would curl her arm around the back of her head to hold her hair in place. She became so accustomed to this that she would subconsciously do it in her sleep. How we teased her about it!) Black Beauty was an all purpose car. Dad would remove the front passenger seat and the back seat so he could take a calf to the auction barn or haul hay to the barn, then he'd sweep her out and put the seats back in and we'd all get dressed up and go for a drive to the city of Clarksburg.

When the older girls graduated from our eighth grade country school, they were bussed to the city to attend Adamston Junior High School and then Victory High School. When Dad had to drive them back to school in the evenings to attend various school activities, they would always have Dad let them off a block away from the school. They were ashamed for the city kids to see our old, windowless car. This made Dad feel so bad he decided to retire Black Beauty for a newer model. Mom had just gotten a new Electrolux sweeper which was advertised to do most anything, even spray paint. She talked Dad into spray painting our "new" used car to look like the new two-tone automobiles that had just come on the market. Dad spent one whole weekend spray painting that car Mom's favorite color, chartreuse, with dark green trim. Oh, we thought it was so beautiful. After all, we had come up in the world. We had a two-tone car with all its windows! We didn't realize it was so unique that you could see us coming two miles away! Looking back now, even the splendor of that new used car could never replace Black Beauty and all the funny, wonderful memories she created. She'll always have a special place in my heart.

We made our own fun in those days. Not having television sets, video games, computers and the like left a lot of time for a kid's mind to wander, and my eldest sister's imagination seemed to work overtime. Like the time her idea got us into big trouble. My dad had rented the garage beside our house to a neighbor. Mr. Leeson was a very dignified gentleman who kept his car in immaculate condition. It was his prized possession. One day after a warm summer rain, as we kids were wading in the mud puddles along our driveway, my sister decided we should decorate Mr. Leeson's car. You can imagine his surprise when he backed his car out of the garage that afternoon to go to his job on the evening shift. His shiny black sedan was covered from top to bottom with large, muddy, yellow, bare feet prints. Not having the time to wash it, he was forced to drive through town displaying our "modern" artwork. I'm sure he must have received many humorous stares. When a very angry Mr. Leeson confronted our dad the next morning, needless to say, we were punished quite severely and ordered never to go near that car again. You can be sure that we never did. Yes, our homemade fun often got us into mischief, but looking back now, I'll bet when all was said and done, in their own private moment, Mom and Dad got quite a laugh over that one.

Over the years, I have recalled so many funny events that occurred during my childhood. It was a great time to be a kid. Even the simplest things seemed special. The neighborhood kids loved coming to our house because Mom would make a huge kettle of steaming cocoa and an old washpan filled to the rim with popcorn. We didn't have all the troubles and worries that plague our society today. True, we didn't have all the modern conveniences either, but maybe that's what made it so special. The world was unspoiled by it all.

I thank God every day for my three sisters Jean, Carole, and Myra, and the wonderful childhood we shared. Most of all, I thank God for such wise and loving parents who made it all possible. What better gift can a parent give a child than the ability to see those common everyday moments as priceless, treasured memories that last a lifetime. Over the years, those memories have warmed my heart and lifted my spirit as they've transported me back to those happy childhood days one more time.

Author: Judith Drumpus Bennett. Mrs. Bennett is a retired employee of Anchor Hocking Glass Company. She says there is nowhere else she would rather call home than our very own "almost Heaven" West Virginia.

124-001-ST-WV-001-1997

I Love West Virginia Auctions

"I'm an auctionholic" reads an occasional ball cap on the head of a habitual auction-goer. I don't have a hat like that, but I should have. West Virginia has wonderful estate auctions, and over the last twenty years or so, I've gone to as many as I can.

I tend to frequent those by certain auctioneers, perhaps because the fliers of future auctions they hand out make it so easy. But after you get accustomed to the distinctive lilt, sometimes almost singing, of a particular auctioneer's voice, others often just don't quite measure up. Over the years, however, I've incorporated a number of the pet phrases of various auctioneers into my own — often unspoken — thoughts:

> "By the each and times five."
> "A dollar-na-half, a cow and a calf."
> "Cheaper'n hog guts."

It's nice to sit in a heated fair barn in winter or an air conditioned fire hall in summer, but the best auctions in my opinion are those that take place on site. I particularly like small farm auctions in which the owners have died or are wanting to sell the place and retire elsewhere. These auctions generally start promptly at 8:30 in the morning selling old shovels, picks, rakes and hoes by the bundle, sometimes for as little as a few dollars, followed by handfuls of screw drivers, wrenches, and pliers. An occasional log chain or "block and tackle" brings $25 to $50. By 10:00, they are hauling out $100 to $200 air compressors, and by 11:00, they have pretty much finished with the one or two tractors and the circle of old machinery, such as the horse-drawn cultivator and dump rake. After that, everybody settles in the front yard for the household goods. If "dealers" are plentiful, the smart auctioneer starts right in with the best things: antique furniture, nice quilts, antique glassware, signed pottery crocks and jugs, and maybe an old school bell. Many of these items bring several hundred dollars.

The real estate sells at noon. After a reverent silence while the auctioneer talks in a normal voice explaining the terms of the sale, the bidding proceeds, starting this time in $5000 or $2500 increments and later narrowing to $1000 to $500, and finally to $250. It takes much longer for the "Sold!" hammer to drop, because the young couple that wanted the farm looks longingly at each other before daring to bid another $500. Sometimes they get it; sometimes they don't. In any case, the real estate bidding is often followed by applause, the locals' welcoming for their new neighbors.

From there, the "merchandise" for bid proceeds from most to least valuable. As the antique dealers and folks who are getting too tired, bored, cold, or hot begin to leave, and as prices begin to drop, the lots get larger and larger. Eventually, near the end, "everything in the box" or "everything on this table" goes for one sum. Sometimes, when a particularly unsavory-looking collection of junk fails to get even a starting bid and someone — who already has enormous piles of boxes around him — offers one dollar, the auctioneer immediately says "Sold," lest the bidder change his mind.

Why do I like auctions so much? West Virginia is still mainly a rural state, and, in my experience, rural-minded people enjoy getting together in a friendly, homey atmosphere that characterizes most of these auctions. The humor is rare but simple and there are rules of politeness that apply. A rolling pin might be called a "husband controller," and everybody laughs. I also like the hot dogs with chili, the pepperoni rolls, the Polish sausages, the pies, and the coffee that are sold by one of the local churches as a fund raiser.

I must confess that the most compelling reason for my love of auctions is the quiet excitement that comes from the thought that I *could* become

the owner of an extremely valuable item by paying next to nothing. Would I, too, find a laundered $100 bill in the pocket of an old shirt in a box of rags? Would that $35 painted oak dresser, if I stripped and refinished it and replaced the hardware, be worth $400? If I started a collection of 1950s aluminum ware, which generally occupies much of the $1 boxes at the end, would it appreciate a few years from now like Griswold cast iron skillets have done in the past couple of years?

What do I have to show for all my efforts? I have a beautiful oak dining room table (expensive) and miscellaneous oak chairs (which cost $1 each). I have lots of other antiques and semi-antiques around the house and garage, like a working 78 rpm Victrola, a large cast-iron apple butter kettle, miscellaneous horse harness parts and hames. I also have enough screws, bolts, and hardware supplies so that I can usually find what I want without going to the store. On the down side, I have acquired 100 player piano rolls with no player piano, more old books and picture frames and screw drivers than I'll ever look at or use, and a few real "clunkers." (How about a greasy, 200-pound spool of used steel cable?)

Have I found my treasure? Not yet, but I'm still looking and enjoying every minute of if.

AUTHOR: Kenneth St. Louis. Ken and his wife Rae Jean Sielen live on twenty acres up the Cassville Hollow, about six miles west of Morgantown. He and Rae Jean are co-founders of Populore Publishing Company.

125-001-ST-WV-001-1997

Tribute To Blanche Geary

Growing up in West Virginia in the 1970s, I was touched by many extraordinary people who influenced my life in profound ways, often ways I didn't appreciate until much later. One such person was Blanche Geary, a woman who babysat me when I was three and four years old. Many years later, my memories of my time with her are fuzzy, but certain images and feelings have stayed with me and have helped shape my life.

I grew up near Cassville, West Virginia, a small community close to Morgantown. Blanche, who lived in the community of New Hill, would pick me up at my house or my parents would drop me off at her place on Mondays, where I would spend the day under her supervision. Life at Blanche's and in the New Hill community was quite different than my life at home, making my days with her new and exciting. As an only child, I wasn't used to the bustle of activity that I experienced with Blanche. For a

Blanche Geary.

three year old, this could have been traumatic, but Blanche's kindness and protectiveness always made me feel at home and at ease. These first positive ventures without my parents in a completely new atmosphere helped me to approach new situations in my life without fear.

Blanche exposed me to certain things that I never would have known otherwise. She was a craftswoman, who fired and painted beautiful ceramic figurines. Though this was an art that required careful and detailed work, she allowed me to work on my own pieces while she created hers. I remember being filled with wonder the first time she drove me to the kilns up on Walnut Hill. I watched in amazement as the soft clay figures became hard and shiny. We spent happy hours working on our ceramics together. Through her patience and positive reinforcement, I felt proud of the final pieces I had seen through to completion (with her help). She let me keep the Easter eggs and bunny that I painted (I would call them abstract art), and she gave me a beautiful angel figurine that I still cherish.

The sense of community I experienced with Blanche was special for me as well. I remember visiting her neighbors with her and drinking Coca-cola out of glass bottles for the first time. I was passed around by strangers, patted on the head, and told I was the cutest thing around. Instead of fear, I always felt surrounded by warmth and comfort.

On one particular occasion I remember accompanying her to the Women's Mission at St. Stephens Baptist Church in Shriver. My family normally went to a fairly unorthodox Presbyterian Church, but, when I experienced the sense of community and the joy of the Baptists, I was entranced. Years later, I remember being told that St. Stephens was a predominately African-American Church and realizing for the first time that I had been a minority there. Probably the most important lesson I learned from Blanche and my time with her was not to focus on or even notice racial differences. Years later when I was confronted with racial tensions at my high school in Pittsburgh, I realized that I just didn't understand such tension, partly due to my positive experiences with Blanche where race was never an issue.

It has been more than fifteen years since I spent my happy times with Blanche Geary at

her house on New Hill. I have lived in several new and exciting places, including Morgantown, Pittsburgh, Australia, Spain, and now Penn State University, but my life-building lessons learned with Blanche are with me still in subtle ways. I thank her for her nurturing care for me.

AUTHOR: Melinda St. Louis. Melinda is a student at Pennsylvania State University, where she is majoring in International Politics and Spanish.

126-001-ST-WV-001-1997

The Forgotten Shotgun

This is a story told to me by my father Clarence E. Nedrow. When he was a tad, eight or nine years old, he lived on the farm on Beech Run Hill, near Albright, West Virginia. (This story was also told to me by a cousin about her father, my Uncle Lloyd A. Nedrow.) Anyway, this story is about one or the other, who went hunting by himself.

It seems that they were sent out in the woods with the family shotgun to kill a squirrel. My father told me it was a "White-Powder Wonder" shotgun and the cartridges were "Ajax Heavies." After going into the woods near the farm and finding a stand of chestnut trees (this was before the blight), Father sat down on a log and waited. After some time he sighted a squirrel, took aim, and fired. He then ran over to his first squirrel and picked it up. After running home and showing his parents the dead squirrel, they only had one question for him. "Where's your gun?"

In all the excitement of taking his first game, he had thrown his shotgun down, forgotten, and had left it out in the woods!

AUTHOR: James Edward Nedrow. Mr. Nedrow is a Lucent Tech Installer for AT&T. His hobbies include electronics, genealogy, and hunting. He is the father of one and resides in his native Shinnston.

127-001-ST-WV-001-1997

Lillie's Legacy

The greenbriars, raspberry bushes, and multi-floral roses were heaped on top of the toppled house. Forgotten and buried for over a quarter of a century, the old house was about to be exhumed.

I started the weed whacker; the motor cut through the air like an outboard. Birds flew

Lillie and Thurman Everly.

away, my snake-hunting dog deserted me, and the cat ran.

The briar missiles cut me as often as I cut them. Whack, whack, whack. I was determined that this farm wouldn't look like an Appalachian dump. We'd neglected it for twenty-seven years. The dump was our fault, not Lillie's.

I knew little about the family who'd lived here. I knew the names from the deed — Lillie and Thurman. Good West Virginia names. Sturdy, unique to a family, tying generations together.

Whack, whack, whack. Weeds whistled past my ears, and green bits clung to my old clothes. A piece of purple glistened through the mangled green. I turned off the weed whacker and pushed aside a raspberry bush.

By the front door of the log house were two beds of lavender irises. How many years had they bloomed for no one? I saw pink. This time I took the grass shears and cut the weeds away. Clip, clip, clip. The weeds parted gently. Flanking the irises were two rambling rose bushes that climbed in confusion over a collapsed door jamb.

Three weeks were spent unearthing Lillie's treasures — daylillies in flame red, a mock orange tree, peonies, and a rose of sharon. Silvery green hens and chickens marched unrestrained across the back yard. Lillie, who was deaf, had color for her eyes.

I cut the weeds away from the daylillies and smiled. Lillie was her name like the flowers she grew.

Author: Haley Elizabeth Garwood.

128-001-ST-WV-001-1997

Television With Granny And Poppy

My grandfather was a West Virginia coal miner. Like so many of the miners, he made most of his purchases at the Company Store. Some years ago, in the spring of 1956, Granny and Poppy drove to the Company Store to buy a television set. This was something that had the neighborhood in a buzz. It had come down the grapevine that they were getting a television, and since their house was the neighborhood meeting place, everyone was looking forward to this event. They had the battery-operated radio that kept the neighborhood informed of local and international events, and then came electricity with all the new-fangled gadgets. So now with the television they would have a picture to go with the stories they were hearing.

As they entered the store, Granny informed Poppy that there was to be no fooling around. They were getting the television and going straight home. Naturally, Poppy met some of the men he worked with and let them know the purpose of his visit to the store. Some of the men told him that they had heard that televisions caused a lot of health problems. "You will lose your hearing and eyesight really fast," they said. Poppy just brushed away their predictions and bought the television anyway.

About six o'clock that evening there must have been about thirty people standing and sitting around to watch the news. It was so strange to see the newscasters that we had only heard before.

After watching other entertainment programs and commercials the evening was over. Poppy shut off the television. Everyone tried to talk at once. They wouldn't have believed it possible if they hadn't seen it with their own eyes. What a wonderful invention!

As with the radio, the television at Granny and Poppy's house was an evening event not to be missed by their friends and neighbors. There was always an open invitation to visit and socialize; the door was always open and you were welcome. Television was progress, and people talked for years about the enjoyment and excitement of seeing history being made as they watched it happen. I will always have fond memories of these times with my grandparents.

Author: Leslie Florence McCauley Downey. Leslie is a care giver, housewife, and author of poems and short stories for children. She has two children and two grandchildren. She resides with her husband Charles in Morgantown.

129-001-ST-WV-001-1997

A Country Church Celebration

For a small Presbyterian country church in Sugar Grove, located six miles from Morgantown between Laurel Point and Cassville, 1985 was quite a year. The church had been organized on Stewart's Run in 1835, and because its parishioners were celebrating the 150th birthday of the founding, it was decided to organize a series of special events. Under the spiritual leadership of their beloved pastor, Reverend Walter H. Rockenstein and his wife Anne, willing participants began plans to celebrate and preserve the rich heritage of the church.

A display of antique artifacts and a bulletin board filled with clippings and pictures drew the interest of visitors. Members worked together to compile and sell a directory of church history, as well as to sell commemorative coasters, notepaper, and pens. As things began to happen, they were captured on camera for recording in a scrapbook to be kept at the church. The media was kept informed through articles and pictures; folks who had never heard of Sugar Grove Church were beginning to! Renovations began which included installing new carpet, a bell, and repairing an 1876 kerosene chandelier and a pump organ manufactured in 1891. The split-rail fence behind the church was rebuilt. For most events, members dressed in clothing of the 1800s.

As interest grew, there were specially-written skits and songs, slide shows, birthday cakes, and the baptism of a fifth-generation infant. Former ministers and members returned to visit at the July Homecoming Picnic and the August Founder's Day worship service, at which time recognition was given to leaders in the church. A gospel sing featured

Mountains In My Horizon

A country church in Sugar Grove.

a local family group, and community talent performed at the Fall Social. Crowds numbered from seventy-five to 100 persons.

A youth delegate represented the church at the General Assembly in Indiana and the highlight of the whole year was the visit of the head of Presbyterian government in the United States, General Assembly Moderator William H. Wilson of McAllen, Texas. Tents were set up in the yard to enable the ladies of the church to serve a soupbean and cornbread dinner to over 100 Grafton Presbytery members who attended. The Clarksburg television station covered that meeting.

Christmas traditions were begun, including a "Trim-A-Tree" Night, a caroling hayride, the annual Christmas program and a Candlelight Worship Service. A local freelance writer, impressed with the church family activities, submitted an article to *Guideposts* magazine, which resulted in the church being presented a $1,000 *Families are Forever* award. The money was applied to the building of an addition behind the church for Sunday School classes and social events. Both the award and the addition were beyond our wildest dreams.

This was an especially meaningful time to me, as many generations of my family had worshipped at that country church. It was a time of renewal involving the whole community — a time of great rejoicing, remembering, sharing, caring, and serving the Lord together. It will remain in my memory as an unforgettable experience!

AUTHOR: *Evelyn T. Kennedy. Mrs. Kennedy is a homemaker and retired funeral home organist and secretary. She and her husband Jack are the parents of three children.*

As a child, I lived in a metropolis. In my native part of the country, cities and suburbs stretched on for miles and miles as did the all-important freeways, networked to the hilt. But, I always longed to get out and away on those freeways — for day drives, weekend camping or boating trips, or extended vacations in the wilderness. Mountains, beaches, deserts, river valleys, and rolling hills — to me, all were welcome changes from the hustle and bustle of big city life.

When I was about ten, my mother, a schoolteacher fond of projects, gently roped my six brothers and sisters and me into an "arty" activity. A local business had a special deal where they would take a child's drawing and have it printed on a white, nine inch plate that could be hung on the wall for display. One rainy Saturday, gathered together at the kitchen table and the two card tables, Mom handed out crayons, paper and minimal instructions. After several long minutes of staring at my blank paper, I remember Mom or a sibling saying, "Just draw something you love." Well that was easy. In no time at all, I was interrupting the others to show them the majestic mountains I'd drawn, with me sitting cross-legged in the foreground admiring their greatness. Yes, I loved mountains and knew it early on.

For several years, my love of mountains was sometimes powerful in its influence. When it came time for summer Girl Scout camp, I signed on for "Singing Pines," the *mountain* camp, without giving the marine camp a second thought. And, I'm embarrassed to say, when it came time to choose which state colleges to apply to, my first choice was simply the one whose campus was located in among mountains and redwoods. I ended up in a place of incredible beauty, aptly nicknamed "The City on a Hill." You might think that my next decision was to find a "mountain state" and settle there. But no, my settling in West Virginia wouldn't come for twenty more years. And interestingly, it came at a time when chasing mountains wasn't at the top of my list.

Rather, when my phone rang March 13, 1993, I was nearing forty and still hoping for love. A call came from West Virginia of all places! It was a man I had met at a speech, language, and hearing conference in Missouri, a few years before. He explained that he was snowed in and somehow got the idea to give me — "a far off woman enjoying clear skies and a moderate temperature" — a call. I listened as he described something I'd never experienced, let alone could imagine: snow just pouring out of the sky, piling up so quickly and heavily you wondered if

Chapter 9: Mountaineer Country

Looking out from our porch.

over an old leaf and considered anew my love of mountains. His weren't the 8,000 foot and higher peaked beauties that were the backdrop for my childhood or subject for my "plate," but there were similarities, mostly having to do with the enticements of high and low land.

Indeed, on my trips to West Virginia I now began to see there were mountains nearly *everywhere*, with towns, farms, houses, schools, and so forth somehow nestled. Amidst the mountains, my friend's home was so picturesque and inviting: a loghouse on a hill; a horse, barn, pond, and woods in the background. And the countryside was spectacular: wild flowers, lightning bugs, creeks, and berries. And people waved when I drove or walked by. "Hmm, what would it be like to live here?" I speculated. Soon I knew! We were married February 26, 1994, at the Shack Presbyterian Church in Pursglove, and settled into our home in Scotts Run.

With my newish home — home place and home state — there has emerged a growing bank of not-to-be-forgotten memories. Vegetables fresh from the garden. Firewood from our own woods. Deer, wild turkey, skunks, groundhogs, and raccoons. And winding backroads. I remember one drive early on, when for about two hours we took the truck up and down and around various hollows. Come to find out, we'd been within about a two-mile radius of our home the whole time. Of course, he knew. I didn't.

There have also been plenty of surprises and new experiences. My first real lightning storm was quite a scare. Was the world coming to an end?! The house shook, sky lit up, wind howled, and clouds let loose. And there was dialect. Our neighbors surprised me by using words I'd never heard used like that before ("Pap," "toboggan," and "backward"); other words I'd never heard pronounced the way they said them ("push," "color," and "piano"). And, some phrases and sentences baffled me. For example, there was a sign — "Bridge freezes before road" — that I kept seeing and finally asked to have explained to me. Other things I saw were new to me too. There were the days I exclaimed, "Look! A red bird on the little oak tree!" Months before I'd been awed by yellow

you'd even be able to plow when and if it ever stopped. And, in subsequent calls, we talked about more than the weather. He told me more about himself, his dreams and interests, quirks, and disappointments. I reciprocated.

Our calls became very frequent, as did our correspondence. We became more and more "serious." I got out my atlas and studied his state. I remembered that I had actually visited West Virginia twice. Once on our family's "Big Trip East," we had stopped at Harper's Ferry, sometime between checking out the Capitol, Boston, and Philadelphia. I was about twelve as we trekked up rocky steps to view the Potomac and then back down to view and ponder the flood markings. Many years later, on business, I visited the Fish and Wildlife Service's National Education Training Center near Kearneysville. My strongest memories from that trip involve "glass." "This is glass heaven," my traveling partner informed me. "Some of the country's best glass artisans had called West Virginia home." So, on breaks from our work, I tagged along to various antique stores as he searched for the perfect addition to his collection of Carnival glass.

Back to the long distance romance… My friend came west to see me a few times and I came east to see him. Between trips, an acquaintance where I worked back home, teased, "You're not going to go move on us and become a mountaineer now are you?!" He had grown up in Pennsylvania and gone to Penn State. He went on, "It's the 'mountain state' don't you know?" I didn't. But it was enough to make West Virginia seem all the more attractive to me. Next time I visited my West Virginia friend I turned

ones. "Did they escape from a zoo or pet shop," I wondered, being accustomed mostly to dark and dull sparrows, crows, and pigeons.

A person unfamiliar with country living once came to visit us. While walking about, he said, wanting to be helpful I believe, "Your horse over there is eating grass... is she sick?" Ha! Now that I lived in the country I knew, horses were *supposed* to eat grass! On a less playful side, I also now knew about porches, and watching, seeing, listening, and hearing. Yup, give me a hot, humid, hazy day, and you'll find me out on the porch swing early in the morning or late at night. Most importantly, though, give me just about any kind of day and you'll find me thinking and singing the praises of a special state with a mountainous horizon.

Author: Rae Jean Sielen. After years on the west coast, in Southern and Northern California and the Pacific Northwest, Rae Jean moved cross country where she lives with her husband Ken St. Louis. With fondness, amazement, and gratitude, she likes to recall the Blizzard of '93 and her happenstance meeting with "Mr. St. Louis," at the top of the Gateway Arch in St. Louis, Missouri. Beverly Farfsing, her mother in California, still has and treasures her seven children's plates.

131-001-ST-WV-001-1997

You Never Know Who You'll Meet At The "Y"

In 1989 I met my future wife Julia. I was at the YMCA with a couple of people who were living at the group home with me, my neighbor, and some employees of the Association for Retarded Citizens (ARC). They were all up there at the gym playing basketball, I think. After they were done we all came out and got ready to head back down to the home. That's when we came out into the lobby and I saw a lady I called Barbara. The first time she just ignored me when I called her Barbara. The second time she said, "My name is not Barbara." I asked her what her name was and she said Julia. Anyway we got to talking and she was somewhat scared at first. After the ARC group stopped going up to the YMCA, and even before then, my mind just got stuck on Julia and I could not get it off of her.

Well, whenever I was up at the YMCA I would look for Julia. We would usually run into each other in the lobby. The first four times that I met Julia, the Coke machine and I had a meeting; the first time I ran into it, the second time I backed into it, the third time I walked into it, and the fourth time I barely missed it. I was nervous.

One time I went back to the pool to see Julia. As I was watching her and after she got out of the pool and was assisted back to the ladies' dressing room, I called out "Julia," and she turned around and looked and wondered who it was. Then I just disappeared out the door that goes into the men's dressing room. I just left without a word.

I spent about three weeks trying to get hold of Julia. Finally I came down to where she lived and asked to come in so I could come up to see her. That was after Memorial Day weekend of 1989. Our courtship lasted about six months.

We got married at the Northview United Methodist Church. There were no printed invitations; it was just word of mouth. My best friend Pat McIntyre was best man. My mom came as well as a friend she was living with. Some of the people I knew and had informed that it was an open church wedding came. My favorite teacher from the West Virginia Children's Home came as did my lawyers from Fairmont. The day that I married Julia was also the day I quit smoking.

Our honeymoon was right there. I was reading cards to my wife. Then we went out to dinner at the Canteen, and when they found out it was our wedding day they gave us a free meal. The day after we went to the Canteen again and bought dinner.

Author: Howard Cobb. This story was taken from a piece prepared as part of a project sponsored by the West Virginia Developmental Disabilities Planning Council. Howard was born in 1956, and became a ward of the state in 1962. Howard says that now, through various legal channels, he is "free." Although Howard and Julia are no longer married, he wanted to share this particular story documenting a special event in his life. Howard currently lives in Pittsburgh, Pennsylvania.

132-001-ST-WV-001-1997

Life's Photographs

I grew up on a farm in West Virginia during the Depression in the 1930s. Money was scarce and we children had to work; I started to hoe corn at age seven. I was a skinny little girl, complaining about sweat bee stings. My elder brother yelled from across the field, "Flash that gooseneck, drown them in your sweat." Then, "Ha, ha!" drifted back over the corn.

The hardships my mother endured are some of my worst memories and hurt the most to expose. Through it all she never complained. If the weather was cold you froze your feet making biscuits at the old kitchen cabinet, and had to break the ice on the water bucket. When things were the darkest and her health began to fail she would sing a few lines of some old hymn, recite a poem she'd learned in school, or talk about her father's experiences in the Civil War.

She left us when I was twenty years old. The Bible says we won't have any remembrance of this life up in Heaven. All former things will be passed away. I believe, though, that God has all power. I think of sitting under a big tree in Heaven, telling my mother about my life and my girls she never got to see. I believe they'll be up there too.

Dad was a strong, hard-working man who worked in the mines. I remember one long winter he drove a 1927 Chevrolet to work. The car didn't have a top, and the distance was twenty miles. I can see him so plain, going up the bank and into the old garage. My brother had also gone to work in the mines and would be in that old topless car with him.

I recall coming in from the field to eat. Mother would have a dish of garden lettuce, cottage cheese, potatoes, beans, applesauce, and maybe a slice of ham or sausage — all from the farm. Her home-churned butter couldn't be beat. We spread it on hot cornbread, made from our own white meal. I remember brown loaves coming out of the iron stove oven and Mom's good vegetable soup. That soup was the only thing I'd eat when I had pneumonia. I remember putting our bare toes on the kitchen stove hearth on a cold fall morning. Times were hard but we all look back at the best and talk about the good ol' days.

Dad pushed his cares back occasionally and danced a little tune. The ditty went like this: "Pack up your troubles in your ol' kit bag and smile." One Sunday — we didn't work on Sunday — Dad said, "How about us all going on a field trip?" I rode on his back, my bare toes fanning the tall foliage. I remember that trip, over sixty years ago, and still believe it helped fuel my great love of the outdoors.

I'm living within a mile of land my great-great-great-grandfather bought and settled in the late 1700s. I would love to know where he was born and where he's buried. There were so many John Mitchells. I feel so close to my ancestors and realize they helped make me what I am today.

Mother talked a lot about "over home." I know so well now where she was looking; I know about a precious time that can never come again. Life's photographs are stored in the heart! No projector will ever be invented that can replay the film, unwind time's clock, or put a memory in motion.

AUTHOR: *Claris Mitchell McDaniel. Mrs. McDaniel was born, grew up, and still resides near Philippi. She's the daughter of Monzel and Daisy Moats Mitchell. She likes to make quilts, write, and read.*

133-001-ST-WV-001-1997

Remembering What Used To Be

My grandmother Billie Marie Pierce Straight, was the daughter of Charles and Bondolyn Jackson Pierce. Granny Straight, as we all called her, was my great friend while I was growing up in the 1970s on the Sugar Grove Road in Laurel Point near Morgantown. She lived just down the road, and she was the one I always went to talk to about things that were bothering me. She was wise but like a friend, talking about things I couldn't discuss with my parents or just whatever we wanted to talk about.

One of Granny's best friends was Dot Fox, my neighbor. In the summer when Dot's granddaughters Tamme, Johnda, and Jo Ann visited her, this was great fun for us all. My sister Billie Jo and the rest of us would ride our bikes down to Granny's to raid the refrigerator for dill pickles. She was glad to see us whenever we came, and we would stay and chat with her for a while. She was always funny and told us jokes. We thought she was so "cool" because she was like one of us.

A happy couple, Billie and Robert.

My mother Becky Straight Layman remembers the time Granny needed a chicken to cook for dinner and no one was at home to kill it for her, so she got the gun and shot it and cooked it. She fixed big meals at harvest time for the teams of threshers who came to thresh the grain. She was a wonderful cook and enjoyed feeding her family. She canned vegetables and meat, and made butter, cottage cheese, candies, cakes, and bread.

Granny's husband Robert Straight and Dot's husband Albert Fox were good friends; they grew up together and left for Army service together in 1944. Dot's memories include those times when she and Granny took "pin-up" pictures of each other to send in their daily letters to their husbands in the service. They each received an allotment of $100.00 a month for a family of a wife and two children.

Rationing was in effect for gas, shoes, and sugar. The older family members would give up their shoe stamps for the children, whose feet grew faster.

Dot's mail came in Granny's mailbox since Dot didn't live on the mail route. One day a letter arrived for Dot from Albert, who had been wounded at the Rhine River crossing. Granny had a terrible feeling that something was wrong so she opened the letter out of concern. It said that Albert's injury had caused the loss of his arm. Granny called Dot to meet her halfway, where they shared the news and cried together.

Billie's "pin-up" photo for Robert serving in the Army.

Granny was very talented. She taught herself to crochet and made beautiful quilts for her family, and she sewed clothes — some from feed sacks, also called "henhouse linen"— for her children, Sandra, Rebecca, Roberta, and Robbie. She taught ceramics at the Scott's Run Settlement House in Osage, and many of her beautiful pieces decorate our homes today. Granny and Robert "Pap" Straight and children were selected as Monongalia County's Farming for Better Living family for the year 1956.

Granny was a wonderful blessing to her family and devoted to her grandchildren and great-grandchildren. She accepted people for who they were and was always there when one of us needed her. When she died on April 1, 1991, I lost a wonderful Grandma, friend, and confidante.

Author: Tawny Layman Hoxter. Tawny wanted to write about her grandmother and asked Dot Fox to share some of her memories as well. Dot was Granny Straight's best friend when Dot moved to Laurel Point from Preston County in 1941.

134-001-ST-WV-001-1997

Defy The Storm

Howard Harold Swick, Sr. Born, Harrison County, 1908. Died, Harrison County, 1991. Coal miner. Dam builder. Farmer, hunter, trapper. My father.

When I was small, and storm clouds from the west darkened Goke Hollow, sending leaves whirling, bending maples and oaks, I looked out the window into the gathering darkness and saw him standing with one hand leaning against a dead crab apple tree on the slope of our side yard. At these times he always stood there, as dark in the unnatural light as the black tree beside him, watching the west as if warning the storm not to bring its fury against his family, his home. He was watching for what he called "tornado lightning," the constant flicker he had once seen lighting the skies before a funnel cloud smashed Shinnston back in '44. At any hint of danger, he would have had us all in the root cellar under the old school house we lived in, but to my young mind, he was the barrier against the storm that made me feel safe.

It was perhaps the only time in childhood I felt safe with my father. My mother had convinced me from my earliest days that my father would harm me to hurt her. I did not know then she was mentally ill, had been diagnosed with a split personality, and her illness led her to paranoia and obsession. I was her greatest obsession, and she was determined not to share my affection with my father or anyone else, so she taught me to fear him.

Dad knew what the doctors had told him about Mom, but he believed marriage was for life. He knew he was not going to be permitted to be the father he might have been to me, but he faced this storm like all the rest: Watching quietly, waiting.

Had my mother's behavior been consistent, Dad would never have been permitted time alone with me, but each autumn she happily permitted me to go off into the woods with this man she swore would harm me, despite the fact he and I were both carrying shotguns in hope of finding squirrels. I went with the fear she had implanted in me gnawing at my mind, but these were the times Dad gave me gifts he wanted me to have.

Beside a stream running orange with acid mine drainage, he would point to tracks in the mud. The small hand prints with sharp claws were left by a 'coon. A 'possum's tail left a thin, snake-like trail. Deer, rabbit, muskrat — everything that used the stream left its mark behind, a mark that let a hunter or trapper know what he could expect to find nearby.

The trees had their own stories to tell. Some made better dens than others, and a hunter needed to know where to look. Shagbark hickory, ash, sweet gum, I learned every tree in the forest as we wandered the hillsides. Dad would cross shale-lined gullies to find trees so I could sample their nuts. He once carved off a piece of draining beech sap to teach me where chewing gum came from. We stopped by an abandoned house where his own father had lived so I could learn the sweet taste of persimmons and learn not to pick them before the first good frost.

On Saturdays, Dad would go to the small mine where he worked to feed the mule that still hauled out ore even in the mid-1960s. Occasionally he took me with him, and on one trip, when I was in seventh grade, he suddenly took out a stick of dynamite, a blasting cap, and wire. Patiently, he taught me how to wire dynamite and told me how to drill rock, pack, and place a blasting charge. Why, I wondered, was he telling me this? I had no intention of working in the mines.

Many years later, I understood, understood about the dynamite and the animal tracks and the need to identify trees and know when to pick nuts and fruit. To survive and support his family, my father had dug eighteen-inch coal lying flat on his back in narrow passageways. He had worked the strip mines he passionately hated when no other jobs were available. He helped build the Grafton Dam, and he kept a garden and butchered hogs. During the Great Coal Depression of the 1950s, he swallowed his pride and accepted commodities from his union — meal, dried milk, flour — and did yard work for our landlord because we couldn't pay the twenty-five dollars a month rent. Had my father grown up in other times, he might have been a teacher instead of a laborer with an eighth-grade education; he knew life had a way of changing a man's plans. Without ever telling me so, he prepared me to be ready to do whatever work was available, to find my own food, to do what was necessary to care for myself and my family.

I've never had to depend on the woods to feed me, nor have I had to wire dynamite or butcher hogs. Not yet anyway. But I've seen jobs end suddenly, watched my savings get wiped out time and again, and I took care of my own wife as cancer slowly drained every ounce of life from her. I have survived, and I have grown whenever a sudden storm has turned my world unnaturally dark and sent my plans sailing away like so many leaves. In each tempest I have seen the image of a tall man standing beside a dead crab apple tree, defiant in the darkness. My father taught me well.

AUTHOR: *Gerald D. Swick. Gerald is a Clarksburg writer and teacher. His work won a Billboard magazine award and was included in a "Best Of" science fiction list.*

135-001-ST-WV-001-1997

The Fuller Brush Man

Many of you who read these words will remember the Fuller Brush man. He came knocking at your door hoping to sell you some of those famous Fuller Brushes. I worked for Fuller Brush off and on for several years. Each Fuller Brush man had a specific territory and went from door to door taking orders. Then the products sold were delivered at a later date.

As a Fuller Brush man I met many nice people and was welcomed into many homes leaving me with many memories. I gave away thousands of those famous door openers — the vegetable brush.

Besides cleaning items, Fuller had a line of cosmetics. One day I was in the home of an older lady whom I expect came here as a young girl from the old country. She had difficulty understanding and speaking the English language. Besides the vegetable brush, I gave her a sample bottle of "Blue Hedge" toilet water. She said, "Toilet water? Do you put it in the toilet?"

"No," I told her, "put a little behind your ear." But I couldn't convince her not to put it in the toilet.

Later, when I delivered the wet mop she had ordered, she said, "You bring me a bottle of the toilet water. I put it in the toilet and it smelled so good."

The next time I stopped at her house she said, "My daughter will not let me buy any more toilet water."

AUTHOR: *David Darwin Calvert. Mr. Calvert is retired and resides in Clarksburg.*

136-001-ST-WV-001-1997

The Purple Heart

The President of the United States of America awards the Purple Heart, established by General George Washington at Newburgh, New York, August 7, 1782. On September 21, 1918, the medal was awarded to my father, Private John A. Darnell, United States Army, for wounds received in action in France. At that time he was also promoted to Staff Sergeant. In 1919, he received a second Purple Heart and other medals.

Dad was always proud of his medals. As children we were also very proud and would ask questions about how he was wounded and so forth. I can remember that I always thought the medals were from a wound in the heart since they called it the Purple Heart. I would ask Dad how his heart was, and if it was still purple. For years I connected his wounds with his heart. Dad would explain that his heart was the same as everyone else's; that was just the name of the medal. I always thought it was beautiful, and still do.

At some point I became aware that the medal was for his being a hero. I had dreams about how he did a great hero's deeds. I was so surprised when I found out that others had received the Purple Heart too. I wondered if their heroic deeds were as great as my father's.

John Albert Darnell gave me his Purple Hearts because I was his oldest child and was interested in them. I promised to treasure them and take good care of them. Dad gave my brother Donald a medal with a ribbon and some star-type pins and ribbons. Today Dad and my brother are deceased, but the medals and the memories serve to preserve them.

Author: Ethel Louise Righman. Louise is a retired nurse. She serves as Regent for the Black Water Chapter of the Daughters of the American Revolution. Her father was from Darnell Hollow, near Morgantown. Her mother was Mabel Virginia Arnold.

137-001-ST-WV-001-1997

The Grand Old Lady Of Morgantown

It was a Victorian house on 229 Grand Street. It had wooden banisters and doors that slid between each room downstairs, a back stairway and lots of closets and fireplaces. It had lattice along the back porch which was always filled with a plethora of morning glories which seemed to grow themselves and blossom such simple beauty of velvet flowers.

As a child in the 1950s, I found secret places in the tall bushes and played on the swings and in the sandbox. On the front steps was the best place to have banana popsicles from the corner store, and on the porch was the sweet smell of honeysuckle and a place to watch the world go by. Across the street was the high school, with the sounds of the band or a football game.

Inside, there were books everywhere and closets filled with coloring books, games, photographs, fragile yearbooks, old *Readers' Digests*, clippings, recycled wrapping paper and even on the third floor, linoleum with game boards right on it and more interesting things in the window seats. In the den, my father David Christopher and his newspapers would be surrounded by cigar smoke.

One afternoon, my sister enticed me into running away. We made it to the top of the street and turned back when it became woods. My parents hadn't even noticed we were gone and we snuck back to our bunk beds. At night, of course, we would read under the covers with flashlights or streak them across the wall, imitating the openings of movies.

It was a magic place, I realize now, a museum. My mom Mary Behner Christopher repaired dolls and rarely threw anything away. So there were dolls everywhere and drawers full of wigs, eyes, lace, and buttons. There was the smell of wood putty and the whir of the sewing machine running late at night, because she sewed dance costumes and rented Santa outfits and Mountaineer dresses. The kitchen table was where we stuffed little animals to sell, where dolls were healed and political events were discussed.

It was a busy place. The phone rang a lot, and many students from other countries stayed in our home. Sometimes there were surprise parties, and my mom was so tolerant allowing me to let my parakeet and his feathers be everywhere. I watched Poochie give birth to seven puppies in the basement, and my oldest sister Margie tried to hide a cat in the attic. There was a wonderful secretary desk in the hallway with all sorts of interesting cubbyholes and drawers of bridge tickets that had tassels on them. Sometimes we would get all the decks of cards out (for there was always a lot of everything) and play endless games of War, and then fling them at each other in a real game of war.

The Grand Old Lady, a museum of memories.

It was there, in the dim light, that romance flourished when I brought my beaux home. It was there Tom and I opened our wedding presents and left in a hail of rice. It was there my daughter Renée as a baby learned to crawl up the steps. How many times were we well into dinner when Mom would jump up and say, "The rolls!" that were forgotten in the oven.

After my father died, the red leather chair looked so empty. When my mom became ill, she sold her dolls and walked painfully up the stairs. The last time she came home from the hospital, it was I who carried her in the door. When she died, the energy of the house departed and I watched furniture being sold. Love left the house.

I wondered if I could ever walk in that house again after the new owners bought it, and where I had lived or visited for forty-one years. It was the only home together my parents ever knew. But what I thought would be a traumatic experience turned into a healing one.

It looked different, of course. Emptier, new furniture and no more dolls, no more costumes stuffed into closets. I realized that the Grand Old Lady had passed into other hands, as caring, I hoped, as my mom's. I couldn't hold onto it forever, but I felt so full of all the good, extraordinary and simple memories, which we always realize too late how special they are. I walked out smiling and at peace.

Author: Bettijane Burger. Mrs. Burger is an English teacher at St. Albans high school.

138-001-ST-WV-001-1997

Happy Memories Of Long Ago

lifford Righman, his dad, and other relatives loved to hunt and fish. Each year when the game law came in, they started out very early with hot coffee and food to supply the entire community of hunters. They were not always successful hunters and fishermen, but they loved to tell their tales. Fishing bait was always the most discussed, as were special places to fish. Each person had his own special place and tall tale to share around the campfire.

The next generation, Clifford's sons Michael and Glenn, took to hunting and fishing naturally. Sometimes they were all successful, each bragging that his game was the largest ever caught or killed. Everything was weighed and measured and checked against the others'. Michael now has twins Mike and Mark. Like their dad, they've joined in the ranks of sportsmen and tellers of tales.

A favorite story to tell is the time Glenn rigged up a buck decoy near the woods they were to hunt and told his brother Michael to go forward and they would branch out. Michael started to the woods and saw the buck in the clearing. He started stalking, and taking careful aim, he shot. But the deer did not fall. He went toward the buck and all his buddies were watching and laughing like nuts. He got teased about cutting his shirt-tail off because he missed such an easy shot at his big buck. He was teased for many years about this.

Author: Dana Ann Swartz Righman. Dana is a secretary and homemaker from Philippi. When not listening to family stories, she studies history, travels, and reads.

139-001-ST-WV-001-1997

My Father's Bootstrap Education

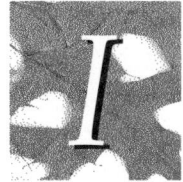

n the foothills of the mountains near Crawley, in Greenbrier County, West Virginia, Emmett Heaster finished eighth grade in 1912, and hung around a couple of years, helping the schoolmaster. Then an official came to Lewisburg, giving state teacher's examinations. Emmett was told he couldn't possibly pass it without a high school education. But he took the test anyway and passed it, and became a schoolteacher at seventeen.

He thought he was set for life, there in the hills, but World War I called him away. He had hardly been outside Greenbrier County in his life. In the Army, he was amazed and stunned by the world beyond his little country enclave. It was his first contact with real city people, real educated people.

Although he was offered the opportunity to go to Officer Candidate School, he was too embarrassed and self-conscious about his backwoods raising, education, and speech. But by the time he mustered out of the Army, he had developed a burning obsession to get a real education.

After his discharge, he worked in the big lumber camps in Greenbrier County, saved some money, went up to Morgantown, in Monongalia County, and enrolled in Morgantown High School. He did maintenance chores in exchange for room and board.

He attended some regular classes, but studied textbooks on his own for other classes, only taking exams with the rest of the class. In one year he managed to complete sixteen and a half credits, with all A's and B's, except for one C in biology. Although he had enough credits to graduate, he did not receive a high school diploma.

However, when he applied for admission to college, the administrators were quite im-

pressed and enrolled him anyway. He worked his way through college, receiving a degree in education from Broaddus College in Philippi, where he also met Georgia Golden, who became his wife the day he graduated. He then became a schoolteacher again, along with his new wife.

For years I thought about going to the Monongalia County Board of Education to see if they could grant him a belated high school diploma, but I kept putting it off. In 1995, at the age of ninety-eight, he passed away, without the diploma, but with a most remarkable educational achievement.

AUTHOR: Dale Heaster. Mr. Heaster is an architect and father of four. He resides in his hometown of Morgantown.

140-001-ST-WV-001-1997

District High School was renamed to Kasson High School. Dorwin Wolfe was appointed the first principal. At that time the teachers were Agnes Haller, Fred Clayton, Delmer Nestor, Belva and Blanch Poling, Ena Shaw, Roselee Poling, Lenore Marsh, Robert Summers, Nellie Nestor, John Nestor, and Hazel Wolfe.

The first principal was Dr. L.S. McDaniel. In addition to his administrative duties, he offered a teacher's training course for college credit. Earl Loughridge walked from Tucker County to attend, also Howard and Floyd Cornwell, James Wilson, Lula Coffman Sturm, Fred Nestor, Hazel Nestor, Ira Wolfe, Pearl Combs, Lillie Moore Richman, and Faye Nestor.

AUTHOR: Agnes Dennison Haller. Mrs. Haller is a retired school teacher from Barbour County. She is now ninety-three. Her hobbies include travel, genealogy, and history. She is the daughter of Andrew and Florence Hardin.

141-001-ST-WV-001-1997

Cove District High School

During 1916 and 1917, N.C. "Tobe" Hardin and his brother-in-law Dallas Wolfe canvassed Cove District, on Route 92 near Philippi, Barbour County, to establish a high school. Their efforts paid off. A three-year high school was built from the donations and labor of local people. The high school met minimum requirements, but was not considered a "first class school." Until 1923, George Coffman, John Lee Righman, and Oliver Wolfe were the three members of the Board of Education. Strather Lohr was secretary of the board. Dallas Wolfe might have been involved, but he joined the Navy.

Children from the following families attended the school in its early years: Hugh Humphrey, Benton Lohr, John Isner, Will Loar, Bradford Miller, Clager Coffman, Ed Skidmore, Walter Hovatter, Strather Lohr, Noble Lohr, John W. Nestor, James Wilson, John Miller, Charley Bolyard, Andy Loar, Andrew S. Hardin, Barney Godwin, Oliver Wolfe, Leo Freeman, Cleophas Marsh, Howard Campbell, Jacob Lutz, Jasper Deahl, George Coffman, Archies and Harry England, George Campbell, John C. Shaw, Pat Ryan, George Colebank, Taylor George, A.S. Lindsey, George Isner, Melvin Polin, L.L. Friend, Blackburn Ware, "Hob" Thompson, George Ford, Ellis Moats, Charley Bolyard, John Nestor, Clay Hardin, John Miller, Claud Freeman, Harold Ritter, Zella Frye, Lige Loar, Blaine Stemple, Dow Howdershelt, Ed Auvil, Barbara Ekis.

Students walked from Valley Furnace, Nestorville, Moatsville, Cove Run, Martin Beulah, Colebank, Boot Jack, Calud, Corinth, Locus Grove, Mt. View. Around 1933, the Cove

Excerpts From My Journal

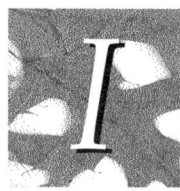

I was born December 18, 1917, in the house I am now living in. My parents were William Alexander Rumble and Gertrude Elizabeth Gibson Rumble. I had a sister Darlie Rebecca, who was born July 18, 1912.

Dad and Granddad Thomas Benton Rumble farmed, and would go for miles on horseback to buy cattle and drive them home. They cut lots of hay on both farms, raised corn, and had horses. They used horses to plow, and cut hay pulling a mowing machine, hay rake and a sweep to sweep the hay into before stacking. They also always raised corn for silage and filled the silo for use in the winter. When the corn was ripe they put it in the corncrib. It was used for feeding the horses and chickens.

The wedding picture of Gertrude and William Rumble, Dorothea's parents.

Chapter 9: Mountaineer Country

Gertrude and William Rumble pose with their daughter Darlie on one of the family's horses.

We raised almost everything we ate, only buying flour, sugar, spices. We had our own corn ground for cornmeal. Mother always raised a good garden, complete with strawberries and raspberries. The family had milk cows, and the women made cottage cheese and butter. The men always had an orchard with a wide variety of good apples — some names I remember: Wolf River, Russet, Pippin, Rambo, York Imperial. In the fall we would pick the apples and put them in a cave and they would supply us all winter. We had a cider mill, and from an overabundance of apples we would make cider. My dad built a cave where we kept apples, potatoes, and cider in barrels in the winter. The cave was built next to the coal bank, and because only the front was exposed to the weather, things stored there wouldn't freeze. Sometimes in the winter we knew a sneaky neighbor visited that cave to taste cider. I guess he didn't realize he left footprints in the snow.

Dad had a stallion named Kilt that he drove around for the purpose of breeding mares. Dad hitched Kilt to a dog cart (a small cart with one passenger seat) and would travel to several counties, sometimes for two or three days at a time before returning home. Other horses we had were Perch and Babe, Beauty and Maude. Bird was another, and Nell was our trusty one. Dandy was a horse Dad bought from gypsies who came around every couple of years wanting to trade. Most people were afraid to deal with them because they had the reputation of being slick traders. But Dandy was a wonderful horse.

I started to school when I was five years old. I was very bashful and would not talk to my teacher Jesse Gwyn. He was a good fellow and had three daughters. I think I just wasn't ready to go to school yet. The next teacher I had was Esrom Sprout. One day he told all the kids to go outside and get their picture taken. Everybody went out but me, and when I was missed he marched me out and stood me in front of him for the picture. I was furious. When he got the picture he gave me one, but I resented the whole episode. Sometime later when I came across that picture, I cut the top of it off. From then on I had Clarence Reppert, Elery Brown, Alice Giles, Charlotte Kramer, and Elmus G. Price for teachers in grade school.

I moved to Fairmont in 1932 to attend East Fairmont High School. I roomed upstairs with Darlie at 707 State Street. During my junior year, 1935, Darlie was teaching at Kinkaid School. That fall she had a fall festival with a box social. Each girl fixed a box with a complete meal in it, wrapped it in pretty paper, and the boxes were auctioned off. Margaret Moran and Clerissa Hathaway came home with me over the weekend, so Mother worked hard all day fixing good food to fill our boxes.

The event was well advertized and there was a big crowd there. Margaret had been

Mountain State Stories Of The People

Newlyweds Dorothea and Vanden King

dating Stanley Vincent, and I guess she marked her box in some way so he would know which was hers. I don't remember who got mine, but Vanden King got Clerissa's. Before the evening was over, Vanden asked me to walk with him in the cake walk and we got the cake.

When people started leaving, Vanden asked me if he could take me home, and I accepted. It was a beautiful fall moonlit night when we walked down the road. When we got home we sat in the swing on the front porch and talked until Mother and Dad came home. When they got there, Vanden said to Mother, "Mrs. Rumble, may I sit in the swing with your daughter?" Mother said "Yes." We soon went into the house and Vanden and Dad and Mother started to get acquainted, probably not suspecting what would happen five years down the road. It wasn't easy for my parents to even think of the time when their two daughters would marry. At the time we met, Vanden was teaching at Layman School at Morgan's Ridge and living with his brother Marner at the Home Place.

Saturday, November 4, 1995 — Day before our fifty-fifth wedding anniversary, if only Vanden were here to celebrate it with me. This is the coldest day we've had this fall. It is quiet, leaves are tumbling down and the birds are checking out their feeding stations. My daughter Karla helped me rig up an old ironing board for a feeder. Already I have seen many bluejays, cardinals, and various little birds. A few snowflakes are falling. I began to sort through our books and maybe will sell some.

Author: Dorothea Cyrena Rumble King. Dorothea graduated from college and taught in Monongalia County. She and Vanden settled in Marion County with their three children. After seventeen years they returned to Dorothea's birthplace.

142-001-ST-WV-001-1997

Editors' Note: Cake walks were done as fundraisers at school festivals and other events. Music was played while couples walked in a circle around the room. In the middle of the circle a blindfolded person stood holding a broom upright. When the music stopped the broom was allowed to fall. The couple the broom dropped in front of won a cake. Each couple paid to participate in the cake walk.

Growing Up In Memorial City

Grafton, West Virginia, is known as "Memorial City" since it is the location of the state's only National Cemetery. One of my earliest recollections is of viewing the annual Memorial Day parade. My parents would take me to see the parade, but the blare of the marching bands was almost too much for me. However, it wasn't long before I was part of the marching groups.

The memorial event began in 1867 with what was called "The Big Strewn of Flowers." On that day the Civil War veterans' graves were decorated with flowers. In later years it became known as Decoration Day, and eventually all the county school children took part, carrying flowers to decorate these and subsequent war veterans' graves.

My participation began in the first grade and continued on until I marched with the Boy Scouts, then the Fire Department, followed by the Army Reserve, and then a few years ago driving some of the dignitaries.

Now when I view the parade it brings back fond memories of the excitement of marching, decorating a grave, rushing off to West Side Elementary school for a free ice cream cone, and finally to the end of the West Side bridge where each year a small carnival was set up. This carnival consisted of two or three stands which were overshadowed by what seemed to me to be a huge merry-go-round and Ferris wheel. These I thoroughly enjoyed.

Memorial Day was eagerly anticipated not particularly for the parade, ice cream cone or even the carnival. It meant "END OF

SCHOOL!!!" No more books until after Labor Day — hurrah!!!

I fondly cherish these memories, and although long since removed from Grafton, I make an attempt each year to return and view with pride one of the longest-lived remembrances of our veterans and the sacrifices they made.

Author: Louis W. Smith. Mr. Smith is a government retiree, currently working on compiling his family history. Although he lives in Maryland, he says, "You still can't take the hills out of the boy!"

143-001-ST-WV-001-1997

A family farm house in Fairview.

Long Ago But Not Forgotten

As I drive from Parkersburg to Charles Town, I fondly remember times forty years ago traveling along old US Route 50 to Fairview, West Virginia, to visit my grandfather. From our eastern panhandle home, Route 50 between Romney and Grafton was very curvy.

I recall our many trips to the farm so vividly. We would turn onto the gravel road Rush Run, turn at the road to the farm, then stop and open the gate which was opposite the Basnettsville Methodist Church where my father attended as a young man. We traveled up a gentle hill. Soon, in the distance, I would get my first glimpse of the farm house straight ahead. We passed a fenced-in field on the left and several small wooden chicken coops on the right along the way. The grain house and barn were next to the farm house, on the right. And in back, in the distance, was a higher hill all around.

At the path of the driveway, the two-story white clapboard house with porches on three sides came closer. On one porch was a wonderful old swing which we thoroughly enjoyed. The house had a big kitchen which was the social center of our activities.

My grandpa was over eighty years of age when I was a child. I recall he spent many hours in bed during our visits, but he still managed to join us at the dinner table for family meals. He seemed so tall, had a full head of white hair, and a white beard. He had big hands like my father's hands.

My sisters, my parents, and I slept in the living room. It was very dark. There was an old pump organ that I attempted to play, but my feet didn't reach the pedals. There were pictures of relatives, taken when they were younger. There was a circular stairway to the bedrooms upstairs: one for the boys — my father and his brothers — and one for Dad's sisters. One night, my sister Lisa and I slept upstairs with Aunt Lizzie. She was a big woman with glasses, curly hair, and a nice smile. Grandpa's bedroom was downstairs, and in it was an old crank telephone.

There are other memories. I can see my aunt making maple butter in a churn, and making cottage cheese. One time, she killed a chicken which we later ate for dinner. Milking cows was something I tried, but never developed the knack for. Also, I remember the dark, damp basement where food they produced in the garden on the farm was stored.

My great-great-great-great-grandfather John Shuman settled in Monongalia County in the 1700s. Grandpa's name was Francis Ellsworth Shuman. Today, my grandpa's house is gone and a new house is there, but I still visit the land that belonged to the Shuman and Haught families long ago.

Author: Norabelle Shuman Corra. Nora is a speech-language pathologist in the public school system. She grew up in Charles Town with her sisters Mimi and Lisa, and her parents Willis and Helen Shuman. She currently resides with her husband Mike in Parkersburg.

144-001-ST-WV-001-1997

The Keeper Of The History

I looked into the forest and there she resided
A grand and formidable salute to life.
This life has made a valuable contribution,
Counted and remembered by those touched.

Flanked by younger straighter trees
Not yet weathered by the experiences of life.
Her strong branches lead the way
    Sheltering and guiding those coming
      after her.

    For it is their task to continue on,

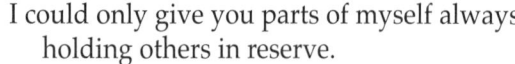

Carrying within them truth, history and the future.
Her limbs have been a haven to her offspring and others,
Cradling young and old in the need of mothering.

Stretching her arms into the canopy above,
Reaching heavenward to grasp the sun,
The life giving rays of nature and spirit
Radiate through her and are reflected to others.

The soft whispers of her delicate leaves
Have gently guided during the storms of life.
Her love is never given by measures,
But flows unhampered by changing seasons.

Life has bent her, twisted, scarred but never broken,
For her roots are deeply seated in the ways of the spirit.
There is heartfelt gratitude from those she has sheltered
To one who has graced our lives so majestically.

When youth was her daily fare,
As is the case with her descendants,
The world was quite a different place.
Great joys and many sorrows have been recorded.

For she is the keeper of the history.
And if she could but only speak,
What secrets would be told?
What mysteries would be unlocked?

For she is the silent guardian of the memories.
The keeper, of the history.

AUTHOR: *Patricia Kiger Morgan. Mrs. Morgan wrote this poem for her father's sister Ruth Kiger Headlee to be included in a scrapbook celebrating Mrs. Headlee's eightieth birthday on October 17, 1994. The poem was inspired by the mighty trees that grow in Coopers Rock State Forest in Preston County. Mrs. Morgan is a native of Morgantown.*

145-001-ST-WV-001-1997

Without History

You came into my life during a time of greatest need.
I had become lost and you helped me find my way.
My constant talking must have been a clue to how empty was my heart.
You were there — open, interested and caring.

I could only give you parts of myself always holding others in reserve.
There was a tentativeness in the beginning as we found our way
Our talks were good and I always felt your love was unconditional.
And so we began to build a daughter mother relationship like no other — without history.

Through the years your presence has been felt — understanding, listening, supporting
Never too busy to care, to come when needed, to sit and talk.
We have built a bond of respect that allows us to enjoy each other,
Without the need to direct, criticize or judge we could enjoy our newly discovered friendship.

I am thankful that I have you to hold our family together and to give us a point of reference.
Of course being a woman of "few words," I always know how you feel about things
But it is my decision whether or not to accept the advice given.
I feel good when we laugh together at ourselves and adorn each other with praise.

Without you to lead us, just think what we would have missed.
What would life be like without candy day?
No more faces burned with cinnamon or scorched fingers.
Think of the skills we would have missed, cutting, measuring, how to spin a thread and "how much is scant?"
But mostly the thick memories of being together, sharing love and laughter and the scents of approaching Christmas.

The traditions that we cherish have come from your caring about our family.
The specially selected gift at the birth of each grandchild and
Christmas Eve has become such a tradition that no one wants to be absent.
Who will receive the hand made "Nana" gift?
And what will it be?

Some years it was the grandchildren, dress-up hats for the boys, dress-up clothes for the girls.
Other years the adults were privileged with hand made quilts, photo albums and furniture.

Humor always plays a part in the evening
A mood ring to replace a thrown away gift,
    argyle socks, Big Al - Big V. Shirts and of course
    the best of all — gold lamé pants

But this is just the tip of our traditions, the
    memories have filled my life for the
    past twenty-six years.
When God gave you to us, He certainly knew
    what He was doing.
You have given us a family, traditions,
    belonging and love.
I hope in return we have filled your life as
    abundantly as you have filled ours.

And now after all this time together
I am privileged to have you as my own
And I like the relationship we've grown
    as we have become daughter and
    mother with history.

AUTHOR: *Patricia Kiger Morgan. Mrs. Morgan wrote this poem as a tribute to her second mother, Jane H. Kiger, who over the past twenty-six years has nurtured their unique family so lovingly.*

146-001-ST-WV-001-1997

Rationed Candy/ Rationed Gum

Just where the Tygart Valley River takes a sweeping bend through the rolling hills beside the Fetterman District of Grafton, West Virginia, at the corner of West Main and Boyd Streets, Mrs. Peters operated a neighborhood grocery store.

During World War II, sugar was rationed. Its purchase required a government-issued coupon, so candy and gum were hard to find. Therefore, at First Ward Elementary School, the playground cry, "Mrs. Peters has bubble gum and candy!" was long-awaited news.

Impatiently, those of us whose families bought at that store waited for classes to end. Then we dashed down the hillside, lining up at her door to await our turn to receive our bag of goodies! No shoving allowed, nor was it needed…for Mrs. Peters had prepackaged for each of us an equal share of her allotment.

How special I felt to know that ahead was a plain, brown paper store-bag with "Charleen" boldly written with black, waxy marking pencil!

That evening I would count out pieces of Kits, Hershey Kisses, Bits-of-Honey and lollipops with that chewy Tootsie chocolate inside as I lay strategies as to how many days each precious paper-wrapped pink bubblegum would need to be chewed to sustain me until we would next hear, "Mrs. Peters has candy! Mrs. Peters has gum!"

Years later, we sang a song, "Does Your Chewing Gum Lose Its Flavor on the Bedpost Overnight?"

Mine did!…unless it fell off and got lost in my hair at night.

But chew it, I did!

AUTHOR: *Charleen Evans-Thomas, Ed.D. Charleen is a retired educator and businesswoman. She grew up in Grafton and is a descendant of early pioneer families of Taylor and Monongalia Counties.*

147-001-ST-WV-001-1997

Memories Of The Rural Mail Carrier

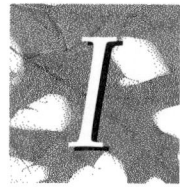

I grew up on a farm in a very rural area of Doddridge County, West Virginia. My memories of the rural mail carrier begin about 1930. The arrival of the mail was one of the eagerly awaited events of the day. Many times my younger sister and I would watch for the "mail boy" to come into sight on the road that passes our house.

In the early thirties the mail was our daily connection to the rest of the world, as we had no radio until the mid-thirties. The mail brought the daily newspaper, weekly papers, and magazines. All were a welcome source of information, as were letters from family, friends, and businesses.

Packages from Sears and Montgomery Ward were very welcome arrivals. Items obtained this way included clothing, household articles, farm supplies, and especially, Christmas presents.

The mail carrier did more than just deliver mail. He really operated a mobile post office. Buying stamps, mailing packages, and any other mail service you needed was as close as your mail box. In 1930 stamps were two cents. The carrier also brought pick-up notices from the railroad for items too large for mail shipment. I especially remember the gasoline-powered washing machine and our first radio that came by train and needed to be picked up.

My mail memories would be incomplete without telling of the dedication of our mail carrier. The carrier I first remember was Ray Conley, a prime example of the postal creed. He lived near our post office at Blandville. His thirty-some mile

L. Meigs Stout, Loutellus Stout's father, awaits the mail at his Doddridge County farm in 1952.

route over dirt or mud roads served over 125 patrons. From the post office it went up Lick Run and down Cain Run to the Hughes River road at Porto Rico (where my home was located), then two miles to the head of Hughes River, down Cove Creek and over the hill to Grove community, back over another hill to Porto Rico, then back a quarter mile through Porto Rico and down Little Tom's Fork to Market community on Route 18. His route ended there, but he still had to go about six miles on this road along Tom's Fork and Meathouse Fork to return to the post office.

He usually arrived at our house around ten o'clock when roads were at their best. He could drive a Model T Ford for six or eight months, and then he had to ride a horse, at times leading a pack horse. This was particularly necessary at Christmas given the extra mail. Sometimes flooding would keep him from making his trip. The Model Ts were succeeded by Model A Fords. With the arrival of the Jeep after World War II, horses were no longer used. In the mid-thirties, Route 18 was paved, but the poor conditions prevailed for the rest of the mail route until after World War II. Several miles of the route had improved roads by the time I left the area in 1963, but there were still several miles that made it necessary to drive a Jeep.

Author: Loutellus Stout. Mr. Stout was born in 1924, and grew up on a farm in Doddridge County. He currently lives in St. Albans and works at the Supreme Court of Appeals of West Virginia.

148-001-ST-WV-001-1997

The Simpson Hotel

During the 1920s Simpson, West Virginia, was a boom town. Coal ran rich and black from the mines in the area. The railroad hauled it away. And the citizens had it made. There were still a good many farms along with the company houses. Roads connected them with all the major routes and towns. They had a train station, post office, schoolhouse, doctor's office, three or four general mercantiles, and the Simpson Hotel.

As hotels go the Simpson Hotel was small and not very luxurious. Rooms and meals were provided for the weary traveler. Eventually the hotel and property came into the hands of my grandfather. It was no longer used as a hotel by that time. Grandfather closed off the upstairs and rented out the first floor to a local family. Yet the old two-story building with its long unpainted wood siding and tin hip roof was a continuous source of speculation among the few youngsters in our small community. We were all sure it was haunted.

When the family who lived there moved on, my family opened up the upstairs and used the hotel for storage. This allowed us kids to start a long tradition of sneaking into the old hotel at night, on dares, of course. Many times during the years of growing up my friends and I were sent screaming from its doors at some sound we just knew was a ghost; many an imagination was sparked along with some genuine mysteries. Even a romance or two blossomed among huddled teens.

The old hotel is gone now. It had become too rickety and had to be torn down. Its foundation, like the ghosts, brings back memories of yesterdays, remembrances not to be forgotten.

Author: William H.D. Shelton. William is a registered nurse. He and his wife Cindy Shelton (Lynch), of Nutter Fort, have been married for eight years. They reside in Simpson.

149-001-ST-WV-001-1997

Losing My Mamaw

It was true she had left me. My mamaw's death was a shock to me even though I knew it was going to happen sooner or later.

I was very close to my mamaw. When I was little, I would follow her around her house "helping" her cook, clean, and weed the garden. I can picture the back porch with the big white swing where we would sit

Mamaw Georgia Ellen Deavers Bolyard, approximately twenty years old, with daughter Eldora Bolyard Nuzum, who became the first woman editor of a daily newspaper in West Virginia — The Elkins Inter-Mountain. *Photo taken around 1929 in Bluemont Cemetery in Grafton.*

What Ever Task Lies To Your Hand, Do It With All Your Might.

— Ecclesiastes 9:10

A short time before 1800 — the exact date is not known — Isaac Van Camp, a settler from Virginia, secured a "land patent" from the governor of Virginia for eight hundred acres of land. That area is now known as Harmony Grove and is located on the west side of the Monongahela River, at a distance of two and three-quarter miles from Morgantown. Van Camp built a one-room log house and moved his family there. This was then called the Van Camp Settlement. The log house was later occupied by the Jolliffe family, the members of which were Van Camp's direct descendants.

In 1954, my family bought property on which to build. My deed states the location as Camp Ridge. The purchase included the original Isaac Van Camp log house. Over the years, about four rooms had been added. Hoping to find out more about the property, I talked with Anna Jolliffe, who lived in the log house. From her, I learned that for many years the water spring on my property had supplied water for every family which had lived in the community. My interest in local history led to more information and eventually, a project.

Early in its history, Harmony Grove had three saw mills: the Michael Kearns, Jr. Mill, near the Monongahela River; the C.W. Ley Mill, located on the U.B. Brown property; and the third on the Jolliffe farm (the Van Camp land). There was also a grist mill on this farm.

In later years, some of the names in the community were: Rawley Evans; French Gainer; Rufus Conn; Jess Knotts; George Jamison; Ben Morgan; James Thompson, a doctor; Henry Cox; and Frank Cox. Ben Morgan went on to become a lawyer, and Frank Cox was also a lawyer and later a judge. The Cox property is the present site of the new Westwood Middle School.

In 1845, the church the community attended burned. There is still a cemetery there called the *old Burnt Church Cemetery*. It was located one mile west of the Van Camp House.

Rufus Conn and his wife Elizabeth gave property to build a new church. The land was at the fork in the road, one road leading to Evans Ferry, the other to Kearns Mill. In October, 1853, the constitution of the Harmony Grove Meeting House was written, and soon after, the building was completed. The meeting house was used for the worship of God and as a union meeting house. During the weekdays, the house was to be used for school.

and color or play Chutes and Ladders. When she started misplacing things and forgetting to do things, we thought it was just age.

When she started getting worse, we decided to put her in a nursing home. Mamaw became happy again for about four years being with people her own age. She was in and out of coherency. Sometimes I would be her sister or my older cousin or sometimes she knew who I was and could carry out a normal conversation. She would forget the conversation took place an hour later. The last year was the worst. She was bedridden and silent.

For a week after the funeral I cried every time someone mentioned her. She meant so much to me that it was hard to let her go. But, I realized that she would want me to remember her before she got Alzheimer's disease. I now recall all the good times we had together and how much she loved me.

AUTHOR: *Jennifer Nicole Whyte. Jennifer is sixteen years old and lives in Cross Lanes. Her grandmother was Georgia Ellen Deavers Bolyard. She was born and lived in Grafton, West Virginia, until four years prior to death when she resided in Elkins. Mamaw Bolyard was a wonderful grandmother who lived from March 12, 1909 to August 27, 1994. Jennifer's papaw was Roy Everett Bolyard.*

150-001-ST-WV-001-1997

Roman Catholics were prohibited from using the house. This is not surprising, for mid-nineteenth century Americans were often quite prejudiced against Roman Catholics. On the first Sabbath of each month the Methodist Episcopals and Methodist Protestants were to use the church. On the second Sabbath the Presbyterians Old Side and Cumberland Presbyterians were able to use it. The third Sabbath was reserved for the Baptist Reformed, and the fourth and fifth Sabbaths were left open to any Protestant minister of good standing in his own church. The Meeting House constitution was signed by Ulysses Camp, secretary and Rawley Evans, president.

The first trustees were Rawley Evans, Jesse Hallard, and John Camp, Sr. If any of the trustees should

Harmony Grove Church, built 1854, listed on the National Register of Historic Places.

"die or remove," the subscribers were to meet and elect another to fill his vacancy. This was done through the years. The property was deeded to the trustees.

On Sundays, people would come from miles around and gather to hear the Sabbath service. In those days, the church was always filled. In addition to being a church, union meeting place, and schoolhouse, the house was used by the community for quilting frolics, apple parings and corn huskings, cider parties, and basket dinners.

In 1867, a one-room school was built near the church. This was a frame structure and was used until 1925, when a brick building was built.

Beginning in 1913, only the Methodists used the church. In 1979, it was closed because of low attendance. This was when I started to work with other members of the community to get it listed on the National Register of Historic Places and to preserve it for the community. I wrote to the Historic Preservation Unit at the Division of Culture and History in Charleston. We did not receive much encouragement. The staff told us there were hundreds of small churches all over West Virginia trying to get on the National Register of Historic Places, of the United States Department of the Interior. They did send forms to fill out, however. It was clear that we needed help — specifically, a historian with expertise in local structures and history.

A call to West Virginia University's Department of History resulted in Dr. Barbara Howe and Dolores Fleming visiting the site. The National Register requires documenting both the architecture and history of a building. Dr. Howe and Ms. Fleming checked out everything from nails and glass in the windows to chimneys. To increase our chances of qualifying for the register, the church needed some work — sound work that was authentic. The foundation of the church — rough-cut, big stones — had shifted. Dr. Howe advised us on the guidelines for the mortar. I remember we had to get sand from a creek bed. As this was being repaired, we could see the floor joists, which were large oak logs, rough hewn only on the top side, and fortunately, these were still in good condition. To think — they have been there since 1854. This was critical for the National Register listing, for this meant that the building retained a high degree of its original integrity.

Dolores Fleming did an enormous amount of survey work to help the case for Harmony Grove. She checked every old church building in the county against the Dodds survey in the 1950s. (Dr. and Mrs. Gideon S. Dodds surveyed Monongalia County's churches between 1949 and 1954, and published their findings in *The 175th Anniversary of the Formation of Monongalia County, West Virginia and Other Relative Historical Data*, 1954.) She proved that Harmony Grove is the oldest intact, unaltered church building in the county.

Dr. Howe suggested that we interview everyone in the community over eighty years old to try to find out as much as possible about the church. We found a lot of history. We learned, for example, that gas lights were installed in 1909, according to some old church records. Later, the church members installed electric lights. There were two wood

CHAPTER 9: MOUNTAINEER COUNTRY

Harmony Grove School class of 1908.

burners for heat; later, they had a gas heater. Mrs. Gillie Camp Willis even had the original constitution written in 1853.

The separation of church and state makes the case for designation of churches extremely difficult. Harmony Grove Meeting House's use as a union meeting house, school, and community center strengthened our application. Enclosed with the nomination form were the required sketch map of the property, a United States Geological Survey map indicating the church, black and white photographs and color slides of the interior and exterior of the church. In addition to answering the questions on the application, we had to provide many other supporting materials.

With the help of Dr. Howe and Ms. Fleming, we made our case and sent our completed application back to Charleston. We were successful! In 1983, the Harmony Grove meeting house was entered into the National Register of Historic Places. In 1985, the church reopened its doors to an interdenominational congregation.

AUTHOR: *Dorothy Moore. Mrs. Moore is the Secretary-Treasurer of Harmony Grove Community Association, Incorporated.*

151-001-ST-WV-001-1997

Home Brew And Ice Wagons

ony took off up the railroad tracks as the police came into the house and began breaking the bottles. Stella was left alone to finish the task, and she ended up overnight in jail.

This was an ethnic family's dilemma as they were discovered in the process of making "home brew." Life in the mining camp was very difficult during the 1930s. The whole country was in the middle of depressed economic times. The varied ethnic families living in the mining camp struggled to keep body and soul together. Without electricity, indoor plumbing, or central heating, life was not very comfortable. Kerosene lamps, outdoor pumps, and coal fired stoves for cooking and heating made life livable.

Life in the camp at Burk, in Preston County, was lived simply. A vibrant community spirit bonded the people and helped them to overcome their difficulties. The children played happily together. The older children taught the younger ones how to swim and to participate in games. Winter was a time of finding makeshift ways to ride on the snow. Some made sleds from a barrel stave and a two-foot piece of lumber. When one family was given a wagon, the other children pushed and pulled the new owners' children around so that they might share a ride.

The railroad track passed through the center of Burk. The children played on the tracks. One child was the watchman and when he yelled, "TRAIN! TRAIN!" all would jump from the tracks. One family had a radio, and in the summer they would open all the windows as neighbors gathered in the yard to listen to a boxing match with Joe Louis.

Each day the Ice Man came by with his wagon filled with large blocks of ice. When he announced his arrival by yelling "ICE MAN, ICE MAN," all the children came running to grab small chunks that fell as he cut large blocks.

The solidarity found in coal camp lives taught the people endurance, and they became resolute in finding ways to better themselves.

AUTHOR: *Jessie Volk. Jessie is a West Virginia University graduate and a native of Morgantown. She assisted in the management of several family businesses. After her three children completed college, she decided to channel her efforts into creative writing.*

152-001-ST-WV-001-1997

A Comforting Change

ontani Semper Liberi. Mountaineers are always free. I don't know if I had heard that at some point in my life, or if my transferring to West Virginia University (WVU) was a fluke. When I packed up the last of my belongings at a small, private college in New England, I only knew I had to leave the superficial community in which I had lived and studied for three years. I did not know where I was going.

I moved back to my home in Upstate New York for a while, but I had to finish my degree.

There are no four-year colleges in that area, and I knew I would have to leave. When I announced my decision to attend WVU, family and friends all asked, "Why WVU?" I guess it did seem like an odd decision, and I had no ready answer. Something about the outdoors drew me, but that alone could hardly be an acceptable explanation. When I left New England, I had studied biology, a strict discipline, in the suffocating environment of an affluent school. I needed more freedom.

I came to WVU in the spring semester, 1996. I changed my major to philosophy, a challenging subject, yet one which allowed — in fact demanded — freer thinking and logical argument. At the same time, I began going outdoors more often. Hikes on the secluded trails in Cooper's Rock State Forest provided a welcome change from the stifling halls of academia which had surrounded me in New England. I began to understand why I had come to West Virginia.

Although I cannot stay in West Virginia after I graduate — family ties draw me back to my home — I will always be grateful for the kindness of the people and the opportunity to share, even if for a short time, in the independence, simplicity, and joys of nature that accompany life in Appalachia.

AUTHOR: *Sarah Bracy. Sarah is a senior at West Virginia University.*

153-001-ST-WV-001-1997

Home Is West Virginia And West Virginia Is Home

I was delivered at home in Morgantown shortly after the Depression, by our neighbor Aunt Ruth Hartley, wife of "Uncle Charlie" Hartley, known as the father of 4-H in West Virginia. Even though my family lived one block from Monongalia General Hospital, my mother had a short labor and was unable to get to the hospital for my birth. As time has elapsed, I've continued to live my life fast-paced. My father laughingly commented, "As you entered this world in a hurry, you haven't changed." He was concerned that I wouldn't stop and smell the roses. His last written words to me were exactly that. Little did he realize those beautiful roses are my West Virginia friends.

My parents, Paul and Inez Wilson (both West Virginia natives), my siblings, and I were part of a close-knit community family. The opportunities afforded me growing up in a middle-class family of six children were positive and many. At a time when family and community values were

Colonel Pauline Shaver, 1997.

strong, the quote "it takes a village to raise a child" certainly had meaning. Church, school, 4-H, and scouting flourished in our lives. I was a member, leader, and an employee in the above activities. My family considered this a way of life.

Times weren't always easy. I remember anxiously waiting for the fresh fruits and vegetables of the spring and summer seasons to grace our tables when the "fruits of our labor" from the previous fall harvest were nearly gone. These fruits included berries and apples from our family's ritual "pickins." The aroma of fresh apple dumplings lingers in my mind. Canning, freezing, pickling, and kraut-making were familiar activities to us.

Raising chickens in the late 1940s was a family affair. We butchered and prepared chickens for use by the Hotel Morgan on a regular basis. My father, a very organized individual, had all of us involved in this task by setting up an assembly line procedure. We also raised turkeys, ducks, and rabbits. My family worked together to plant a "victory garden." One spring when my father was too ill to plant the garden, neighborhood residents and church members, many of whom were Air Raid Wardens during World War II under my father's watchful eye, supervised and helped us get the garden seeded. As proud West Virginians, we humbly accepted this labor of love.

It was not unusual for all of us to work and earn money which we contributed to the family. Our jobs included glass blowing, strawberry picking, baby-sitting, and delivering newspapers. There was a time when my father said he supported six schools all at once — West Virginia University (WVU), Morgantown High School, West Virginia Wesleyan College, Suncrest Junior High, St. Mary's School of Nursing, and Flatts Grade School. Pitching together was the norm.

We West Virginians come together for community work, fun, and projects. There were barn raisings, wedding serenades, and box lunch socials to raise money for school projects. One I vividly remember resulted in the purchase of a school bell for the two-room Flatts Elementary School. This school was located at the corner of the Van Voorhis and Chestnut Ridge Road intersection. My father

CHAPTER 9: MOUNTAINEER COUNTRY

shared some of his memories of the event with the Monongalia County Board of Education president, and his account was part of the dedication ceremony for the new North Elementary School where the bell was placed. Flatts School was later demolished to make way for "city growth."

Certainly much growth and many more changes have taken place since I grew up in Morgantown. The house I was born in on Christy Street has now been moved up the street, also to provide growing space for the city. A favorite feature of the house were the beautiful plaster castings adorning ceilings and trim. These plaster castings were made in Italian rubber molds. They have maintained their beauty through the years. The molds were found in a storage area under the front porch eaves and had disintegrated from the heat.

Despite the certainty of changing times, I tried to instill in my children many of the same values my community family taught me. My children worked on 4-H projects, raised rabbits, waitressed, delivered newspapers, and held whitewater rafting jobs. Their successes have resulted in special recognition. Joy, a "Desert Stormer" Army paratrooper earned a Bronze Star; Mark is a chef; and Patricia is an assistant to a WVU provost. Mark's talents, combined with working with Big Brothers, resulted in the building of cross-country ski trails at Coopers Rock State Forest in Preston County and picnic tables at state parks.

My life has been enriched by the experiences I've had, the people I've met, and the places I've been in this special state. I have never once regretted living in West Virginia. I take every opportunity to share the never-ending beauty of the hills with out-of-state visitors who travel with me as I work with Army National Guard soldiers. It's nice to visit other states and countries, but I always feel home is West Virginia and West Virginia is home.

AUTHOR: Colonel Pauline Wilson Shaver. Col. Shaver is an Army Occupational Health Officer. She has nearly thirty-five years of professional and community service in West Virginia. She is the mother of Joy Elizabeth Shaver, Mark Shaver, and Patricia Cook. She has three grandchildren.

154-001-ST-WV-001-1997

Halloween party in the Thornhill family room, October 31, 1981.

A Favorite Time Of The Year

Autumn was one of my favorite times as a child, the air was clean and crisp, there were plenty of leaves to rake up and pounce in, and there was that anticipation of the holiday season. This began for children of course, with Halloween, that great candy-getting holiday that gave us all an excuse to dress up in really weird outfits, perform outlandish tricks just to scare each other, and consume unnatural amounts of sugar. We, as children loved it. Our mothers, however, did not.

Yet in spite of all the speeches about corroded teeth, our moms still loved to see us get dolled up for their cameras before our big nights of candy collecting. And really, we didn't mind the attention. And we certainly didn't mind getting candy from our friends and neighbors. Halloween was a happy time. It marked a great harvest of sweets for children just as it marked a great harvest of apples and other late crops for farmers.

One of my favorite Halloween traditions was the party my parents threw for our family. It was quite a time of merry-making. All of my aunts, uncles, and cousins came and filled our house with laughter and tricks. My dad spent days decorating the basement with cobwebs, skeletons, and spiders. I didn't think it needed all those touches to be scary; I was terrified by it anyway.

While Dad worked in the basement, Mom worked in the kitchen, making all kinds of goodies for the party. It made the house smell wonderful, and it made my mouth water just to think about tasting those peanut butter cookies with Hershey kisses on top, and creamy chocolate fudge pieces made with marshmallow cream. While they worked on party staples, my sister and I worked on details. We dusted, and swept, and mopped everything in sight.

After cleaning the house to the point of hospital sterility, I was always exhausted and Mom knew it. But horror of horrors, she

expected me to take a nap! This was just unheard of — I was afraid my cousins might arrive early and start having fun without me. Even though I was almost falling asleep anyway, I would hole myself up under the dining room table and my poor mother would have to drag me out to get me to go to bed. And eventually I did.

When I awoke, it was time to get dressed and ready for the party. I was so excited to see the guests start arriving; I knew that we would soon be talking and laughing and having fun. Dad came downstairs to start the music and we kids started playing games. My older cousins always teased me and told ghost stories to scare me — it was their form of affection. The adults sat on the couches and talked, told stories, and caught up on who was doing what. At the pinnacle of the evening, Mom brought the treats downstairs and we all dove for them, trying to see who could get the most at one time. We loved eating those divine treats. Soon after this, everyone had to return to their homes and get ready for their own celebrations. As I went to bed after those parties, I kept thinking back over all the evening's events, savoring them.

I hold these memories of Halloween parties dear in my mind because they were such special times for our family. It wasn't nearly as hectic as Thanksgiving or Christmas, which is why I now think everyone was able to just settle down and have a good time. There was no real purpose to these celebrations except for the family to just get together. We were able to focus on each other, and enjoy each other's company. These were special times in my family; they brought us together in joking and in laughter, and in all the warmth of being inside together when the days get shorter and the nights get colder. This is why I loved those Halloween parties so much, and it's also why autumn is still my favorite season.

Author: Melissa Thornhill. Melissa is a student at West Virginia University. She grew up in Shinnston.

155-001-ST-WV-001-1997

Grand Are The Grandchildren

hat is important to me? My grandchildren! Presently I have six and a seventh on the way. From August 23, 1972, the day the eldest, Jay, was born, through the present, my grandchildren have been a constant source of joy and pride. Through them and with them, their grandad Gerald and I have had experiences we would have never had the opportunity to have without them. There's Jay Auvil, twenty-four years old, Tonya Auvil Gripper, twenty-one, Lacoa Corder and Ben Auvil, both eighteen, L.G. Corder, sixteen, and little Alexis Auvil, three.

We've followed them to numerous ballgames, all the way from T-Ball through high school and Legion ball. There have been gymnastic meets, band and choir concerts, cheerleading events, school parties and trips, and drama events. There have been track meets, cross country meets, soccer games, wrestling matches, banquets, awards, horse shows, and on and on, with "Mammy," (the name Jay gave me when he was learning to talk, and it still sticks), and Grandad sitting there, sometimes with tears of joy, but always so proud.

Cherished great-granddaughter Alexis Auvil.

Jay, who gave us our first great-grandchild, is in the Navy and married to our new granddaughter-in-law Kim. Tonya, who will soon present us with another great-grandchild, gave us our first grandson-in-law Eddie Gripper. Lacoa and Ben just graduated from high school and are attending Marshall and West Virginia University. L.G. is a junior in high school, and little Alexis is a live wire at three.

Their grandad and I are both sixty-nine years old, and we're looking forward to more grand times with our grandchildren. Thank you, God, for making us grandparents.

Author: Edith Ware. Mrs. Ware is a homemaker in Belington. She says that when she learned she could write about what was most important to her, there was no question about what she would share: stories about her grandchildren.

156-001-ST-WV-001-1997

Generations

iane Hutchinson Parker is the most courageous woman to ever cross my path. Well, she didn't just cross my path. She brought me into this world. She ignited my imagination, instructed and corrected me. She and my father, Paul Edward Parker, are the two greatest influences in my life. They are my family.

The author of the story, "The Family,"

CHAPTER 9: MOUNTAINEER COUNTRY

beginning on the following page, is my maternal grandmother Ray Pefley Hutchinson, and the setting is Sonnencroft. Clyde and Lyda Hutchinson, her in-laws, visited the Scottish castle Inverness during one of their many trips around the world and it became the inspiration for Sonnencroft. The patriarch, Clyde, was one of the state's most influential coal barons. Since the Hutchinson's had eight boys, it seemed appropriate to name their family home Sonnencroft or "home of many sons." In 1912, construction began on the twenty-eight room Fairmont landmark of red tile and stucco. Sonnencroft's "coming out" party was held on New Year's Eve 1914, and four hundred guests attended.

Minnie Reinhart Ringgold wrote to a mutual friend in January 1926 about her many holidays spent at Sonnencroft:

June 1914, at Sonnencroft. Clyde Effington and Lyda Watkins Hutchinson flank their sons (top to bottom): Claude Effington, Brooks Swearingen, Bernard Lee, Frank Ehlen, Harold Herbert, Paul Mason, Robert Jay, and James Jeremiah.

"When one's thoughts are turned to Sonnencroft one immediately starts thinking also of Queens and Castles, fairy godmothers and Princes and all of the other wonderful things that go to make up the beautiful illusions and dreams of youth…for while Mrs. Hutchinson's affections find their fullest expression and safest anchor in her own family, they do not end there, and there is probably no home in West Virginia whose latch string is more surely 'out' to relatives, friends and the stranger within the gate than Sonnencroft's. Indeed one is impressed with the fact that Mr. and Mrs. Hutchinson find their chief happiness in sharing their pleasures with others…" (Times-West Virginian, December 8, 1985, with permission.)

Sonnencroft tragically stood vacant after the Great Depression and the death of Mr. Hutchinson forced its sale. It was finally demolished in May 1960, never to see another legendary party. But in the twenty years of its heyday, many guests celebrated the holidays with their gracious hosts inside the gray, ivy-clad walls of the castle.

Ray Pefley Hutchinson was a native of Boise, Idaho and a member of a pioneer family. She was born January 4, 1897, to Ray and Lucinda Gumbert Pefley. Her grandfathers were both active in developing the politics of the West: Peter J. Pefley as a member of the first legislature of Idaho and a mayor of Boise, and George Gumbert as a county commissioner.

Ray was graduated from Boise High School in 1914, then attended Mount Vernon Seminary in Washington, DC, and was graduated in 1916. She met my grandfather while visiting mutual friends in Morgantown and married him in September 1917 at St. Michael's Episcopal Cathedral in Boise.

Once settled in West Virginia, Ray became active in the community. She was a charter member of the Junior League of Fairmont, a member of the Huguenot Society of West Virginia, president of the Green Hill's Garden Club of Fairmont, president of the Women's Guild of Christ Episcopal Church, and served on the Woman's Parish Board, and as an officer of the Altar Guild and Rose Guild.

My maternal grandfather, Brooks Swearingen Hutchinson, was born in Monongalia County on July 10, 1888, to Clyde Effington Hutchinson and Lyda Watkins Hutchinson. Brooks was the second of the eight sons. The family moved to Marion County when Brooks was young and he later attended Staunton Military Academy.

Brooks went on to earn an AB degree from West Virginia University (WVU) in 1909. He was very active in student life at WVU as a member of Delta Tau Delta and Delta Chi fraternities and belonged to two honorary societies — Sphinx and Mountain. He was also elected Student Body President and lettered as a right end on the WVU football team.

Brooks was also quite active at Yale University College of Law, and was graduated in 1912. He was a member of Book and Gavel and the Phi Alpha Delta legal fraternity.

He returned to Fairmont to practice law and was admitted to the Circuit Court of Marion County in 1913. Brooks was a member of the Marion County Bar Association for more than half a century, and was honored in 1965 for fifty years of service. This legacy continues with my father, Paul, and my brother, Eddie, who are current members of the Marion County Bar Association.

Throughout his career, Brooks served as president of: Rich Creek Coal Company; Empire Fuel Company; Oakland Coal Company; Hutchinson - Arnold Coke Company; Hugheston Gas Coal Corporation; Rayland Corporation; Annapolis Company; and Mountain City Drug Company. He was vice president of the West Virginia Coal and Coke Company, and of Kanawha Coals of Charleston.

From 1925 to 1947, Brooks served as chairman of the Fairmont Chapter of the American Red Cross. He was also the president of the board for the Fairmont Field Club. For several years he served as president of the Delta Tau Delta Corporation, the house corporation for WVU's chapter, and he was instrumental in constructing Morgantown's fraternity house. From 1942 to 1949, he served as chief rent enforcement attorney for West Virginia. He was a member of Christ Episcopal Church and a thirty-second degree Scottish Rite Mason.

In November of 1958, Brooks and Ray moved to Hawaii to be close to their daughters Elaine and Sylvia and their families. Ray died August 18, 1967, while visiting my family in Fairmont. I can't help but believe that Grandmommy wanted to come home to die. Brooks died on February 11, 1971, in Honolulu.

Elaine was their first child, born January 24, 1922. On March 27, 1953, she married Captain George Pullen Peed also of Fairmont. She lived an exciting Navy officer's family life, enjoyed with their three handsome sons: George Pullen Peed, III, Brooks Hutchinson Peed, and Robert Fleming Peed. Aunt Elaine passed away June 26, 1989.

Second was Sylvia Jane, born October 15th, who later married Kenneth Paul Derby. They had two adorable children, Kenneth and Diana. Aunt Sylvia is recently retired from a management career with Quantus airlines. She continues to travel the world, loves spending time with her friends and grandchildren, and never forgets a birthday!

My mother, Diane (with the French pronunciation), born December 30th, was the youngest. Ray named each of her daughters with soft names — nothing that could be said too harshly. Mother held forth in Fairmont for the family and followed in her mother's footsteps.

Diane married Paul Edward Parker, Jr., in November 1952. Paul was graduated from WVU School of Law in 1951, and recently retired as a practicing attorney in Marion County and the state of West Virginia. Finishing her studies as a newlywed, Diane was graduated from Fairmont State College with a degree in elementary education.

Diane served as president of the Junior League of Fairmont and chaired various committees before going sustaining. She served as president of Green Hill's Garden Club and on the Altar Guild of Christ Episcopal Church, as did my grandmother. Diane also served two terms as the president of the Fairmont General Hospital Association. Never tiring, my mother remains an inspiration. Above all else, Diane Hutchinson Parker is a true lady who prides herself on volunteerism and community service as well as providing a welcoming home for family and friends.

My brother, Paul Edward Parker, III, "Eddie," was named after our father and grandfather. Eddie married Jan Carpenter in 1980. Jan is also a Fairmonter and graduate of WVU. They have two beautiful, talented, athletic sons, Brooks Edward Parker and Brett Russell Parker. Eddie has practiced as an attorney since graduation from WVU School of Law in 1980, and is currently with the firm of Jackson and Kelly in Fairmont.

I was named for my mother's two sisters. After graduating from WVU with an undergraduate and a Master's degree in Rehabilitation Counseling, I pursued a career in private rehabilitation services. I am now marketing the state for HealthSouth MountainView Rehabilitation Hospital in Morgantown and am proud to have helped open the hospital in 1991.

Now that you have some family history, here is Ray's intimate view of the Hutchinson family and Sonnencroft: weddings and holidays and the end of an era.

The Family

I was an only child, but when I married Brooks Swearingen Hutchinson I acquired a family of a mother and father, seven brothers, three sisters-in-law, and numerous nieces and nephews. I literally became a member of the family. There were no conferences in corners, everything was discussed openly, and my opinion asked and listened to. Mother rejoiced at each son's marriage and took us to her heart, for she had always wanted a daughter. The home of all these boys was an immense house in Fairmont, West Virginia, which looked like a medieval castle. Terraced gardens, rose arbors, pools filled with

Chapter 9: Mountaineer Country

June 1954, Diane and Paul Parker, and Ray Pefley Hutchinson in front of Mt. Lake Hotel, Mt. Lake Park, Maryland.

fish, surrounded it. Inside all was cheer and comfort — not merely a house, but a home — dominated by a mother who was the spirit of Ceres.

A large family is delightful at all times, but at Christmas it is the most thrilling. The excitement began with decorating the whole house with holly, mistletoe, and red candles. A great wreath was hung in the huge hall to welcome everyone. Logs of gigantic proportions were blazing in the living room fireplace. Everything in readiness for the welcome of those who were living out of town.

First Frank and Bonnie with their two little boys arrived from their home in the southern part of the state. The first arrival was the most quiet, for as more and more of the clan gathered, more hilarious were the greetings.

Next morning, Paul, a student at Yale, came dashing into the breakfast room — kissing everyone — glad to get home. Then Bob and Jimmy, the youngest, from military school and quite dashing in their uniforms. Many bear hugs and kisses again. Harold and Margaret drove up about dinner time. The whole family trooped out to meet them and help them unload their luggage. The next day brought Katherine and Lee with their two children. Many hugs and kisses for the babies. Many admiring comments on how tall Helen, the oldest grandchild, had grown. And how fat the baby was. Such joy to be together again.

In the dining room, with its tapestried walls and ivory wood-work, its clusters of long windows, looking over the terraced Italian garden, hours were spent at the long dining table. Sipping coffee, cracking nuts — anything to delay the departure of an impatient one. The most closely knitted family. Loyal to the last degree to each other. Each secretly admiring all the rest. Everyone more or less clever in the art of conversation. A word would start the ball rolling around the table, each adding a pun or a joke. Everyone laughing as though it was the funniest in the world.

Mother at the foot of the table, always calm, always pleasant, never impatient. A large, handsome woman with soft brown eyes and beautiful black hair, and that best of all gifts, a sense of humor. Tolerance is a word I always associate with her — and kindliness.

Father at the head of the table. A sturdy man, with ruddy complexion, grey eyes, and iron grey hair. A perfect model for Rembrandt. A man keen, clever, vital, impetuous. Not talking much, but listening to everything. When he did have something to say, everyone else was all attention. A man who has cut and hewn the granite of life, from the farm boy to a well-known, respected financier throughout the East. A veritable Viking in business.

Henry, the butler, in his spotless white coat, passing the plates quietly, answering a dozen demands at once, coming in for his share of jokes and questions, especially from the younger boys.

Much reminiscing of happy times from the oldest to the youngest. Times when Brooks and Lee roomed together at the University and were right and left ends on the football team. Then with much laughter, "Do you remember the time Jimmy slept in the newest automobile all night so that Bob wouldn't get it first?" More teasing of Jimmy. "Why do you always sign your letters home to Mother and Father 'Yours truly, Jimmy'?" Jimmy blushes and there is more laughter.

When the three youngest have rushed away to keep engagements, and we can't linger at the dining table any longer, some drift into the conservatory, where soft lights are reflected in the fountain pool. Some of us wander to the music room and sounds of harmony, in spirit at least, are heard through the halls. Some go to the library, some to the billiard room for a game. But not for long do they separate. Soon the large armchairs on either side of the huge fireplace in the living room are filled. The davenport in front of the fire is easily accommodating six people.

Mother is sitting by the table so that the light from the lamp falls on the sweater she is knitting. She knits slowly and methodically. The

Sonnencroft in its heyday.

sweater will probably be outgrown by the child it is intended for and fit a much younger one when it is finally finished! Mother is always busy. This great room reflects her personality with its warmth and cheer of mulberry velour draperies, harmonizing chintzes on the furniture, and lamp shades of golden silk. The huge fireplace of bronzed tile, topped by a mantle six feet above the floor, over which hangs a beautiful picture of the Canterbury Pilgrims. Great bronze lights flank either side, casting a soft glow over all. A copper kettle hangs on a crane and slowly steams from the heat of the fire.

Father sits at one side under a standing lamp. The *New York Times* strewn all around him on the floor. He is so impatient to find just the part he wants to read, or having finished a section, to the floor it goes. He reads and listens at the same time. Sometimes breaking into the conversation to read us some article which especially interests him. Then again he puts down the paper, holds his glasses in his hand, listens to us, makes some comment to the point or asks that some remark be repeated. Sometimes he gives his short, hardy laugh then back to his paper.

Katherine and Lee are occupying one chair much to the pretended disgust of everyone else. They were childhood sweethearts long before they were married and never got over their honeymoon days. Katherine is tall and slender, with sparkling brown eyes and bronze-gold hair. Vivacious, friendly, interesting personality. Lee is one of the two blondes of the family. Hail-fellow-well-met, popular with everyone. Simply radiating good humor. Katherine says no one ever knows he has a surname.

Bonnie, blue-eyed with beautiful blonde, wavy hair, sits in a big armchair, looking dreamily into the fire. She is a quiet, relaxed southern type. She reads everything in sight. Taking life as it comes without struggle or striving for more than it has to give her. Adoring Frank, who is her exact opposite. He is tall, dark, domineering. Most certainly the undisputed head of his small family. He never allowed Bonnie to pack a trunk or even a suitcase, or choose a curtain for their home. But she likes that, so they get along perfectly together.

I am sitting next to Frank on the davenport. Suffice it to say that I am also blonde. All these boys, so far, have preferred blondes. Brooks sits next to me. He is dark, and of course most handsome in my eyes. He is not so tall but just the right height for me. He is broad-shouldered, powerful looking. When I say he has a disposition just like Mother's I can say nothing better. He is the personification of thoughtfulness, kindness, and loyalty. That old adage about a good son making a good husband is true in this case. He is the oldest of the boys now, and the younger ones look up to him as a model and take their troubles to him more often than to Father. I, who am so prejudiced, should not be writing this.

Margaret sits on a stool, toasting her back to the fire. She looks almost as small as one of the children. She has chestnut hair and blue-grey eyes. She is always well-groomed, immaculate. Excitable, energetic, nervous type, with a keen sense of humor. Always ready to get down on the floor and play dolls or spin tops with the children, who adore her. She was from a small family like myself, and at first it was difficult for her to realize that she had married this whole family, not just Harold. This is exactly what we all did, much to our surprise. But not one of these boys could be separated from the rest.

Harold sits in a chair near her. Calm, quiet, brown eyes gazing at the fire, while he smokes a cigarette. We often laugh and remark that it's a good thing Margaret and Frank didn't marry, for their wills are eternally clashing while Bonnie and Harold would simply have drifted lazily with the tide. As it is, each has someone to spur him on.

It all comes back to me how much fun we had at Margaret and Harold's wedding. Her home was in a small town in the southern part of the state. Harold, at that time, was superintendent at one of Father's mines. He and another boy had a rambling old house at their disposal, so we all landed en masse for a house-party the day before the wedding. The family had not been together for quite some time so everyone was hilarious. We laughed and giggled until it was disgraceful. We danced until we were worn out, then played bridge. At dinner, the dining table wasn't large enough to accommodate all of us, so Bonnie and Jimmy had to sit at a small table at one side. They pretended to be infants and such antics as they performed!

When Brooks and I were married, a good part of the family came out to my home in Idaho for the wedding. They almost went with us on our honeymoon, as we all took the same route through the Canadian Rockies. They followed us to Portland, Oregon, and spent a few hours with us, then preceded us to Seattle. When we arrived at the hotel, we found the bridal suite of rooms engaged for us and filled with roses! And we had hoped to fool everyone as to our being bride and groom! We were well advertised in Lake Louise and Banff, too, but from there on they left us while we lingered in that paradise.

Lee was the first son to marry, then Frank. Both weddings before I joined the family. Now we always urge the younger boys to marry a girl who lives far away so we will have a long journey to the wedding!

Paul, Robert and Jimmy are unmarrieds, as yet. Mother always spoke of them as her second generation. There are five years between Harold and Paul. The latter is the other blonde besides Lee. Very fiery temper, impetuous. Flinging a golf club for yards after a bad shot. Then very sorry for such a display. Loveable and charming, nevertheless rather a devil-may-care spirit. Yet he would leave a golf game early to rush home and hold the tiniest baby in the family before it was put to bed! Quite a Don Juan with the girls. His very indifference seems to attract them all the more.

Robert — but how could anyone describe him? Driving the whole family to distraction with scrapes he seems unable to avoid. Everyone worrying because of their very fondness for him. Endearing himself to the children until it was understood that Bobby was their favorite. The most witty, good-natured, clever person. He would don a white cap and apron and immediately become an excited French chef, demanding our wishes as to Sunday night supper. Or he would rough up his hair imitating the Russian artist who had just painted my portrait: "Ah, ze great art, ze great beauty. Ze broad curve of ze brush." Much to the delight of all.

Jimmy was the baby. Tall, dark, and handsome. A perfect understudy for Richard Barthelmess of movie fame. Very quiet and retiring. He looked after Robert like a hen with one chick. When Robert wasn't around, Jimmy could be extremely witty, but when Robert was present, he was only a foil for Robert's jokes.

Mother's father lives here, too. He sits in an armchair by the fire. A patriarch of ninety winters. A giant man with sparkling sea-blue eyes, and hair of heavy silver. He is deaf and sits for hours watching us. We thought to interest him in jigsaw puzzles, but after trying to fit several pieces together he would laugh, shake his head, and declare that it simply could not be done. Again and again, he would ask Brooks how he ever met me for my home was in Idaho. It was always a wonder to him why Brooks had to go so far from home to get a wife!

But, it's Christmas Eve. Around nine o'clock, after the children are asleep, a regal Christmas tree is brought in filling the room with the pungent, teasing odor of pine. Mother brings down the ornaments and tells just how long each has been in the family. We decorate all evening and then find the lights don't work, as usual. After many suggestions to Frank, always perched at the top of the ladder holding forth with side-splitting soliloquies, the tree is arrayed in all its glory. The mantle is hung with a row of stockings in graduated sizes from the largest to a tiny one for the baby. Toys have to be inspected and enjoyed as they are placed under the tree for their true recipients. All the packages are shaken with wild guesses as to the contents.

Finally, we repair to the kitchen to raid the icebox. Coffee and sandwiches appear as if by magic. Then Mother appears to guard Christmas dinner and reminds us that it is after midnight. Everyone shouts "Merry Christmas!"

Great excitement next morning. Always the first to greet us as we rushed downstairs was Father, who slipped a gold piece to each of us. We girls always gave him a hearty kiss, which seemingly embarrassed but really delighted him. Children scattered with toys all over the floor. Red and green tissue paper, ribbons of silver and gold, litter the room with delighted abandon.

Dinner is announced all too soon. The table is a wonderland. The centerpiece, a mirrored lake surrounded by snow and pine trees with Santa Claus in a tiny reindeer-drawn sleigh. The dinner, too, was a culinary perfection. From the bouillon to the flaming plum-pudding. Robert jokingly fusses with Henry by casually remarking "That pudding isn't burning very brightly, Henry. Are you sure you put *all* the brandy in it?"

By this time, the guests are arriving and the living room is aglow with soft lights and roaring fire. Boxes of chocolates and bowls of nuts, figs and dates, are passed to all. Much laughter and music echoes throughout the halls.

Evening comes and the children are dragged reluctantly to bed. The last one remarks, as he yawns and rubs his eyes, "I wish Christmas would come every day." So thought we all, as tired but deliciously comfortable we gather in the warmth of the fire.

The words which we pass in the leaded glass window on the landing as we trail upstairs to bed seem perfect: "East or West, Home is Best."

There is the strength of womankind in these memories. The strength of mothers and daughters. The strength of family. Perhaps the true essence and heart of these mountains is matriarchal. The soft, powerful, feminine voices resonating through the hills. Echoing through the generations. Leading and teaching each of us the way to live our lives.

Our right to a life of love, beauty, diversity, freedom. Freedom to be the best of our past. Freedom to make the best of our time. Freedom to add to the very best of our state's future! "Mountaineers are always free" reverberates in every aspect of our souls. Our family is scattered now throughout the world. Several generations carrying a part of West Virginia with them wherever they go.

My parents have always stayed in West Virginia. My brother and his wife strayed to Pittsburgh, Pennsylvania, briefly. I moved to Baltimore, Maryland, and Charlotte, North Carolina, for a few years. Yet, we all came home. Home to West Virginia. Home to our families.

The person that I have become is a direct result of Paul and Diane's loving coaxing and a bit of unrehearsed coercion! I am a happy, successful and loving human being. I enjoy life. I enjoy my parents and want to spend as much time with them as possible. I love them for all that they are and all that they have allowed me to be.

Mother and Daddy, I just wanted to tell you how very much I love you! This writing is my attempt to document a small part of our history.

It is with highest respect and admiration that I dedicate these musings to my parents, to family, to West Virginia!

Authors: Ray Pefley Hutchinson and Sylvia E. Parker. Ray wrote the segment entitled "The Family." Sylvia, her granddaughter and author of the foreword and conclusion, has treasured the stories written and passed down by Ray.

157-001-ST-WV-001-1997

Nestorville United Methodist Church

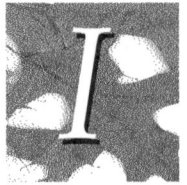

In many small towns, churches came about through the sheer determination of local residents who generously donated land and labor. This is certainly true of two early churches in Nestorville, Barbour County.

Nestorville was named for a family of settlers, the Nestors. William Nestor, son of George Nestor and a grandson of Jacob Nestor, built the first log cabin home on the banks of Teter Creek. It was built near the Righman water mill, where Bill Nestor, Jesse L. Righman, Andrew Righman, Albert Righman, and Clifford and Louise Righman were millers. The mill was destroyed by a tornado in 1942. The first Methodist Protestant church building in the area was built on land purchased from James S. and Hulda Nestor. The church was Mt. Olivet, built in 1871. It is no longer standing.

The Methodist Protestant Church in Barbour County originated when the Reverend I.A. Barnes introduced the principles of this church in 1842-1843. The organization first met in the log home of Jonas Nestor until the members built their first house of worship on Glade Run. When that building burned, the members met in the Camp Valley schoolhouse on land donated by Jesse L. Righman, until they built Mt. Olivet. Jesse L. Righman also gave land for a cemetery to be used by the church. Others who helped build the church were Jesse's sons Charles and Andrew Jackson; John D. Godwin and family; John Marsh and his sons Calvin, Isaac, and Loyal. The church's first members were the Reverend and Mrs. I.A. Barnes; John McIntire and family; George Nestor and family; Jonas Nestor and family. The first trustees were Aaron Phillips, Jesse L. Righman, James P. Fitzwater, and Elijah Phillips.

The building of St. John's Evangelical United Brethren Church in Nestorville also came about through generosity. It was built in 1889, and the congregation formally established on September 20, 1889. St. John's sits on a knoll with a cemetery behind it on land purchased for one dollar from John and Amelia Hoffman (sometimes spelled Huffman), Germans from Pennsylvania who had bought several hundred acres from John Wesley Ridenour (b. 1855, m. Mary Roseatha Carpenter) for a homestead. The Hoffman family lived in a two-story log cabin. There were seven sons and five daughters. The sons Jacob, Sanford, Isaac, Robert, Grannele, and Stingley, as well as John Wesley Ridenour, helped build and maintain the church and cemetery.

St. John's was built with hand-hewn sills and sleepers roofed with oak shingles, later replaced with metal. The floors were oak, and the ceiling and weather boarding was poplar. The nails were antique square pointed. In its early years, the men painted the church white. According to the journal of Gay Marsh, "while driving on the road near Tacy you may see St. John Church shining through the green trees, with its coat of white paint."

The women tended the inside of the church. They cleaned the globes of the oil lamps, scrubbed the floors with split brooms made from a hickory sapling and lye soap made from wood ashes, and used white sand on the floors. The Hoffmans were very good singers, and the organist was Minnie Hoffman Burner.

The first trustees of St. John's were R.G., E.F, and Sanford Hoffman. In 1921, Floyd and Rotha Marsh donated additional land to be added to the cemetery. Trustees at that time were J.N. and Jonas Hoffman, and S. T. Humphreys.

St. John's Church is a historic landmark — with the original benches and pulpit in place — used for funerals, reunions and community affairs. The church remains important to many residents of the area. Dr. Herbert Waters of Alderson-Broaddus College did a wood block print of the church, copies of which are proudly owned by several local families. In September 1989, Bud and Beulah England held a picnic to celebrate the 100th Anniversary of St. John's. It was said that folks could almost hear "the echoes of a fire and brimstone sermon."

Substantial in both churches were Allen Chambers "Chame" and Dora Poling Wilson. Chame was song leader and taught shaped notes. He was a member of the United Methodist Church for over forty years. He passed away March 1, 1967, at age ninety-three. Dora passed away March 29, 1960, at age eighty-one.

In 1969, the denominations of Mt. Olivet and St. John's, along with the United Brethren Church in Nestorville, united. The Reverend Gary Edwards was the first minister. Known as the United Methodist Church, or simply the Nestorville Church, the building stands on the site of the former United Brethren Church. The directory in front was built by Arthur Wilson, and the creche by Kenneth Marsh. Reverend William Smith is currently minister of the united church, which has a membership of ninety-one, many of whom have ties to the early settlers of Nestorville and the founders and builders of St. Olivet and St. John's.

AUTHOR: Betty Marsh. Mrs. Marsh's grandmother, Gay Marsh, who was the granddaughter of Stingley Hoffman, great-granddaughter of John Hoffman and William Nestor, attended St. John's when she was a little girl. Many details about the church come from her notes. Additional information is from Clementa Proudfoot, Stanley Mick, and Ronnie Righman.

158-001-ST-WV-001-1997

Chapter 10
Young Authors

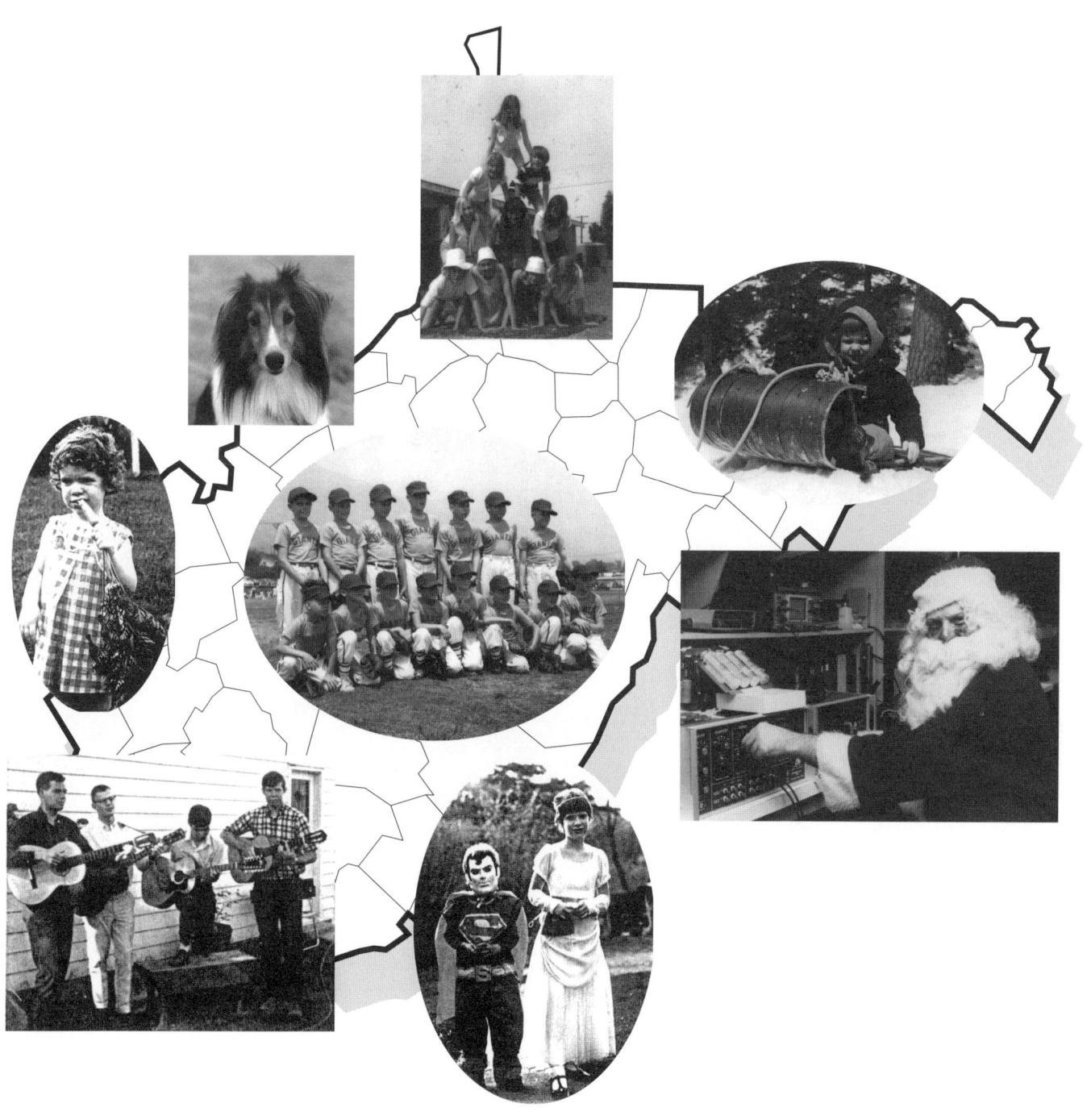

Introduction

Throughout this project, we have been lucky to share in the authors' sense of accomplishment. This is particularly true of the young writers in this special section. Several teachers contacted us about including some stories from their students in this book, and we agreed that it would be a nice addition. The narratives in this chapter are mostly stories as requested or assigned by those teachers. However, as you will read, each student interpreted the assignment in his or her own way.

Many students interviewed relatives: parents, grandparents, and sometimes great-grandparents. Others wrote about family stories that have been passed down for years, some going back several generations. A number of students chose to write on their own observations and experiences. As we read through the submissions, we saw many parallels to the adult writings in terms of subjects. Respect of the hardships of the "good old days," a love of family, an appreciation of fun and pranks, tragic losses, and mishaps are topics that can be found throughout this book. But the stories in this section give us a glimpse at a perspective that often only teachers and students' parents get to see: the children's.

We believe it is important to encourage children to write down their observations and experiences. It inspires in them an interest in language. It helps them communicate more effectively. It is educational. It is also a wonderful method of preservation. When a child is eight years old, he can remember things that happened to him when he was two or three, events that he will not recall even when he is ten. And at ten years old, we may well remember the last name of our best friend from the first grade, but how often do we remember that name when we are fifty-nine? Imagine how nice it would be if when we retired we could reflect on life by looking through a collection of written memories which we recorded over our lifetime and started at an early age. How much more would we remember? How many faces would come back to us? How many lessons could we relearn?

The stories in this section reflect the changing times. If the stories had been written by the interview*ees* as children rather than the interview*ers*, certainly we would read different bylines. Talking on the phone, rollerblading, playing Nintendo, and skateboarding are relatively recent phenomena. After reviewing the difficulties of her grandmother's life, one young author wrote, "She (grandma) said those were the good old days. I am glad that I don't live back in those times though, because I believe these are the good days." If that author is interviewed by her grandchild someday, what will the grandchild's story and byline say about the times?

Life in West Virginia has changed rapidly over the past few decades. But as this chapter shows, some themes remain constant. Hunting and camping skills, making molasses, preparing wild mushrooms, and learning about nature are all part of a collective knowledge that continues to be passed down through generations of West Virginians.

My Grandmother And Lye Soap

In the mid 1930s at Man, West Virginia, my great-grandmother Bessie Clay, who is now deceased, always made lye soap for her family. I interviewed her daughter, Evelyn Brumfield, my grandmother. Evelyn is sixty-six years old and lives at Whitman.

The one thing that stands out in her childhood memories is watching her mother make lye soap. Although she was not allowed to help, she loved to watch her mother so she could see the finished product.

All she could remember was that the soap was made out of raw, fat meat and lye. You had to cook it for a long period of time, pour it into pans, and then cut it into bars. The lye soap was mainly used for washing clothes.

My grandmother also said that every time she tried to help, her mother scolded her. It was too dangerous for small children to be around the boiling pot.

Author: Brittany Nicole Adkins. Brittany is the daughter of Kenneth and Tammy Adkins. She has two brothers, Kenny, Jr., and Michael. She enjoys talking on the telephone, watching movies, swimming, and cheerleading.

159-001-ST-WV-001-1997

A Winter To Remember

It was late evening early in the fall, just after my parents had finished building the house. They heard a few booms echoing in the hills, one after the other. My dad called our neighbor and asked them if they had heard the booming. They said they had. They had Dad's shotgun and he told them to meet him at the bridge with it. He said he was nervous walking down to the bridge. He got his shotgun and went back to the house, where he sat with Mom. The booms continued for about an hour; then they stopped. My dad never heard them again. Now he thinks he knows what they were. They were rocks cracking from the cold.

In the winter that year, Mom and Dad were watching television, and through the window they saw a young cow wander by. They started to call people they knew to see if anyone knew where the cow came from. Nobody knew right then, but they said they'd check around. Meanwhile, the cow decided that the outhouse was a cozy place. Then the owners of the cow got in touch with Mom and Dad and said that because there was so much snow, they couldn't come and get the cow. They asked if it was okay if they could bring in some hay and the cow could stay. So they brought down the hay, and the cow stayed in the outhouse. After about a week, the owners came to get the cow. No one was any the worse for wear except maybe the outhouse, which fell down.

Author: Eamon Barker. Eamon is the son of Lynne and Jerry Barker, and the brother of Rafael, of Sissonville. He is a bookworm who also enjoys drawing and creating.

160-001-ST-WV-001-1997

Papaw Edd

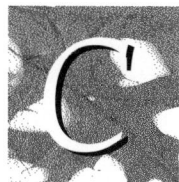

Clarence Edward Aldridge, Papaw Edd, lived in Blair, West Virginia, all of his life. When he grew up in Blair, he got married to Wilma Jean. They had nine kids in one big house.

On June 18, 1992, Papaw Edd went looking for berries. He hadn't gone far when a bear came out from behind the berry bush. At first Papaw Edd was scared, but then the bear came right to him. He was shocked! Then he pet the bear. He wasn't scared at all.

The story was in the *Logan Banner* with a picture that my momaw took. It had Papaw and the bear standing beside each other. It was amazing. He left the bear on the train tracks. He never saw the bear again.

Author: Amanda Ann Aldridge. Amanda is the only daughter of Roy and Teresa Aldridge of Sharples. She enjoys cheerleading and riding her four-wheeler. She is in the fifth grade.

161-001-ST-WV-001-1997

Growing Up In The 1940s

What my mommaw Annabelle Butcher remembers most about growing up in Crawley Creek, Logan County, is her mom boiling their clothes. First she would build an open fire outside. She would use a big iron kettle to boil their clothes in.

She used lye soap made from hog fat and lye. This made the clothes come really clean. Then she put the clothes in to boil and used a wooden paddle to stir them after they boiled. She took them out and washed them in their Maytag wringer washing machine. After they got through washing, she put them in a tub of rinse water to rinse. Then she hung

them on an outside line to dry. Things that needed to be starched would be put in separate water with Satina. This made the clothes smell really good. It was hard work, but they always had clean clothes to wear.

What my mommaw liked most of all was every evening her mom would cook supper, and after they ate, they would go out on the porch to wait for her dad to come home from work. She would sit in her mom's lap every evening, until she was fourteen years old. Then her sister made fun of her. She said she was too big to sit in her mother's lap.

AUTHOR: Kristin Farley. Kristin attends Chapmanville Middle School. Her hobbies include music, racing, and watching movies.

162-001-ST-WV-001-1997

The Early Life Of Dianna Adams

Dianna Adams was born February 21, 1954, the fourth of five children, three boys and two girls. She was also the first born in a hospital. She lived in a two-story house on Harts Creek. Heat came from two fireplaces and a cookstove in the kitchen. The toilet was outside.

Her father Freeman Adams was a coal miner. He had to walk three miles to catch a ride to the mine with a neighbor. Her mother Anna Mae Adams was an at-home mom. She kept herself busy by cooking, cleaning, gardening, feeding the animals, washing laundry, and watching her youngest son Glenn.

Dianna was the only first grader in a one-room schoolhouse. She walked two miles to and from school with her older brothers Neal and Terry. Her grandmother Anna Adams was the teacher of the Upper Trace School. Dianna's older sister Delores had to board with John and Dorothy Brumfield so she could ride a bus to school in Chapmanville.

In the second grade her family moved to Airport Road in Chapmanville. She completed the second grade at West Grade School. Then she moved back to Harts and attended Hugh Dingess Elementary for grades three through seven.

Dianna's fondest memories are of making apple butter and attending quilting bees.

AUTHOR: Clarissa Nicole Fekete. Clarissa is twelve years old and attends Chapmanville Middle School. Dianna is her mother.

163-001-ST-WV-001-1997

Grandma's Good Old Days

When I asked my grandma what she remembered most about her childhood, her answer was "I remember the terrible winters we had, and how hard it was to get to school."

She was born in the town of Chapmanville, West Virginia, and everyone went to the same school. She would have to walk to and from school no matter what the weather was, because there weren't any buses. She lived about two miles from the school up a hollow behind the old post office in Chapmanville. It was pitch dark when she would leave in the morning to get to school. School lunches didn't exist; she had to pack her lunch or walk back home. Sometimes the snow would be so deep that her legs would feel frozen before she ever got to school.

The winter months got really bad. At home, the only heat they had to sit by to get their feet warm was a coal stove. Sometimes that would be hard to do with six brothers and sisters.

She believes that the hard times she had then, made her more thankful because she learned how to appreciate every good thing that has happened in her life. She says those were the good old days. I am glad that I don't live back in those times though, because I believe these are the good days.

AUTHOR: Jennifer Bryant. Jennifer is a seventh grade student and member of the cheerleading squad at Chapmanville Middle School. She has one younger brother, Jordan, who is in the second grade.

164-001-ST-WV-001-1997

A Day In The Life Of My Grandfather

My grandfather Virgil James Tackette was born on September 4, 1921, in Floyd County, Kentucky. However, three years later, his family moved to Big Creek in Logan County. Therefore, most of his childhood memories are of times spent in this location.

When I asked my grandfather what he remembered most about his childhood, he replied, "I remember playing in the snow with my brothers." He was the seventh son of eight. His brothers were Willis, Grover, Webster, John, Luke, Fred, and Penny.

"We would go sleigh riding all day and have huge snowball fights. After we got tired we would go inside, where a big cup of cocoa

and a warm plate of homemade gingerbread biscuits would be waiting." The brothers would build a fire and talk about their day.

The next day they would wake up at 8:00 A.M. and bundle up in warm clothes. They would go back outside and play all day again. Perhaps today they would skate on the frozen creek near their house.

My grandfather said his winter days with his brothers in Logan County were probably the best days of his life.

AUTHOR: Jilleyn Gabrielle Gore. Jill is the daughter of Cathy and Gary Gore of Chapmanville. She likes hiking, playing the piano, reading, bowling, and playing with computers.

165-001-ST-WV-001-1997

Polly Hall And Harvey Gore

Polly Hall and Harvey Gore lived about two miles from where I live now, seven miles from Chapmanville in Logan County. They were my great-great-great-grandparents. In the late 1800s, they made their living by farming and making railroad ties.

They made railroad ties by going in the mountains and cutting down large trees with a crosscut saw. They pulled them down to a clearing with mules. Then they cut them into the lengths that the railroad ordered. They would hew them out, which means taking an ax and cutting them until they were flat on top and bottom so the rails could be placed on them.

After they got a load of railroad ties cut and hewn, which would sometimes take days or even weeks, they would load as many upon a wagon as they thought four to six mules could pull. Then they would start their journey toward the Guyandotte River. They had to travel about seven miles of rough roads and steep hills. This was hard on the mules. It took all day to get there.

When they got to the river they would take a big sledge hammer with their initials embedded on it and hit each tie. They did this so they could tell theirs apart from hundreds of others. This was because lots of people made railroad ties. They would unload them and let them slide down a chute into the river with hundreds of other ties that were already there. The ties didn't float away because the river was dammed up with them. When the river reached the right depth the railroad got as many ties as they wanted, then they let them float down the river to reach their destination.

AUTHOR: Ashley D. Gore. Ashley is the daughter of Danny and Katrina Gore. She has one brother, Casey. She enjoys horseback riding and rollerblading.

166-001-ST-WV-001-1997

Making Lye Soap

When my grandmother Janie Spangler was growing up in Cow Creek, Logan County, West Virginia, she would watch her mother make lye soap. It took her many hours to make the soap. Most of the soap made was used for washing clothes.

The first step in the procedure for making lye soap is to take hog fat and lye and put it in a big pot of boiling water for a long period of time. When it gets really thick you know it's ready to take out of the boiling water and put into pans.

The second step in the procedure for making the soap is to cut the soap into blocks after it cools.

My grandmother always loved watching her mother make lye soap even though she was never allowed to help because of the boiling water.

AUTHOR: Crystal Dawn Spangler. Crystal is the oldest sister in a family of three girls. Her father is a West Virginia State Trooper. She enjoys cheerleading, bike riding, and hanging out with her friends.

167-001-ST-WV-001-1997

Molliemunchers

Molliemunchers are mushrooms that grow in the mountains. They are not poisonous. They look like a halfway closed umbrella. They are black, autumn brown, and white. They come in all different sizes. They have rugged edges and a smooth base (stem).

Molliemunchers grow on the side of the mountain where the sun rises. They grow in shaded areas on soft ground in higher elevations. Molliemunchers grow from March 20th up until the first or second week of May.

To fix the molliemunchers you have to wash and split them vertically down the middle. Then roll them in egg, milk, and flour. Finally, you deep fry or just fry until golden brown. Molliemunchers taste like fish or hushpuppies.

I like molliemunchers. They taste very good. I also like hunting them. My dad and I always make a bet who can find the most. He usually beats me, but I beat him sometimes, if I am lucky. He has a better eye than I do. I will get better at it.

AUTHOR: Shelly Marie Bell Carter. Shelly is twelve years old. Her parents are Kennard and Lori Workman Carter. She likes to play Nintendo and ride her four wheeler.

168-001-ST-WV-001-1997

Soccer Kid

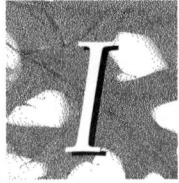

I would like to tell about my experiences as a soccer player with the Summersville Soccer League. I started when I was four years old. I have no concept of what I am supposed to do except to kick a ball and chase it up and down the field. Sometimes we are lucky and kick it into the net. The coach's son Kent is good at kicking it in the net. I am good at running after the ball. One time I did score a goal. Someone kicked the ball and it hit me and bounced into the net. There is one guy on the team who gets tangled in the net all the time. One day two coaches had to stop the game and untangle him.

I like soccer, but Dad yells at me too much. He thinks I should stay on top of the ball all the time, but I have other interests. For example, when Mom brings the video camera, I have to pose for the pictures. My grandfather and grandmother come to all my games. My sister comes too. She sits on a blanket and pays no attention to the game. My best friend Chance plays soccer. He is on my team. One girl on the team always tackles the ball and picks it up when it comes near her. Dad doesn't yell at her. Dad says Mom is a soccer mom. I guess she is, because I play soccer. I almost forgot, I enjoy the snacks after the games. Someone always brings something to drink and something fun to eat.

Author: Zachary Damon Hanshaw. Zachary is the five year old son of Damon and Sandy Hanshaw of Canvas. He has one sister, Whitney Nicole. His hobbies are T-Ball, soccer, coloring, and painting.

169-001-ST-WV-001-1997

My Grandma

When my Grandma Lucy Dingess was a young woman she was a cook at Hugh Dingess Grade School. She cooked a lot at home too. She would get up in the mornings and make a big breakfast with all kinds of different things to eat. She made a lot because she had to make sure there was enough to feed all the men that worked in the fields and who cut timber.

In between working and cooking she had to take care of the garden, do the planting, hoe and weed the garden, and do the canning. She also had to slop the hogs, feed the chickens, take care of the horses, milk the cows, churn the butter, keep fresh milk to drink, and make buttermilk. She used to carry 100-pound bags of chop to feed chickens.

In the meantime, she raised three boys, and kept house. She used to take in boarders to make ends meet.

Grandma made homemade quilts too. She would take pieces of old clothing and make patchwork quilts. She also would take pieces of material to make patterns. Then she would sew them together to form the top. Next, she would use more material to make the back. She then would put something in between the front and back. She would either use a frame or old sewing machine to quilt them together.

She used to make apple butter from apples from the apple tree in her front yard.

My grandma is an older lady now. She cannot do things like she used to. She is eighty-six years old and we all love her very much. My grandma is a special person, and if more people were like her, the world would be a better place.

Author: Amanda Kay Dingess. Amanda attends Chapmanville Middle School. She enjoys reading, swimming, and having fun.

170-001-ST-WV-001-1997

The Mountain Lion

One cold December morning Dad, Jeremiah, and I were going deer hunting. The snow was deep and dry. The moon just glistened on the snow. It was five o'clock in the morning, I believe. It was only five degrees outside. We started the truck to get the heater hot. We were going up on Jenuer's.

We got out of the truck, loaded our guns and split up. Dad was using a 30-06, and Jeremiah and I were using 270s. Dad and I went in the holler and Jeremiah went up on the ridge. It was kind of hard walking in two feet of snow. Dad found some tracks going up the hill and said they were mountain lion tracks.

We saw a buck and I shot and hit him. Dad whistled for Jeremiah — no answer. Dad said he was too far off. We followed the blood trail. I felt like something was watching us from the trees. Dad stopped! Dad was in Vietnam for two years so he has good instincts. He got out his 45-caliber pistol and cocked it! I saw something running at us and it jumped. Dad shot twice. When I opened my eyes there lay a huge mountain lion. Just ten feet from the mountain lion was my deer, and it was a very nice one.

Author: Joshua William Jones. Josh is the son of Judith and Gary Jones. He has two brothers, Jeremiah and Joseph. He lives in Islands Branch, Sissonville, where he hunts, fishes, and collects all kinds of things.

171-001-ST-WV-001-1997

The Greenbrier River Trail

In the summer of 1996, my parents and I were going to go visit my cousins Brandon, Erin, and Leigh Ann Duckworth at Watoga State Park in Greenbrier County. They had rented a cabin there and had invited us to stay the weekend with them. When we got there it was late, so we just went to sleep as soon as we lay down.

The next day we decided to go on a bike ride. We were going to ride on an eight mile stretch of the Greenbrier River Trail. We loaded up the bikes and headed for the trail. We were having a hard time finding the trail. We drove around for about two hours. Then we found a closed logging road. My Uncle Rick looked at the map and saw that this road would take us to the trail.

We unloaded the bikes and started down the hill. All the way down the hill we had to hold our brakes. I flipped my bike going down the hill, but I wasn't hurt. After we got off the hill we found the trail.

For about a mile or two on the trail nothing really happened. Then my mom Kathy wrecked on her bike and scraped her knee up. It then turned out that a lot of the trail had been washed out by a flood. We had to push our bikes for a long way.

After we finished the trail we enjoyed a Pepsi and a bag of chips. When we got back to the cabin we had spaghetti and meatballs. We then just sat by the fire and talked. It was a pretty good trip after all.

Author: Jeffery Duffield. At age twelve, Jeffery is the youngest of three children. He enjoys practicing the guitar and playing Doom on his computer. He lives in Sharples.

172-001-ST-WV-001-1997

Interview With Mabel Lucas

Schools were only one room in the 1920s. Everybody went to school in grades primer through eighth. When you finished the eighth grade you could take a test, and if you made a certain grade you taught school.

We had six months of school each year. We went from nine o'clock in the morning until four in the afternoon and studied reading, writing, English, arithmetic, spelling, geography, and agriculture. Sometimes we would go for a nature hike and study trees.

The school had wooden floors that lay on big rocks. Most schools had a pot-bellied stove for heat. There were no lights because people had never heard of electricity.

To write, some people used slates and slate pencils. Others had a rough tablet of paper and a penny pencil. We had a quill pen to dip in a bottle of ink and write with. The ink was made from elderberries, pokeberries, and spicewood berries.

We had ciphering matches and spelling bees. Parents could spell and cipher with us if they wanted to. Many parents could not read, spell, or do arithmetic, but they enjoyed watching the children.

There were no sports for competition. We played a game called round town which is similar to baseball. We made our own balls out of yarn. Bats were made from boards. The most fun we had was going out to get walnuts, chestnuts, and hickory nuts for Christmas treats.

There were no breakfasts or lunches at school. You carried your lunch in a four-pound lard bucket. Lunch was often cold beans and cornbread. If you had milk cows, you might have milk and cornbread. Sometimes you would have a baked potato or some kind of meat, usually pork or beef.

Most parents farmed for a living. A few might cut timber for sawmills. You lived on what you raised on the farm and any meats you could hunt. When apples were ripe we would have apple peelings. Neighbors came and helped peel apples. The next day we would make a run of apple butter.

We had corn shuckings when corn was gathered in. Neighbors came and helped shuck corn. If the boys found a red ear they could kiss their girlfriends.

Author: Matt Lucas. Matt is Mabel's grandson and wrote this story in her words.

173-001-ST-WV-001-1997

A Peaceful Picnic

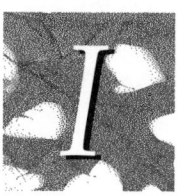

In the summer of 1996, my family took a trip to Pete Dalton Rock. This is a huge rock that is moss covered, with a stream running through the middle of it.

We took a basket full of goodies and snacks up to this rock to have a picnic. We played tag, ten-step, and hide 'n' seek. But the best part of the day was when we sat down to eat. It was so peaceful. You could not hear the traffic sounds that are in the big city. Just quietness. This is what I like best about West Virginia.

Author: Malindia Hensley. Malindia is in the seventh grade and enjoys rock collecting.

174-001-ST-WV-001-1997

When Great-Grandma Was Little

When I asked my great-grandmother Vena Crisp what she remembered about growing up near Charleston in the late 1920s and 1930s, she said that she hated when her father would come in her room at five o'clock to awake her to do her chores. Some of her chores included feeding chickens and collecting their eggs. She also had to do stuff like feeding the hogs, lighting the stove, and helping the young children with their homework.

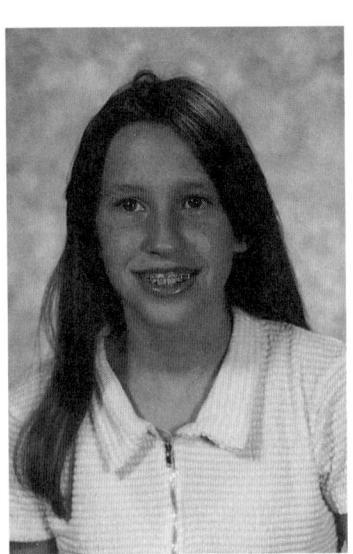

Ashley Adkins, 1996.

After she finished with all of her daily chores, she would walk down the road to the schoolhouse. She said, "The old schools were in one room. I remember when I felt as if I could faint, because of the hot room. I also remember when the boys were separated from the girls. They had to stay on one side of the room and the girls had to stay on another."

Every Sunday she said that the family dressed in their best and finest clothing and went to church in a wagon.

My great-grandmother said another event was when her father died. "Everyone joined in to hear the preacher say the prayer. I remember I cried and cried."

She remembers when everyone gathered for family reunions. She said, "Our small cottage in Pipestem, near Bluefield, was always so crowded. I also remember I didn't like one of my cousins and my mother punished me, because she said I was being rude."

My great-grandmother's family would can strawberries. She said that they messed up one whole quart of strawberries, and she had to go pick some more out of the garden.

AUTHOR: Ashley Adkins. Ashley is in the seventh grade at Chapmanville Middle School. She enjoys rollerblading, talking on the telephone, watching television, and especially writing.

175-001-ST-WV-001-1997

The Devil Made Him Do It

When my dad Travis Baldwin was little, in the 1950s, he did all kinds of horrible things. This is one of them. Once he had a fight with his sister Nancy in the bathroom and she shoved him really hard. He fell down into the bathtub and hit his head against the faucet. She waited for him to get back up, but when he didn't, she started to cry. At that moment she thought that she had killed him, and she said that if he came back to life she would give him her allowance for a whole month.

Of course my dad, being the little devil that he was, was just lying there pretending the whole time. So my dad got his sister's allowance for a month and he spent it at the grocery store on candy and Cokes. But after his sister found out that she had been had, she felt really awful.

AUTHOR: Daniel Whittington Baldwin. Daniel is a Charleston native whose interests are James Bond novels and movies, scouting, and collecting comics.

176-001-ST-WV-001-1997

An Average Day For My Grandparents

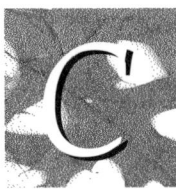

Children in the early 1900s had it pretty rough. That's when my grandparents Tom and Lema Garrett grew up in Chapmanville, Logan County. They had more work than today's kids ever have to do in a day.

They would get up around five A.M. and eat breakfast. Afterwards they would wash dishes. Then they would get ready for school and pack their lunch in their dinner bucket.

Every day they would have to walk one mile to the schoolhouse. The schools were not like they are today. Back then they were one or two rooms. Every room had one teacher with fifty to seventy-five students ranging from first to eighth grade.

During the day they would learn about reading, writing, arithmetic, history, geography, and English. They had three breaks, two fifteen minute recesses and a noon hour break. They would play games like roundhouse — which is much like baseball — marbles, and antney over. Antney over is a game in which you break up into two teams and the teams get on opposite sides of the schoolhouse. You throw the ball over the side and the other team tries to

catch it and catch as many people on the other team as they can.

After school was over they would make their way back home. When they got home, their supper was waiting for them. After they ate supper they would have to do their evening chores, such as getting coal and wood for the fire, feeding the animals, milking the cows, and washing dishes.

After the evening chores my grandmother would go to bed with her seven brothers and sisters in their four room home. She would go to bed at eight P.M. My grandfather and his brother and sister didn't have to go to bed until midnight. He would go opossum hunting, check his traps, or he would just go down the road and talk to his friends.

Author: Seth Cyfers. Seth is the son of David and Virginia Cyfers of Chapmanville. His hobbies are sports, listening to music, riding his four-wheeler, and hunting.

177-001-ST-WV-001-1997

Mountains

The mountains in West Virginia are so beautiful. There are mountains everywhere you look. All the mountains are different from each other. They have different heights.

When it snows in West Virginia the snow is so nice on the top of the mountains. There is more snow on the high mountains than on the lower ones.

There are many mountains around my home. All you have to do is look out the doors and you will see a mountain. Sometimes you can see deer come out of them.

In the summer people might climb the mountains. People might even take pictures of them. There are various mountains in West Virginia. If you ever climb a mountain here in West Virginia, then you would say that the mountains are great. I think they are beautiful.

Author: Jennifer Dingess. Jennifer lives in Chapmanville. She likes talking on the phone and spending time with her friends.

178-001-ST-WV-001-1997

Making Molasses

I remember hearing about making molasses. My Uncle Harold Dingess told me about how they made molasses. He said that they would start out by taking the stalks of cane and putting them in a big pile. Then they would get their machine that squishes the stuff and makes the syrup. Then they got a wash tub and filled it with water and boiled it. Next they would put the cane through that machine and make it into a syrup. They poured the water out of the tub to make sure that it was sterilized. They put the syrup in it and boiled it. There was a bad film of goo on the top of the syrup when it was finished. They took that off.

"Now," he said, "that's how you make molasses."

Author: John David Dingess. John lives in Harts. He has two brothers, Will and Bobby. His mom works for the Health Department and his dad raises cows. He likes to hunt and fish.

179-001-ST-WV-001-1997

One Of The Best Days Of My Life

One day my sister, father, and I went hunting. I go hunting a lot but my older sister doesn't. She doesn't know what to look for or what to do.

We went to my grandfather's house at three o'clock that morning. He owns a little over 200 acres of land in southern West Virginia. We arrived at the house and went in. We spent about twenty minutes drinking coffee, talking to my grandparents, and getting ready.

We set out into the woods and I brought my grandfather's 30/30. Dad and I led the way. First we climbed a hill and sat on a rock cliff. We looked over a valley with a pond on it. About an hour later we started to move to a new location. We went over a lot of dead trees and trails. Then finally we got to the spot. We sat down on a huge, mossy rock and looked out into the woods. Now we were behind the pond but couldn't see it.

We waited there for a good fifty minutes and walked around to the other side of the pond. We sat down near a huge oak tree. We were not there ten minutes when we saw two does walking near us. We sat and watched them prance around watching us for at least an hour.

Finally they left, and so did we. We walked back to the truck, unloaded the guns and hopped in. When we got back to the house we told our grandparents.

Even though we didn't kill anything, I still spent one of the best days of my life that day.

Author: Jeremy Wells. Jeremy is thirteen years old. He enjoys playing basketball and Nintendo games.

180-001-ST-WV-001-1997

Fox Hunting

When my dad Wade Workman was growing up, my grandfather, the late Bennie Workman, used to take him fox hunting.

Fox hunting is where hunters take their dogs with them and the dogs would chase the fox. The fastest dog is the pack leader. The object is to chase the fox, not harm or kill it.

My dad remembers one time when he was eleven and his dad took him fox hunting. They were with one of his dad's hunting friends Odell and they were going to Lick Creek. As they were going up an old logging road in Odell's truck, they came across a rattlesnake on the side of the road. His dad got out of the truck and shot the snake! Then Odell got out of the truck to remove the rattle from the snake. All of a sudden, the snake moved! It scared them all.

They proceeded on to the hunting camp where they set the dogs loose. The dogs jumped a fox and chased it until the next morning.

My grandfather kept his dogs at home. He often took them hunting in the mountains. My dad liked fox hunting, and he loved to guess which dog was in the lead.

My dad still remembers all the times my grandfather took him hunting and he enjoyed all of the hunting trips.

AUTHOR: *Alicia Workman. Alicia is the twelve year old daughter of Wade and Linda Workman of Chapmanville. She is in the seventh grade and attends Chapmanville Middle School.*

181-001-ST-WV-001-1997

My Mountain Grandma

I have sat in Dulcie Baker's cozy, warm kitchen eating homemade biscuits and listening to wonderful stories of the past since I was a little girl. My mountain grandma has told me some amazing stories over the years.

Dulcie Baker grew up in the Asbury-Blue Sulphur area of Greenbrier County back in a hollow with few neighbors. She was born May 3, 1908. As a young child she went to work with her mother Ida, who worked cleaning and cooking for the richer people in their community.

In 1915, Dulcie went to school for the first time. The school was called Lake View. To get to school Dulcie had to walk a mile, but she walked it with the neighbor boy Thomas and his sister. Her first teacher was Carrie Link. Miss Link gave her a Christmas card that Dulcie still has! When she went to school, students only went for three months a year. So school was a very special time for the children. One year her uncle taught at her school and he brought her a special present: a pencil and pad of paper.

After elementary school Dulcie decided to go to high school, though she was one of the only ones from her school. Her high school education was at Smoot High School. During high school she stayed with her aunt and uncle. She then went to college at the Alderson Baptist Junior College to complete her teaching certificate.

Her first job was in the same elementary school she had attended. So for this job she stayed at home. Though her earnings were not much, they helped her family. Her second job was in Saw Mill Hollow, where she had trouble with lice. Almost everyone had it, and she had to send the children home to get rid of the lice. Her last job was on Keeney's Knob. She walked from the boarding house to school in the deepest snow she had ever seen.

AUTHOR: *Mesha Maren-Hogan. Mesha is twelve years old, and in the sixth grade. She is an avid reader and writer, and is interested in history.*

182-001-ST-WV-001-1997

Grandma Emmie Remembers War

My grandma Emmie Low Brown Bowling didn't grow up in one spot because she had to move to wherever her father Everett Brown could find work in West Virginia. Grandma grew up with eight brothers and sisters. I asked her what she liked to do when she was little and she told me she liked to go into the mountains and sleigh ride in the winter.

I also asked her what went on in her childhood, and she answered that the first and main thing she remembered was World War II. She told me that three of her brothers, Charles, Nathan, and Clyde were in the war. Charles was wounded by a gunshot. Her sister Virginia worked as a riveter in a factory in Ohio. Grandma explained to me that when a siren blew it meant for the town to turn off every light in their house. This was done because if the enemy wanted to bomb the place where she was staying, they couldn't see the town.

Since you had to give your money up for

CHAPTER 10: YOUNG AUTHORS

the war, you got tokens that you picked up at the post office. The tokens could buy you stuff instead of paying for it with money. Grandma told me she remembered having to buy shoes with the tokens before school started.

When a family member died in the war, a taxi cab would come with a telegram. Grandma said that she remembered her mom sitting on the porch waiting for a taxi cab to come by. Every time she saw one she prayed and trembled.

I asked her how her family stored food in the winter, and she said they canned vegetables and kept food in their ice box and their refrigerator. Every other day the ice man would come, and grandma's parents would buy ice.

My grandma had an interesting childhood. It would have been hard living like she did.

AUTHOR: Casey Maran Bowling. Casey's parents are Rick and Tammy Bowling of Chapmanville. He has one sister, Erin. Casey's hobbies include baseball, basketball, and football.

183-001-ST-WV-001-1997

My Grandparents' House

My grandparents' house was very nice, and the people in it were also. When I was little I went up there all the time when my parents went to work. I would play outside and in the garden. My grandpa would always be in the garden working. I had most of my birthday parties in the house. We would have holiday dinner there and family get-togethers.

When my grandma and grandpa died, the house was torn down. The hill was empty for a long time. Someone decided to build a restaurant there. Now there is a Wendy's where my grandparents' house used to be.

It's hard to go by and eat at Wendy's knowing that my grandparents' house used to be there.

Christina Kessell, 1996.

AUTHOR: Christina Kessell. Christina is in the sixth grade at Sissonville Middle School. She likes to play basketball and soccer. Her grandparents were Alfred (d. 4/5/88) and Mary Atkisson (d. 2/23/92).

184-001-ST-WV-001-1997

The Cow On Coco Road

Laura F. Pitzer Ross was born February 4, 1864, in the state that would later be West Virginia. She married my great-great-grandfather James Ross and moved by train to Elk Lick Creek where they founded a little town. James opened a general store and a Post Office and named the town Coco. Both my great-grandfather Jerry O. Ross and my grandmother Dottie Ross Lynch were born there.

Great-great-grandma Ross became a midwife out of necessity. In the year 1898, she was walking up Coco Road after visiting the neighbor's house to deliver a baby. It was late at night, and she was tired and in a hurry to get home. Up ahead she saw something big and black lying down in the trail. It was a two-horse trail, so it wasn't very big. She couldn't tell what the thing was because the moonlight was barely hitting it. As she approached it she picked up her skirt to step over. As she got one foot over, it raised up. It was a cow. Great-great-grandma Ross rode the cow all the way home.

AUTHOR: Amber Smith. Amber is from Charleston. Her hobbies include music, dancing, reading, and writing short stories. This is a true story from the Ross family.

185-001-ST-WV-001-1997

The War

Edward Light, my popaw, was in World War II. He was born April 1, 1922. He worked hard every minute, and never quit on anything. He had to go to training camp, but didn't have to quit school. The school he went to was Logan. He lived in Sharples on a big hill.

When he went to war he survived. He was very strong and brave. Because he did so well, he got many awards. Also when he was in the war, he got shot in the ribs and had two of his fingers shot off.

His wife Irene Light was a nurse, and is also my momaw. When Popaw got shot my momaw took care of him in a hospital bed. Then about eight months later he didn't have to be in the Army anymore. Everybody was glad that he didn't have to be in the Army because he was getting shot and everything.

Then he got better and started to chew tobacco and smoke. Everybody told him to quit, but he didn't listen. He got cancer. My mom took me up there where he lived because we wanted to see him. He looked very, very, very sick. Then on December 31, 1989, he died. We had a funeral, and everybody was sad.

Author: Jacob Smith. Jacob attends Sharples Elementary School.

186-001-ST-WV-001-1997

How Pecks Mill Got Its Name

Ned Peck owned an old mill on the Guyandotte River, near what we now call Pecks Mill. The old mill had ground mostly corn and wheat. Mill workers would make corn meal every day because flour and meal weren't sold in stores. Farmers and customers would come from distant places to have corn ground into meal.

The old mill no longer exists today, because corn meal is sold in grocery stores. If the mill did exist, there would not be much business. Although the mill is gone, many members of the Peck family have become prominent people in the area.

Author: Jennifer Smith. Jennifer submitted this story, told by Nancy Risko, her great-grandmother. Jennifer is the daughter of Alan and Vicki Smith of Chapmanville. She has one sister, Angela.

187-001-ST-WV-001-1997

Hidden Objects

This story happened a long time ago, in the 1950s. My dad still remembers, though. My father's family couldn't find my Grandma Johnson's pop and cigarettes. Such things were scarce for a poor Pinch, West Virginia, farm family, so Grandma would find hiding places for her "supply," which everyone would try to find. They were all bewildered.

My Grandma Johnson had hidden her cans of pop and cigarettes in the oven. She had forgotten about them by the next day and started baking things in the oven.

Everyone was out of the room; they all heard a loud "Boom!" The house filled with cigarette smoke. The cigarettes and pop cans had blown up. Grandma Johnson never hid her stuff there again.

Author: Erica Johnson. Erica is the daughter of John and Janet Johnson of Charleston. She is a student at Sissonville Middle School.

188-001-ST-WV-001-1997

A Town's Loss

As a kid, my dad grew up in Holden, West Virginia. He was about ten years old when he and his friends were playing a game called hidden trial, now known as spotlight. There was a boy who was playing with my dad and his friends. He was going to hide up at an old power station. My dad said no one could find him until the next morning. They found him up at the old power station lying there dead. My dad didn't find out until he saw the evening paper that day. He was one of my dad's best friends. My dad said he was sad for a long time. He said it was a great loss for the whole town of Holden.

Author: Brandon John Picklesimer. Brandon is the son of Mike and Margaret Picklesimer of Chapmanville. He has one brother and one sister. He likes to play sports.

189-001-ST-WV-001-1997

My Grandmother

My grandmother Irene Spry Dingess was born and raised in Logan, West Virginia. She lived in a community called Mud Fork. She came from a very large family of twelve children. There were four boys and eight girls. Her parents were the late Ira Spry and Martha Queen Spry. She is the eleventh child out of twelve. There are two boys and four girls living today.

I asked her what she remembered most about her childhood. She remembered sharing a bed with her sisters. She said there were two at the head of the bed and two at the foot of the bed. Also, the children helped with different chores at home.

One of the best times was when she went to the produce market with her family. The produce market was where Honeycut car dealership is today. Her parents would buy six to eight bushels of peaches, which they would take home and peel and slice. Her mother would make a syrup to pour on the peaches. Then they would seal the fruit in jars and place the jars of peaches in a tub of water. They would put rags between the jars so that if they hit together they would not break. Her father would make a big fire in which to sit the wash tub. The peaches had to cook this way for several hours.

She said they also canned green beans this same way. She said that everyone in the family helped in preparing the peaches and the beans. The one thing that stands out in her mind about her childhood is how everyone worked together to do everything as a family.

Today my grandmother still cans food. She may not can the food the old-fashioned way, but she and her sisters still help each other can the peaches and the beans.

Author: Kara Brooke Meeks. Kara is a seventh grade student at Chapmanville Middle School. She enjoys cheerleading and playing softball.

Working In The Coal Mines

A long time ago, back in 1939, my great-grandfather Okey Thaxton worked hard as a coal miner in the West Virginia hills. Back in those days you had to make a living and support your family the best way that you could.

My great-grandfather used to get up early and

Okey Thaxton.

head off to the coal mines, usually before daylight, to dig and load coal onto the coal carts. My great-grandmother Mable Thaxton would pack his lunch in an old lunch pail, usually with biscuits and homemade apple butter.

My grandmother has told me the story many times about how he would come home

Matthew Foster, 1996.

late in the evening after working in the mines, covered with nothing but soot from coal. Sometimes you could see nothing but the whites of his eyes.

The mines were not safe, they just looked like big holes dug in the side of the mountain. The walls and ceiling were held up by old wood braced together to try and prevent it from falling in. The only light miners had to see and work by was from the lights attached to their hard hats and from old Coleman lamps that hung inside the mines.

One summer the wood gave out and the mine collapsed. My grandfather made it out alive, but our family friend Paul Moore died that day. He was crushed by the wood and the ceiling of the mine. My grandfather died from black lung which is a disease caused from breathing the coal dust in the mines.

Author: Matthew Foster. Matthew is eleven years old and lives in Charleston. He is a lover of all sports, particularly football, baseball, and basketball.

Growing Up On My Farm

On my farm is where I have lived for twelve years. I have grown up learning how to help feed the cows and eventually I will learn to drive the John Deere tractor.

There are a lot of fun jobs, and a few of them are based on what time of year it is. Spring and summer is the time to cut hay. Sometime around fall we chop corn in a cornfield with a piece of equipment that is called a corn-chopper. It is connected to and pulled behind our tractor. In winter there is not much to do but feed the cattle and water them because the creeks or streams from the hills freeze up. Much of my family's Christmas time is spent just sitting around the fire and enjoying Christmas at home.

Now, most of my time is occupied by school, church, and other activities. What time I have left after doing those things, I spend around my farm.

Author: Matthew Mullins. Matthew lives in Harts. His hobby is playing the piano.

Hurt And Scared

When my dad was eleven years old and his brother Jim was nine, they were both riding the same bike to an old mine site at Whitman, West Virginia. When they got there they were playing on a mine locomotive with a trolley pole. My uncle Jim was in the operator's deck. My dad grabbed hold of the trolley pole and swung on the pole to get off the locomotive. Jim's hand was underneath the pole where the hinge was. When my dad pulled the trolley pole down to the ground it came down on Jim's finger. Jim screamed and my dad went to see what was wrong with him. When he checked Jim's hand he saw that the ring finger of his left hand was cut all the way through on the first joint but was still attached by a piece of skin.

Jim and my dad were very scared about what happened. Dad tried to get Jim on the bicycle to get him to help, but he was out of control. Jim took off on the bicycle and my dad ran behind him. They went half a mile until they came to a house. The people living there were on the front porch. They got in the car and took Jim another half mile down the road to where they lived. My grandparents took Jim to the hospital where the doctor sewed his finger back on.

AUTHOR: Andrew Mullins. Andrew is twelve years old and attends Chapmanville Middle School.

193-001-ST-WV-001-1997

Life In The Past

My great-grandmother tells me that many years ago purchases were made at the company store. These stores were owned by the area coal companies.

Clothes were made. They were not bought. You would make the clothes from fabric you bought at a mercantile store by the yard. After one child outgrew the clothes, they would be passed down to another child. These clothes were passed down until they were completely worn out.

In the summer families would grow everything they would need until the next summer. They would can a lot of things. They stored their canned food in cellars. They would raise their meats, too. At the end of summer they would kill the animals. Then they cut and cleaned the meat and stored it in a smokehouse along with clothing, cotton, and wool. They would live on that all winter.

People heated their houses with fire wood and coal. Sometimes they would use oil lamps for a form of lighting.

Houses were not like they are now. About ten people would live in a three room house. Kids would sleep in one room. They had hard wood floors that you could see the ground through. They would have cracks in the walls. It was very cold in the winter. The snow and rain would come in the houses.

People would carry water to drink, bathe in, and to do household chores with. The water came from streams. Sometimes they would have to carry water one mile or more. It was hard work to carry water that far.

AUTHOR: Gary Lee Jeffrey. Gary is the son of Lettie and Gary Lee Jeffrey, Sr., of Logan. He has one brother, Tyler Ray. He enjoys riding bikes, playing sports, and hiking.

194-001-ST-WV-001-1997

My Granny

My grandmother Violet Lambert is the daughter of Thelma and Luther Dempsey. She was born at Harts, West Virginia, in Lincoln County, on March 21, 1932. She is an only child. She remembers sleeping in a feather bed.

The one thing that stands out in her mind is walking a mile to a one-room schoolhouse, and wearing boy shoes. She said a big wood stove in the school was used to heat up the room, and they had outside toilets.

She said she would have to go to a country store once in awhile after school and carry twenty-five pound bags of flour one mile back home. Now she drives herself to the store instead of walking.

AUTHOR: Ashley Jeanette Varney. Ashley lives in Chapmanville with her parents Ivan and Sabrina, and her sister Selena Nicole. She enjoys cheerleading and listening to music.

195-001-ST-WV-001-1997

My Grandma Bryant

My story is about my grandma. Her name is Vonnie Bryant. She is the daughter of the late Harriet and Troy Adams. My grandma lived on a farm, so she worked most of her life. She told me she loves the sport baseball. My grandma likes to pick and can berries. She also likes to can other stuff like green beans and other vegetables.

She likes to cook fried chicken and potatoes. My grandma is from Shively, West Virginia. She's been married for fifty years to James Newcome Bryant.

Grandma had three brothers and six sisters. She has thirteen kids, seven boys and six girls. She has twenty-eight grandchildren and six great-grandchildren. She told me that my great-grandmother used to drink and sell moonshine. She remembers having to get coal from the coal mines to keep her house warm in the winter. My grandma would describe herself as a blue-eyed old lady.

AUTHOR: Jarrod Russell Bryant. Jarrod is the son of Ernie and Christine Bryant of Pecks Mill. He has one brother and five sisters. He enjoys playing basketball.

196-001-ST-WV-001-1997

Camping At Pipestem

During the summer of 1995, my cousin, my parents, and I went on a week-long camping trip to Pipestem State Park. We arrived at 4:00 P.M. The first thing that I did was to set up my tent and then help my parents set up their tent and tarp. After I helped them, I went on a walk into the woods with my cousin Jeff Scott. We followed a winding trail up the mountain. We heard the birds chirp as we were walking. Suddenly we noticed that we were on a horse trail, as a horse came running down the path with a man on it waving at us. About thirty minutes later we came back out of the woods and onto the path at the beginning of the campground. We stayed all week and it rained, but we had fun.

AUTHOR: John Gancs. John is a student at Sissonville Middle School. He likes skateboarding, playing video games, reading comic books, card collecting, and listening to music.

197-001-ST-WV-001-1997

When My Grandmother Was Little

My grandmother Lillie said when she was little her brothers, sisters, and parents lived in a three-room log cabin in Logan County. She said it was cold in the winter, but they survived. My grandmother said it was warm in the summer like it is now.

She said when she and her sisters were little they would pick buckets of berries. They would make pies with the berries they picked. She said her dad would say, "That was the best pie that I have ever eaten." My grandmother said that it always made her happy to hear her father say that.

She said when it was schooltime she had to walk to school. Later she had to walk home for lunch and then walk back to school. She said it felt so good to go home at the end of the day.

She said there were no cars back then; all they had were horses and buggies. She said even though she did not have much she was happy.

AUTHOR: Alisha Dawn Sparks. Alisha is twelve years old and enjoys reading. She attends Chapmanville Middle School.

198-001-ST-WV-001-1997

A Man Named Rabbit

This story is about my papaw Edgar Roe Miller and how he got his nickname "Rabbit." In 1927, Edgar was fifteen years old. He lived in Boone County, in Madison.

Edgar's father was Theodore Miller, a bridge builder, tinkerer, and inventor. He had five sons that helped him, and one day there was a bridge to build. But Edgar decided to go hunting. He got his hat, shotgun, and his old dog and went up the hollow.

His dog picked up a scent of a rabbit at a brush pile, stuck his nose in and flushed it out. The rabbit took off running for a hole in a beech tree. Edgar tried everything to get the rabbit out of the hole, and finally he went after Theodore's blasting powder. He dumped most of it into the knothole, then put a little line out to set it off with.

Jonathan Edgar Anthony, 1996.

He had an oily rag in his pocket which he figured would be his fuse. He struck a match and lit his fuse. As soon as the rag left his hand, he knew he had messed up. He overthrew past the line of powder and straight into the knothole. The last thing Edgar saw was a fireball at the base of the beech tree.

He woke up about fifty feet down the hill. His skin was hanging off his body. He got up and made his way back home. His mother saw him and let out a scream. She found Edgar burnt and nearly naked holding a scorched and scared old hound dog. Edgar's flesh was hanging in blackened strips.

Edgar's mother got a sheet, some scissors, and lots of homemade salve. She trimmed off the loose skin from his head, arms, chest, and legs. She spread the salve everywhere, then wrapped the sheet around him. She put him to bed and sent for the doctor. An old Model-T Ford rattled to a stop, carrying Edgar's daddy and the doctor.

The doctor never laid a hand on Edgar, just walked around the bed and looked. He finally said, "You've done exactly what I would have done," and left.

Edgar lived without so much as a scar. Ever since that day he's been "Rabbit Miller."

Author: Jonathan Edgar Anthony. Jonathan is from Dobra, Logan County. He is in the fifth grade at Sharples Elementary School. His hobbies include basketball and drawing. His parents are Joe and Cynthia Anthony.

199-001-ST-WV-001-1997

When Ruthie Was Young

hen Ruthie Moore, a family friend, was a young girl, she went to a one-room schoolhouse in Kanawha County called Snowhill. School started at 9:00 A.M. and ended at 2:00 P.M. Every morning she walked two miles to the school. There were outhouses, or "outdoor johnny houses" at Snowhill. There was also an outside water pump. They would carry buckets of water inside to put in a stone cooler.

In school, Ruthie learned math, reading, and spelling. On the long walk home, Ruthie and five boys — including her brother Arlie — walked together. Sometimes they teased her and threw rocks at her. One day, she hit Arlie over the head with her metal lunch bucket. They stopped teasing her, but she still went home crying because her bucket had a big dent.

Ruthie Moore of Sissonville, West Virginia.

When she was a little older Ruthie went to a pie social at Camp Creek School. At a pie social, there is dancing, music and fun; everyone brings a pie. Johnny Wright and the Tennessee Hillbillies played. She sang and tap-danced with the group. They said Ruthie should go to Nashville and perform, but her dad said no.

Ruthie, like most other children in her neighborhood, lived on a farm. She had no indoor plumbing, so they had an "outdoor johnny house." She had to wash her clothes on a washboard. On her farm they grew corn, tomatoes, cucumbers, parsnips, and lettuce. They had cows. Butter was made in a stone churn. For fun, Ruthie, her siblings, and friends would play "Go Around the Mulberry Bush," hide-and-seek, jump rope, badminton, and marbles.

Author: Kathryn Leigh Erb. Kathy lives in Sissonville with her parents and three of her sisters. She enjoys painting, drawing, singing, and playing the trombone.

200-001-ST-WV-001-1997

The Huge Sandbox

hen I was six years old, my neighbor Jessica Adkins and I would play in an old metal tube. It was filled with sand. We called it our "huge sandbox." We would get our toys and walk there everyday. But one day when we got there it was gone. We thought we were lost at first, but we weren't. It was really gone. So, we went to my house to ask my mom about it. She said they were coal mining up there and they had to move it. We felt really bad.

The next few days we were bored. We didn't have anything to do. We thought we would go walk up in the mountains. Then we saw something really bad. We saw our huge sandbox crushed! Our eyes filled with tears. We went home with our heads down.

Five years later, we were eleven. Jessica went to another school and we never saw each other. I know Jessica will never forget our huge sandbox, and I know I won't either.

Author: Kendra Burgess. Kendra is the daughter of C.R. and Mary Burgess. She is in the fifth grade at Sharples Elementary School. She has visited all fifty states, Mexico, and Canada.

201-001-ST-WV-001-1997

My Family

t all starts with my cousins Margaret and Bill when they went to a Dairy Queen many years back. Bill was about five and Margaret was three. Bill asked for a plain cone, while Margaret asked for "one with somethin' in it." From that you can tell that the Hensons are a great family. The Mondays, my mother's family, are great too. The only time either family's

gatherings were serious were funerals. Even at those times most of us remained optimistic. The greatest thing, though, is that our families get along very well. Both sides pitched in when we remodeled the house. My dad built the staircase before he started on the second floor, so the big joke going around was "The Stairway to Nowhere." Also, my mom, uncle, and grandpa stepped through the roof.

There is no doubt that my family's fun ways have passed down to my generation. My cousin Jimmy and I share the same hobbies: joking and pulling pranks. One of my favorite pranks was when he and I pushed my sister's bed in front of her door and unscrewed her doorknob. My sister's response: "How are we going to get the glue off??" I hope these traits pass down to the next generation.

AUTHOR: Andy Henson. Andy is the oldest of three children. He lives in Sissonville and likes to play soccer.

Beethoven

My dog's name is Beethoven. He is a black Lab. His feet are white. We have had him since he was six weeks old. He has run away only once. The people that gave him to us found him. They brought him back to us while we were playing outside.

Phyllis Drake, Joshua Collins, and puppy Beethoven.

Now he is almost a year old. He weighs about sixty pounds, maybe more. He is very strong.

Our next door neighbors are Roy and Phyllis Drake. Their dog Alex is twelve years old and he has cancer in his back. Recently he slipped and fell in the creek. Beethoven kept barking and running to the creek until they came out and followed him to the creek and saw Alex.

The day after that my brothers were at the bus stop and a black Chow that is really mean came and Beethoven chased him away.

Beethoven is really a special dog to the Collins family.

AUTHOR: Anthony Dale Collins. Anthony is the oldest of five children. He is in the sixth grade at Sissonville Middle School. He likes building models and collecting cards, particularly those of Dale Earnhardt.

The Big Garden

When my Papa Billy Smutko was young he had a big garden in Mifflin, that was about one acre of corn and other vegetables. This was a victory garden. All families were asked to grow one because the second World War was going on.

One time Papa grew a corn stalk that was fourteen feet tall, and had corn on it one foot long. The next day, they went to pick it and someone had stolen it all! They tried to save the stalk, but it had rotted. They didn't get to keep any of it to show. He said it was the biggest cornstalk anyone had ever grown.

Papa had three brothers to help him, but two of them went to the second World War. Soon he was the only child at his house to work on the farm. Then he left for the war.

AUTHOR: Michael Smutko. Michael lives with his family in Mifflin. He is ten years old and enjoys basketball, hunting, fishing, baseball, and martial arts. Michael's papa, Billy Smutko, is one of eight children born to Hungarian immigrant parents and grew up in Mifflin during the 1930s. This is one of his papa's stories as told to him.

Uncle Fain

My Uncle Fain was incredibly lucky and a real prankster. The most famous incident was when my father grew vegetables and entered them in the Nicholas County Fair. My father entered his green beans. My Uncle Fain took the liberty of entering some of the same beans but under his name. My father won third place for his beans, but my uncle won the Grand Prize for my father's green beans. My uncle claimed the reason he won was the way he displayed the beans he entered.

Another story my father tells is about the

time he sent away for the Roy Rogers Fan Club. He had to send in three cereal box tops and a quarter. He waited weeks for the letter. He checked the mailbox every day except for the one day Uncle Fain beat him to the mailbox and got the package. When my father came home, he found that Fain had written his own name on the membership card in ink!

AUTHOR: William Crichton Miller, III. William is the son of Bill and Betsy Miller of Pocatalico. He has one sister, Jessica. His hobbies include soccer and "tinkering with things."

205-001-ST-WV-001-1997

West Virginian Through And Through

y great-grandmother Ruby Barker Ratliff was born at home in Logan County, West Virginia, at Pecks Mill on March 9, 1918. She grew up on Mill Creek with her two sisters and three brothers. Her parents were Noah and Leva Whitt Barker.

As a child, for fun she jumped rope, played hopscotch and ball. She went to school in a one-room building. The little school was heated by a coal stove. There were about thirty kids in the school. She and her brothers and sisters had to walk to school on a dirt road. They took their lunch to school in a lard bucket.

Since they were the oldest, Mamaw Ruby and her brother Norman used to work in the corn fields while the rest of the kids worked in the house.

Mamaw Ruby loved growing up in West Virginia. She has always lived somewhere in the state. Once she lived at Henlawson where Chief Logan Park is now located. She has also lived at Pecks Mill, Ethel, and Mill Creek.

She was married to Alex Ratliff at the age of sixteen, and had her first child, Ethel, at the age of twenty-two. Her son Ronnie died at the age of three from cancer. Her youngest child, Carol, was born at home on Mill Creek where Ruby still lives.

AUTHOR: Bridgett Alexandra McNeely. Bridgett is the daughter of Greg and Rebecca McNeely of Pecks Mill. She has a sister, Jennifer, and a brother, Travis. Her hobbies are softball, fishing, and talking on the telephone.

206-001-ST-WV-001-1997

Christmas Traditions

y great-grandmother Judith Sych Walters said what she remembers most is during Christmas how she, her little sister, and her dad used to hike up into the mountains looking for the perfect Christmas tree. While they were looking for a tree, my great-great-grandmother popped popcorn and baked cookies. She would bake some hard so they could poke holes in them and string them on the tree.

When they came back with the tree, they all helped put it up in the main room. Then they put the popcorn and cookies on the tree, along with a paper chain which they always made weeks before.

Emily Walters, 1996.

Then they hung their old stockings on the backs of chairs, and went to bed. When they woke up they usually found fruit in their stockings and carefully wrapped rag dolls or sewing kits.

The gifts which they received may not seem like a lot today, but to them it was.

AUTHOR: Emily Gray Walters. Emily attends Chapmanville Middle School. She enjoys shopping and being with her friends.

207-001-ST-WV-001-1997

Mill Creek Grade School, 1927. Top row (L-R), Belva Stowers, Inez White, Elda Collins, Ruby Barker, Pearl Harrison, Nancy Stowers, Elva Collins. Middle row (L-R), Teacher Eva Barker, Elmer Collins, Avery Collins, Willard Collins, Clarence Stowers, Orville Barker, Alex Ratliff. Front row (L-R), Nesta White, Gladys Barker, Norman Barker, Ethel Cabell, Mildred Collins.

Appendix I

APPENDIX I

The Project

Coming Home...Few events can rival reunions as storytelling havens. Reunions were a major focus of Homecoming '96, and that's what got the ball rolling for *Mountain State Stories of the People*. West Virginians would definitely be "in the mood" for story swapping. As a publishing company whose focus is the preservation of stories of everyday people, that presented an opportunity too good to pass up.

In early 1996, Populore Publishing Company owners discussed the project idea with the state's Homecoming '96 office in Charleston. The office was pleased with the initiative, and the *Mountain State Stories of the People* project was designated an official state-wide Homecoming '96 project. Additionally, then-Governor Gaston Caperton — who championed Homecoming '96 — agreed to submit a story and provide a foreword for the book.

Anyone with a story to share about West Virginia was invited to participate in *Mountain State Stories of the People*. A brochure distributed around the state sought true, original stories that celebrate or honor significant West Virginia experiences or places; memories of growing up in the state; native West Virginians, living or not; people who have moved to the state; highlights of a Homecoming '96 activity; and individual, community, or state traditions and accomplishments.

Mountain State Stories of the People was a grassroots project from the beginning. Although partly promoted through mailings to Homecoming Chairs and Committees throughout the state, in the end it was word of mouth and personal contact at fairs, festivals, and workshops that attracted most of the narratives.

The overall goal of the project was to promote story preservation. To that end, a *Put it in Writing* workshop was held on July 20, 1996, at Jackson's Mill near Weston. The day-long event was designed to help people brainstorm for ideas and write true, short, representative, stories that could, if the author chose, be included in the final *Mountain State* book. Over thirty people participated in the workshop, and another was held in St. Albans on September 9, 1996. Popular additions to both workshops were storytellers who shared entertaining tales and anecdotes. A third, mini-workshop, was held at a retirement home. Resident-participants enjoyed reminiscing about the "good old days" and educating the project's coordinator on terms, customs, and home remedies with which she was unfamiliar.

For this project and its general activities, Populore is a "cooperative publisher." Our role is to be the organizer and clearinghouse for stories and to arrange for and oversee a book's printing and binding. Although Populore does not want to publish anything known to be false or made-up, we do not formally verify or research the stories submitted. Rather, general knowledge and common sense guide us in seeking clarification or additional details from authors. In the end, each author (in the case of minors, a parent) attests to the truth of his or her story.

The authors cooperatively share the expense of layout, editing, and so on, and they are willing to do so to ensure the preservation of their story in a book. It is much like the members of a family sharing the cost of self-publishing a family history, only the contributors are strangers sharing a common goal. They do not need to manage or hassle with the problems of self-publishing such as the time commitment and expense, preparing a full "book's worth" of material, printer negotiations and oversight, and distribution of completed books. Populore presents an easy, satisfying, and cost effective alternative.

Appendix II

APPENDIX II

Ideas And Resources

I Like What I Read! How Can I Get Involved?

At Populore, we get excited each time someone tells us, "I've been wanting my mother to write these stories down for years. I'm so glad she finally did it." At the office, and since we've been presenting workshops, we've been asked many questions about how to encourage, motivate, and help people preserve stories. This section contains some hints and resources we have found to be helpful.

Family reunions (or class and community reunions) are ideal places to gather stories. A special time and place can be set aside for sharing memories of places, events, and people. Writing can be time consuming, and because oral storytelling is more entertaining and attractive to a larger group, videotaped or tape recorded gatherings can be successful. If using a tape recorder, have the person telling the story hold the tape recorder's microphone, and set friendly guidelines designating who is allowed to speak. The stories can be transcribed later and sent to all reunion participants, who might be able to fill in gaps or add important information like dates and names. After even one reunion, quite a history can be assembled.

Start a newsletter and encourage recipients to submit stories. Extended families can keep up on one another despite the miles that may separate them, and genealogical information and family stories can be shared. The responsibility for assembling/editing the newsletter can be passed around, and everyone can share in the cost of copying and mailing.

Individuals and families can promote story preservation by sending out holiday update letters detailing important events from the year instead of regular cards. Job promotions, personal milestones, the baby's first tooth, or the older kids' progress in their dance and music lessons can be recorded. Another approach might be to include some memories or a story from the past — from the writer's childhood or even a story he or she remembers hearing from a relative years back. Illustrate the letter with a photograph or piece of original art.

Family histories make priceless gifts. We all love the stories Grandma and Grandpa, aunts and uncles tell, but too often we only hear them on special occasions. Sitting down and writing out stories, tape recording or videotaping *yourself* reminiscing can be an economical, fun, practical gift for current and future generations, preserving precious information about ancestors and where they came from, the "family homeplace," their daily lives, and the marriages, births, and deaths. It can also be a wonderful tribute to people, living or not, who have played important roles in your life.

Encourage the young to write. Children will learn a lot if they sit down and "interview" an older relative or community member. Besides engaging in an educational activity, they will participate in a strong family-oriented project, and they will improve their communication and writing skills.

We live in a fast-paced, technologically oriented world. Families and friends have less and less time to spend together. Storytelling and preservation is a good way to make the most of that time. If you get really stuck, there are a number of excellent resource books, fill-in-the-blank history forms and family trees (your own is provided in the next Appendix), and a growing supply of computer software, websites, and on-line genealogy groups that can help you out.

Readers who want to know more about West Virginia history or genealogy can visit the state's **Cultural Center,** in the State Capitol Complex in Charleston. The Archives and History Section is the state's genealogy research center, containing printed and microfilmed collections of family, local, and state genealogy and history materials.

The *Mining Your History Foundation* sends its members a quarterly newsletter of informative articles and updates on genealogical and historical topics related to West Virginia. For membership information, write to:

> *Mining Your History Foundation*
> Archives and History, The Cultural Center
> 1900 Kanawha Boulevard East, Charleston, WV 25305-0300

For specific local history information, visit your local community or college **library** for a listing of West Virginia's historical/genealogical societies.

Populore Publishing Company offers its 220 page *Put It In Writing Guide For Populore Narratives* to spur your story gathering efforts. Also, we collect stories on a continuous basis for our *Populore Narratives: Stories of the People* books (the "Heritage Series") and at various times may be collecting stories for a special project book such as *Mountain State Stories of the People.* For information on the *Guide*, the Heritage Series and other projects, or to visit our office, contact:

> Populore Publishing Company
> P.O. Box 4382, Morgantown, WV 26504
> (304) 296-7867 or e-mail: stories@populore.com

Readers interested in gaining or improving writing skills can contact **West Virginia Writers, Inc.** Members receive a quarterly newsletter listing upcoming events, workshops, and conferences. Articles contain hints, opportunities, and more for the aspiring and professional writer. Write to:

> West Virginia Writers, Inc.
> P.O. Box 5205, Charleston, WV 25361

Appendix III

Mountain State Stories Of The People

Our Great-Grandchildren: Our Grandchildren: Our Children:

*Some of my family's history is preserved in this book.
See pages(s): _____*

Appendix III

Who's Who

My Name

- My Father
  - My Grandfather
    - My Great-Grandfather
    - My Great-Grandmother
  - My Grandmother
    - My Great-Grandfather
    - My Great-Grandmother
- My Mother
  - My Grandfather
    - My Great-Grandfather
    - My Great-Grandmother
  - My Grandmother
    - My Great-Grandfather
    - My Great-Grandmother

Tips

Fill in as much information as you can. A little is better than none at all.

Beneath each name list the dates and locations of the person's birth and death.

Use women's maiden names.

Modify this form to accommodate siblings, step-children and step-parents.

Spouse

- Spouse's Father
  - Spouse's Grandfather
    - Spouse's Great-Grandfather
    - Spouse's Great-Grandmother
  - Spouse's Grandmother
    - Spouse's Great-Grandfather
    - Spouse's Great-Grandmother
- Spouse's Mother
  - Spouse's Grandfather
    - Spouse's Great-Grandfather
    - Spouse's Great-Grandmother
  - Spouse's Grandmother
    - Spouse's Great-Grandfather
    - Spouse's Great-Grandmother

Index

A

Abbott
  Wilson **83**
Accurso
  Riccardo 99
Adams
  Anna 146
  Anna Mae 146
  Dianna **146**
  Freeman 146
  Harriet 156
  Troy 156
Adamston Junior High School 107
Adkins
  Ashley <u>150</u>
  Brittany Nicole 145
  Jessica 158
  Kenneth 145
  Tammy 145
Afflictions
  Alzheimer's Disease 106, 126–127
  Black lung 155
  Blindness 33, 43
  Burns 157–158
  Cancer 153–154, 160
  Deafness 110
  Dyslexia 34–35
  Illnesses 22, 25–26
    Children 59, 82
  Injuries 33, **156**
  Learning disability 34–35
Albright 110
Alderson 35
Alderson Baptist Junior College 152
Alderson-Broaddus College 139
Aldridge
  Amanda Ann 145
  Clarence Edward 145
  Roy 145
  Teresa 145
  Wilma Jean 145
Allen
  Alta 78
  George 78
  Roberta Eleanor. *See* Escue
Alma 14
Alta **78**
Alzheimer's Disease. *See* Afflictions

Ambler
  Eliza 34
Amick **60**
Amma 27
Ancestors. *See* Family
Anderson
  Geneva. *See* Wynne
Anger. *See* Emotions
Animals. *See also* Pets
  Bear 57–58, 69–70, 145
  Cat 80–81
  Cow 145, 153
  Deer 23-24, 148, 151
  Dog 12
    Hunting <u>12</u>, 152
  Fox 152
  Horse 36–37
  Mountain lion **148**
  Mule 147
  Panther 56–57
  Pig 82
  Rabbit 157–158
  Rattlesnake 152
  Skunk 105
  Squirrel 110
Anniversary. *See* Life events
Anthony
  Cynthia 158
  Joe 158
  Jonathan Edgar <u>157</u>, 158
Antietam 85
Appalachia. *See* Places
Arbanas
  Charles E. 55
Arizona
  Sedona 83
Arnold
  Mabel Virginia 118
Arriving. *See* Newcomer
Arthurdale 103
Asbury-Blue Sulphur 152
Ashley
  Katie 27
Athens 84, 89
Atkisson
  Alfred 153
  Mary 153
Auctions. *See* Recreation
Aunt. *See* Family
Austin
  Juanita. *See* Basham
Austria 27
Automobiles. *See* Vehicles
Autumn. *See* Seasons

Auvil
  Alexis <u>132</u>
  Ben 132
  Ed 120
  Jay 132
  Tonya. *See* Gripper
Avondale 16

B

Babysitting. *See* Occupations
Bailey
  Kenneth, Captain 48
Bainbridge
  Helen Rosella Martin <u>33–34</u>
  Richard C. 34, 78, 85
Baker
  Dulcie **152**
Baking. *See* Skills
Baldwin
  Daniel Whittington 150
  Travis **150**
Baptism. *See* Life events
Barker
  Eamon 145
  Eva <u>160</u>
  Gladys <u>160</u>
  Jerry 145
  Leva Whitt 160
  Lynne 145
  Noah 160
  Norman <u>160</u>
  Orville <u>160</u>
  Ruby. *See* Ratliff
Barkey
  Mildred 35
Barn. *See* Places
Barnes
  Denver 67
  Dewey 67
  I. A., Rev. 138
Bartrum
  Dr. 68
Baseball. *See* Sports
Basham
  Juanita Austin Dove Shepard Eades Eads Lilly **77-78**
Basketball. *See* Sports
Basnettsville Methodist Church 123
Bavaria 62
Bear. *See* Animals; Pets
Bearsville 13

Beauty. *See* West Virginia
Beck
  Lucille Monfradi 33
Beckley 34, 71
Beech Run Hill 110
Behner
  Mary. *See* Christopher
Belington 132
Bell Creek 85
Belle (WV) 40
Belva 78
Bennett
  Annary 55
  Billy <u>55</u>, 66
  Judith Drumpus 108
  Samuel **55–56**
Berries. *See* Food
Beverly 91
Bickford
  Albert 104
  Alice. *See* Farley
Bicycling. *See* Recreation
Big Cabell Creek 52
Big Creek 146
Big Laurel Creek 69
Birth. *See* Life events
Birthday. *See* Life events
Blackberries. *See* Food
Blackdamp 79
Blair 145
Blair's Ridge 12
Blake
  Bertha <u>52</u>
  Haze <u>52</u>
  Jim <u>52</u>
Blandville 125
Blindness. *See* Afflictions
Blizzard. *See* Disasters
Bloomingrose 31
Bluefield 33, 79, 84, 150
Bluestone River 82
Boggs
  Henry C. **23–24**
Bolyard
  Charley 120
  Eldora. *See* Nuzum
  Georgia Ellen Deavers **126–127**
  Roy Everett 127
Booger Hole 51
Boot Jack 120
Borror
  Barbra 89
Bosnia 47

Name in bold indicates "Author" • Page number in bold indicates "Featured" • Underlined page number indicates "Photo"

Bostics 60
Bowden
    Margaret 31
Bowles
    Earlie Iman **38–39**
Bowling
    Casey Maran 153
    Emmie Low Brown **152–153**
    Rick 153
    Tammy 153
Boyles
    Clyde <u>79</u>
    Velva 79
Brace
    Priscilla H. Escue 45
Bracy
    Sarah 130
Brake
    Elizabeth Weatherholt 72
Brawley's Hollow 31
Brawner
    Dr. 67
Bread. *See* Food
Breitmeier
    David 19
    Evelyn Reynolds. *See* Carr
    John 19
    Thomas 19
Brewer
    Grace 103
    Okey 103
Broaddus College 120
Brohard 23
Brooks 77
Brother. *See* Family
Brown
    Alice. *See* Juergens
    Charlie 58
    Clara 56
    Dudley <u>59</u>
    Elery 121
    Elizabeth Huff <u>59</u>
    Eugene <u>59</u>
    Everett 152
    Flavius Hugh, Sr. <u>59</u>
    Flavius, Jr. <u>59</u>
    Morrison <u>59</u>
    Paul <u>59</u>
    Pearl 58
    Robert <u>59</u>
    U. B. 127
    William <u>59</u>
Brownie camp 23
Browning Lambert Mountain 82
Brownton 6
Brumfield
    Dorothy 146
    Evelyn 145
    John 146
Bryant
    Christine 157
    Emma Wiseman **61**
    Ernie 157
    James Newcome 156
    Jarrod Russell 157
    Jennifer 146

    Ken <u>61</u>
    Nancy A. Huffman <u>61</u>
    Steven <u>61</u>
    Vonnie **156–157**
Buck
    Ed 63
    Pearl S. **86**
Buckhannon 72
Buffalo Hollow 47
Bull Fork 56, 67
Bunker Hill 45
Bunner
    Sandra 105
Burger
    Bettijane 119
Burgess
    C. R. 158
    Kendra 158
    Mary 158
Burial 12
Burk 129
Burke Mountain 83
Burlington 93
Burner
    Minnie Hoffman 139
Bush
    Carl "Doc" 66
    Gertrude 66
Butcher
    Annabelle 145–146
Butchersville 65
Butler
    Booze 58
    Gladys 58
Byrd
    Robert C. 55

C

Cabell
    Ethel <u>160</u>
Cabin. *See* Places
Cain Run 126
Caldwell
    Ralph 52
    Ted 52
California 61
Calud 120
Calvert
    David Darwin 117
Camp
    Gillie. *See* Willis
    John, Sr. 128
    Ulysses 128
Camp Creek School 158
Camp Run Hollow 5
Camp Valley School 138
Campbell
    George 120
    Howard 120
    Iva Margaret. *See* Taylor
    Kathryn 32
Campbells Creek 38
Camping. *See* Recreation
Cancer. *See* Afflictions
Candy. *See* Foods
Cannelton 48

Canning. *See* Skills
Canvas 61, 148
Caperton
    Gaston 34–35
    Gaston, Gov. 47
    W.G. 34–35
Carpendale 95
Carpenter
    Jan. *See* Parker
    Mary Roseatha 139
    Missy. *See* McKeny
    Phyllis J., SAC 104
    Vivian Tichner 104
    W. E. 73
    William H. 104
Carpenter's Fork 57
Carpentry. *See* Occupations
Carr
    Dora Foster 38
    Evelyn Reynolds Breitmeier 19
    Gladys <u>38</u>
    John L 38
    June <u>38</u>
    Osie <u>38</u>
Carroll
    Glenna 79
    Leatha Stonestreet 50
Carte
    Brantie 58
    Hattie 58
Carter
    Bertha Inez 32
    Hairm Jackson 32
    Harry Leroy 32
    Kennard 147
    Lillie Mae 32
    Lori Workman 147
    Shelly Marie Bell 147
Cary
    John **80–81**
    Mary 81
Cassville 109, 111
Cassville Hollow 109
Cat. *See* Animals; Pets
Cavallero
    Nicki 82
Cavendish
    Bonnie 58
    Lura 58
Cedar Creek 85
Centuries
    19th. *See* Life
    20th. *See* Life
Ceramics. *See* Skills
Ceredo 47
Champe
    Carrie Jo. *See* Huffman
Chapman
    Ella 58
    Elva <u>52</u>
    George 58
Chapmanville 146, 147, 148, 150, 151, 152, 153, 154, 155, 156, 157, 160
Character. *See* Characteristics
Characteristics

Charitable 31–32
    Determined 33, 34–35, 48–49, 51, 59, 62-63, 77, 99–100, 119–120, 128-129, 152
    Generous 11, 31–32, 43–44, 44, 65–69, 86, 130–131
    Hard working 5–7, 11, 13, 22, 25–26, 35–36, 39, 41–42, 85, 89–90, 95, 107–108, 114–115, 125–126, 128-129, 148, 150 -151, 152, 153–154, 156
    Helpful 35–36
    Heroic 117–118, 153–154
    Honorable 122–123
    Imaginative 23–24, 36
    Insightful 77, 123–124
    Instinctive 148
    Loyal 51, 62–63
    Mischievous 80, 89, 107–108, 150, 158–159, 159–160
    Naive 91
    Patient 56, 91–92
    Proud 49, 51, 78, 85, 99, 130–131
    Religious 11, 25–26
    Resourceful 20–21, 23–24, 36, 37–38, 57–58, 69–70, 80, 156
    Respected 49, 52, 65, 124–125, 132–138
    Self reliant 11, 32–33, 43, 55–56, 59, 85, 89–90
    Strong 22, 59, 123–124
    Tolerant 60, 109–110
Charity. *See* Characteristics
Charles Town 100, 123
Charleston 27, 28, 31, 33, 35, 37, 38, 39, 40, 43, 44, 58, 62, 95, 150, 155
Cheat Mountain 94
Cheerful. *See* Characteristics
Chelyan 31
Cherry River 62, <u>**64**</u>
Chief Logan Park 160
Children. *See* Family
China 86
Christmas. *See* Holidays
Christopher
    David 118
    Mary Behner 118
Church. *See also* History 114, 127–128, 138–139
    Anniversary 111–112
Church Hollow 82
City. *See* History; Life
Civil War. *See* Wars
Clarksburg 107, 117
Clay
    Bessie 145
Clayton

INDEX

Fred 120
Cleavenger 5
Clendenin 37, 71
Cleveland 5
Clinchfield 5
Clothing 14, 44, 84
Coal
   Mines. *See also* Disasters 155
   Mining **5–7**, 39, 79, 155
   Strikes 46
Coal camp. *See* Life
Cobb
   Howard 114
Coco 153
Coffman
   Carla 57
   Clager 120
   George 120
   Larry 57
   Lula. *See* Sturm
   Mona 57
   Terry 57
Colebank 120
   George 120
Collins
   Anthony Dale 159
   Avery 160
   Elda 160
   Elmer 160
   Elva 160
   Joshua 159
   Mildred 160
   Willard 160
Colorado
   Boulder 93
Combs
   Pearl 120
Community
   Sense of 12–13, 25, 42, 65–69, 108–109, 109–110, 111, 111–112, 129, 130–131
   Service 133–134
   Values 5–7, 55, 65–69
Company store. *See* Life
Comstock
   Jim 63, 86
Concern. *See* Emotions
Conflict. *See* Emotions
Conley
   Ray 125
Conn
   Elizabeth 127
   Rufus 127
Connecticut 31
Consolidated Coal 106
Cook
   Patricia 131
Cooper
   Asa 67
   Reta 66, 67
Coopers Rock State Forest 124, 130, 131
Coplin

Dr. 23
Corbett
   Maxine 63, 64
Corder
   L. G. 132
   Lacoa 132
Corinth 120
Corkrean
   Nell C. 81
Corn meal. *See* Food
Cornwell
   Floyd 120
   Howard 120
Corra
   Norabelle Shuman 123
Cottle
   Bernard H. 58
   Dennet 58
   Emmett 58
   Marie 58
   Mary Sue Taylor 58
   Rilla 58
Coulter 58
Counties
   Kentucky
      Floyd 146
   Other
      Culpepper 51
   Pennsylvania
      Bucks 86
   Virginia
      Berkeley 45
   West Virginia
      Barbour 5–7, 114–115, 117–118, 119, 120, 132, 138–139
      Boone 31–32, 32, 38, 40–41, 41, 41–42, 157
      Braxton 24, 50, 56, 57
      Cabell 24, 43, 51, 52, 62
      Calhoun 68
      Clay 24, 69, 70–71
      Doddridge 14, 73, 125–126
      Fayette 33, 58, 78, 81, 84–85, 85–86
      Gilmer 55, 55–56, 56 65–69
      Greenbrier 24, 51, 73, 80–81, 119, 149, 152
      Hampshire 89, 89–90
      Harrison 73, 107–108, 114, 116–117, 117, 131–132
      Jackson 19, 22, 24
      Jefferson 99, 99–100
      Kanawha 24, 31, 32–33, 33, 33–34, 35-35, 36, 36 - 37, 37, 37–38, 38, 38–39, 39, 39–40, 42, 43, 44, 45, 45–48, 48–49, 49, 50–51, 145, 148, 150, 153, 154, 155, 157, 158-159, 159
      Lewis 65, 72–73
      Lincoln 156

Logan 43–44, 44, 47, 126, 145, 145–146, 146-147, 147, 148, 149, 150, 151, 152, 152-153, 153-154, 154, 154-155, 155, 156, 156-157, 157, 157-158, 158, 159, 160
Marion 103, 104, 105-106, 106, 122, 123, 132-138
Marshall 12–13, 13
Mason 24, 51
McDowell 82, 83
Mercer 79, 79–80, 82, 82–83, 84, 85, 86
Mineral 89, 93, 95
Monongalia 108–109, 109, 109–110, 111, 111-112, 112–114, 115–116, 118–119, 119-120, 120-122, 123, 123-124, 124-125, 125, 127-129, 129–130, 130-131, 133
Monroe 83–84
Nicholas 51, 56–57, 57-58, 58, 59, 60, 60-61, 61, 62-63, 64, 69-70, 71, 71-72, 148, 159-160
Pendleton 92–93
Pleasants 24
Pocahontas 95–96
Preston 103, 103–104, 104–105, 110, 110–111, 116, 124, 129, 131
Putnam 36, 37, 48, 51, 62
Raleigh 43, 83
Randolph 90–91, 91, 91–92, 93–94, 94–95, 95
Ritchie 22–23, 23, 24, 27–28
Roane 23–24, 24, 24–25, 27
Summers 77, 77–78, 78
Taylor 105, 122–123, 125, 126-127
Tucker 120
Tyler 13–16
Wayne 24
Webster 24, 51, 62, 94
Wetzel 11, 12, 16
Wood 19, 20, 20–21, 22, 24, 25, 25–26, 26-27
Wyoming 79, 80
Country. *See* Life
Courageous.
   See Characteristics
Cove Creek 126
Cove District High School **120**
Cove Run 120
Cow. *See* Animals
Cow Creek 147

Cox
   Andrew Taylor 50
   Benjamin Dorsey 50
   Frank 127
   Gene 31
   Henry 127
   James Ranson 50
   Stephen William 50
Craigsville 69
Cranberry Glades 63
Cranberry River 62
Crawley 119
Crawley Creek 145
Crisp
   Vena **150**
Criss
   Charlie 104
   Minnie 104
Crites Mountain 56
Crook
   Elizabeth Ann "Annie" Eades 78
Cross Lanes 127
Crosslanes 24
Crupperneck 51
Cunningham
   Audrey 67
   Bill 67
   Connie 44
   Daniel Webster **44**
   Marie 66
   Stan **44**
Customs
   Marriage 103–104
   Separation of boys and girls 150
Cyfers
   David 151
   Seth 151
   Virginia 151

D

Dadisman
   JoAnn Danks 103
Dailey
   Commie 52
   Ethel 52
   Jasper 52
Danks
   JoAnn. *See* Dadisman
Danville 41
Darnell
   John Albert **117–118**
Darnell Hollow 118
Davis
   Alma 19
   Amoret Coralee 28
   Arthur 19
   Donna Ellen Smith 28
   Eloise. *See* Warfield
   George Orville 25–26
   Jerry 26
   Maw 39
   Thelma. *See* Nolan
Davis Run 14
Davy

Name in bold indicates "Author" • Page number in bold indicates "Featured" • Underlined page number indicates "Photo"

Freeda 89–90
  Robert 90
Dawson
  Addie **69**
Deafness. *See* Afflictions
Deahl
  Jasper 120
Death. *See* Life events
Deavers
  Georgia Ellen. *See* Bolyard
Deer. *See* Animals
Deitz
  Elizabeth Murray 60
DeKalb 55, 56, 65
Delaware 44
Dempsey
  Luther 156
  Thelma 156
Denial. *See* Emotions
Dennison
  Agnes. *See* Haller
Depression, The. *See* Life
Derby
  Kenneth Paul 134
Determination.
  See Characteristics
Dial
  Wylene 94
Dialect. *See* West Virginia
Dilley
  Rachael. *See* Sharp
Dingess
  Amanda Kay 148
  Harold 151
  Irene Spry 154–155
  Jennifer 151
  John David 151
  Lucy **148**
Disasters
  Blizzard 71–72, 112
  Flood 58
    Buffalo Hollow 47
    Williamson 47
  Mine 105–106, 155
    Fire 5–7
  Tornado 116
Discipline 52
Discrimination 6
Diseases. *See* Afflictions
Ditcher. *See* Occupations
Dobra 158
Doctor. *See* Occupations
Dodd
  Laura "Alice". *See* Samples
Dodds
  Gideon S. 128
Dog. *See* Animals; Pets
Donaldson
  Bruce 63
Dooley
  Maria 63
Dorsey
  L. Richard, II 36
Dove
  Juanita Austin. *See* Basham
Downey
  Leslie Florence McCauley
111
Drake
  Phyllis 159
  Roy 159
Drumpus
  Judith. *See* Bennett
Dry Creek 83
Duckworth
  Brandon 149
  Erin 149
  Leigh Ann 149
Duffield
  Jeffery 149
Dunbar 32, 33
Duskey
  Sandra. *See* Hanshaw
Dyslexia. *See* Afflictions

E

Eades
  Elizabeth Ann "Annie". *See*
    Crook
  Juanita Austin Dove
    Shepard. *See* Basham
Eads
  Juanita Austin Dove
    Shepard Eades. *See*
    Basham
  Margaret Louise. *See*
    Temple
  Monroe Darrow 78
Easter. *See* Holidays
Eatons 19
Education 20, 22, 43–44,
  56, 57, 84, 119–120,
  120, 129–130,
  152, 158. *See also*
    Occupations; School;
    Schoolhouse
Edwards
  Gary, Rev. 139
Ekis
  Barbara 120
Eldridge
  Carrie 51
Elizabeth 23
Elk Lick Creek 153
Elkins 90, 127
Elliott
  Jane 23
  Robyn. *See* Lindamood
Ellis Fork 55
Ellis Island 27
Ellyson
  Avon 66
  Kim 68
  Ruth 68
Emelene
  John 48
Emerson
  Rita 27
Emmons 48
Emotions
  Conflict 81, 86
  Excitement 64, 93,
    108–109, 110, 111
Fear 38–39, 40–41,
  150, 152, 152–153, 156
Friendship 43, 90–91,
  105, 115–116, 124–125
Fun 64, 157
Grief 5–7, 12, 154
Happiness 36, 83–84,
  93, 146–147, 148, 151
Hope 43–44, 92–93, 99–100
Loneliness 104–105
Love 12, 24, 33–34,
  48, 49, 50–51,
  59, 77, 105–106, 112–114,
  118–119, 124–125,
  126–127, 130, 131,
  132, 132–138, 148
Pride 132
Romance 19, 24, **112–
  114**, **114**, 120–122
Sadness 33–34, 35–36,
  105–106, 106, 126–127,
  153–154, 158
Satisfaction 12
Security 38–39, 50–51
England
  Archies 120
  Beulah 139
  Bud 139
  Harry 120
Engle
  Henry Everett 68
Era. *See* Life
Erb
  Kathryn Leigh 158
Escue
  Buell B. 45
  Deborah 19
  Eleanor 45
  Norris 45
  Priscilla H.. *See* Brace
  Roberta Eleanor Allen 36
Ethel 160
Evans
  Rawley 127
Evans Ferry 127
Evans-Thomas
  Charleen 125
Everhart
  Aida J. Mainella 105-106
Everly
  Lillie **110–111**
  Thurman **110–111**
Excitement. *See* Emotions
Extension Homemakers
  Belles 19, **26–27**

F

Fairmont 103, 106, 121, 133
Fairview 104, 123
Family. *See also*
  History; Stories
  Ancestors 31, 44, **51**,
    55–56, 147, 153
  Aunt 83–84, **91–92**, 123–124
  Brother 25
  Children 36, **42**
Daughter 71–72
Father 12, 13, 19, 22,
  25, 33, 35–36, 38–39,
  52, 79, 82–83, 105–106,
  107–108, 116–117,
  117–118, 119–120,
  148, 150, 152, 154,
  159-160
Father-in-law 27
Grandchildren **132**
Grandfather 23–24, 27–28,
  40-41, 41–42, 48, 49,
  56-57, 69–70, 81, 85,
  95, 145, 146-147, 153–154,
  157-158
Grandmother 23, 32–33,
  41, 60, 62, 77, 81,
  89, 93, 115–116,
  126–127, 145, 145–146,
  146, 147, 148, 149, 152,
  153–154, 154, 154–155,
  156, 156–157, **157**
Grandparents
  19, **39**, 111, 150–151, 153
Great-grandfather 155
Great-grandmother
  145, 150, 156, 160
Heritage 41, **51**, 95–96,
  104, 119, 123
Interdependence 5–7,
  20, 39–40, 85–86,
  124–125, **132-138**,
  154–155
Mother 11, 13–16, 20,
  23, 31–32, 32, 33–34,
  38, 57, 59, 61, 69,
  77–78, 106, 107–108,
  124–125, 146
Parents 120–122
Reunion 78, 150
Siblings 107–108, 120–122
Sister 38
Son **21**
Uncle 83–84, 151, 159–160
Values 35–36, 38, 50–51,
  51, 55–56, 59, 71,
  77–78, 130–131, 131–132,
  132–138
Farfsing
  Beverly 114
Farley
  Alice Bickford 104–105
  Donald 105
  Kristin 146
Farm. *See* Life
Farmington 106
Farrow Hill 19
Father. *See* Family
Fear. *See* Emotions
Feed sacks 14, 107, 115–116
Feelings. *See* Emotions
Fekete
  Clarissa Nicole 146
Fellowsville 104
Ferguson
  Grace **89**
Ferrell

INDEX

Maude. *See* McMillan
Ottie May **13–16**
Peggy June. *See* Smith
Sam **13–16**
Festivals 26–27, 62–63, 93, 120–122
Fetterman District 125
Fire. *See* Disasters
Fitzsimmons
  Juanita 13
Fitzwater
  Becky 58
  Billy 58
  James P. 138
  Preston 71
Flatts Elementary School 130
Fleming
  Dolores 128
  Jack 82
Fling
  Rugie. *See* McGee
Flood. *See* Disasters
Florida 24
  Deltona 39
  Ocala 39
  Vero Beach 37
Fluharty
  Billie 15
Folklore 32–33, 69. *See also* Stories
Food
  Berries 145, 157
  Blackberries 57–58
  Bread **37**
  Corn meal 154
  Lunches 149
  Mulberries 103
  Mushrooms
    Molliemunchers **147**
  Other 19, 39, 107–108, 125
  Preserving 11, 152–153
Ford
  George 120
Forks of Elk 51
Forman
  John 103
Forren
  Virginia. *See* Hudson
Fort Beeler 13
Fortney
  Willis 104
Fortney's Mill 103
Foster
  Matthew 155
Four-H (4-H) 72–73, 130
Fox. *See* Animals
Fox
  Albert 115
  Dot 115
France 33, 117
Freedom 27
Freeman
  Claud 120
  Leo 120
French and Indian War. *See* Wars
Friend

L. L. 120
Friendship. *See* Emotions
Frye
  Catherine Sue 39
  Zella 120
Frymier
  Gladys 67
Fun. *See* Emotions

G

Gad 58
Gainer
  French 127
  Patrick, Dr. 67
Gallagher 33
Galloway 5
Gamoca 33, 78
Gancs
  John 157
Garden. *See* Places
Gardening. *See* Skills
Garland
  Todd 62
Garrett
  Lema 150–151
  Tom 150–151
Garten
  Bada Lee. *See* Parkins
Garwood
  Haley Elizabeth 111
Gassaway High School 57
Gauley Bridge 33, 78, 85
Gear
  Macel G. Pickens 94, 95
Geary
  Blanche **109–110**
Generations. *See* Family; Life
Generosity. *See* Characteristics
George
  Ruth Gaynell Morgan **11**
  Taylor 120
George's Run 15
Germany 50
Getschman
  Bob 6
Ghost. *See* Stories
Gibson
  Gertrude Elizabeth. *See* Rumble
Gift 33–34, **44**
Gilchrist
  Charles 73
  Joy 73
Giles
  Alice 121
Glade Run 138
Gladesville 103
Glenville 26, 55
Gluck
  Joe 67
Godwin
  Barney 120
  John D. 138
Goff
  Daisy 51
Goke Hollow 116

Good old days. *See* Life; Nostalgia
Gore
  Ashley D. 147
  Cathy 147
  Danny 147
  Gary 147
  Harvey **147**
  Jilleyn Gabrielle 147
  Katrina 147
Gould
  Janet 86
Graduation. *See* Life events
Grafton 117, 122, 123, 125, 127
Grandchildren. *See* Family
Grandfather. *See* Family
Grandmother. *See* Family
Grandparents. *See* Family
Grantsville 68
Gratitude **44**, 56, 57, 129–130, 132
Great Britain 45
Great-grandparents. *See* Family
Greenbrier River Trail 149
Gregory
  Jack 37
  Martha 37, 39
Greynolds
  Grant 66
Grief. *See* Emotions
Griffith
  Edith Parker 21
Grimm
  Ann Sams 27
Gripper
  Eddie 132
  Tonya Auvil 132
Grove 126
Gumbert
  George 133
  Lucinda. *See* Pefley
Guns 44, 110, 145, 148, 151
Guyandotte River 147, 154
Gwyn
  Jesse 121

H

Hackney
  Al **43**
Hadden
  Mary 72
Haiti 47
Hale
  Hattie **43–44**
Hall
  Polly **147**
Hallard
  Jesse 128
Haller
  Agnes Dennison 120
Halloween. *See* Holidays
Hanna
  Joe 58
  Lora 58

Mark 58
Pauline 58
Hanshaw
  Damon 72, 148
  Sandra Duskey 72
  Sandy 148
  Whitney Nicole 71–72, 148
  Zachary Damon 72, **148**
Hant 57
Happiness. *See* Emotions
Harbour
  Clarice "Kate" Kirtley 62
Hard working. *See* Characteristics
Hardin
  Andrew 120
  Andrew S. 120
  Clay 120
  Florence 120
  N. C. "Tobe" 120
Hardman
  Asa. *See* Maxwell
  Earl 67
  Elizabeth 66
  Karl 67
  Lona 67
  Virginia 39
Hardship 11, 114–115, 129, 146
Hare
  Zillah 66
Harmony Grove 127
Harmony Grove Church 127-129
Harmony Grove School 127-129
Harper's Ferry 113
Harris
  Theodore F. 86
Harrison
  Pearl 160
Harrisville 22, 23
Hartley
  Charlie 72, 130
  Ruth 130
Hartman
  Edward 89
Harts 146, 151, 155, 156
Harts Creek 146
Hastings 11
Hatfield
  Ellison 44
Hatfield-McCoy feud 44
Hathaway
  Clerissa 121
Hawaii 134
Hawk's Nest 31
Hay 70–71
Haying. *See* Old methods
Headlee
  Ruth Kiger **123–124**
Heaster
  Dale 120
  Emmett 119–120
Heflin

Name in bold indicates "Author" • **Page number in bold indicates "Featured"** • **Underlined page number indicates "Photo"**

Harry B. 67
Heim
  Colene 27, 57
  Fred **27**
  Jim 27
  Mary 27
Heirloom 44, 62
Helms
  Cathy A. Sizemore 84
Helpful. *See* Characteristics
Henlawson 160
Hensley
  Malindia 149
Henson
  Andy 158–159
Hensons 158
Heritage. *See* Family; West Virginia
Heroic. *See* Characteristics
Hewitt
  Mike 63
Hill
  Kay Young 22
Hills. *See* West Virginia
Hinkle
  Phyllis 61
Hinkle Mountain 62
Historic landmark. *See* Places
History *See also*
    Family; Stories; West Virginia
  Church 127-129, 138–139
  City 62–63
  Family 13–16, 34–35, 44, 48, 55–56
  School 120
  West Virginia 31, 58, 72–73
Hoffman
  Amelia 139
  E. F. 139
  Grannele 139
  Isaac 139
  J. N. 139
  Jacob 139
  John 139
  Jonas 139
  Minnie. *See* Burner
  R. G. 139
  Robert 139
  Sanford 139
  Stingley 139
Holbert 104
Holden 154
Holidays
  Christmas 16, 33–34, 41–42, 81, **134–138**, 155, 160
    Tree **82–83**
  Easter 16
  Halloween **131–132**
  Memorial Day **122–123**
  Thanksgiving 82
Hollow. *See* Places
Home. *See* Family; Places; West Virginia
Home brew 129
Home remedies

11, 19, 82, 157–158
Homecoming. *See* West Virginia
Honest. *See* Characteristics
Honor. *See* Characteristics
Hope. *See* Emotions
Horse. *See* Animals
Hospitality. *See* Characteristics
Hotel. *See* Places
House. *See* Places
Hovatter
  Walter 120
Howdershelt
  Dow 120
Howe
  Barbara 128
Howery
  Fletcher 31
  John L. 31
Hoxter
  Tawny Layman 115
Huber
  Frances. *See* Kiefer
Hudson
  Virginia Forren 81
Huff
  Elizabeth. *See* Brown
Huffman. *See also* Hoffman
  Carrie Jo Champe 61
  Henry A. 61
  Nancy A. *See* Bryant
Hugarts 58
Hugh Dingess Elementary 146, 148
Hughes
  Christina O'Dell **85–86**
  Francis Tincher 85
  Michael 86
  Robert **85–86**
Hughes River 126
Humor. *See* Stories
Humphrey
  Hugh 120
Humphreys
  S. T. 139
Hungary 5, 159
Hunting 12, **23–24,** 110, 119, 149, **151, 152,** 157-158
Huntington 32
Hurricane 36, 48, 51
Hutchinson
  Bernard Lee 133-137
  Brooks Swearingen 133–137
  Claude Effington 133–137
  Clyde Effington 133–137
  Diane. *See* Parker
  Elaine 134
  Frank Ehlen 133–137
  Harold Herbert 133–137
  James Jeremiah 133–137
  Lyda Watkins 133–137
  Paul Mason 133-137
  Ray Pefley 133–138, 135, 138
  Robert Jay 133–137
  Sylvia Jane 134

Huttonsville 94

I

Ice man. *See* Occupations
Ice skating. *See* Recreation
Idaho
  Boise 133
  Lapwai 82
Illnesses. *See* Afflictions
Imagination.
  See Characteristics
Immigrants. *See* Newcomer
Impulsive. *See* Characteristics
Independence 103. *See also* Characteristics
Industry. *See* Occupations; West Virginia
Ingenuity. *See* Characteristics
Injuries. *See* Afflictions
Ink making. *See* Old methods
Insight. *See* Characteristics
Islands Branch 148
Isner
  George 120
  John 120
Iuka 13

J

Jackson
  Bondolyn. *See* Pierce
  Butsy **19**
  Daddy Bob **19**
  Edward 72
  Margaret 23
  Marsha **23**
  Thomas J. "Stonewall" 72
Jackson's Mill 72–73
Jacobson
  Elizabeth 59
James
  Isa. *See* Somerville
  Janet 66
Jamison
  George 127
Japan 34
Jarrett
  Zella 40–41
Jarvis
  Phyllis Williams 48, 51, 71
  Sally 27
Jeffrey
  Gary Lee 156
  Gary Lee, Sr. 156
  Lettie 156
Job's Temple 55
Johnson
  Erica 154
  Janet 154
  John 154
Jolliffe
  Anna 127
Jones
  Gary 148
  Joshua William 148
  Judith 148

Jordansville 65
Journalism. *See* Occupations
Joy. *See* Emotions
Juergens
  Alice Brown 59

K

Kanawha City Elementary 62
Kanawha Valley 39
Kansas 84
  Kansas City 105
Kasson High School 120
Kearneysville 113
Kearns
  Michael, Jr. 127
Keeney's Knob 152
Kendrick
  William "Teepi" 72
Kennedy
  Evelyn T. 112
  John F. 62
Kennison Mountain 63
Keslers Cross Lanes 58
Kessell
  Christina 153
Ketterman
  Beverly Sue 93
Kiefer
  Frances Huber 62
Kiger
  Jane H. **124–125**
  Patricia. *See* Morgan
  Ruth. *See* Headlee
Kindness. *See* Characteristics
King
  Dorothea Cyrena Rumble 120–122
  James B. 58
  Vanden **120–122**
Kingwood 47
Kirtley
  Clarice "Kate". *See* Harbour
Knotts
  Jess 127
Knowledge. *See also* Skills
  Practical 32–33, 116–117
Korean War. *See* Wars
Kramer
  Charlotte 121
Kuhens
  Charles **12**
  Karen 12
Kump
  Governor 80
Kurucz
  Andy 5
  Andy, Jr. 5
  Deborah Lynn 5
  Donna Jean 5

L

Lake View School 152
Lambert
  Violet **156**
Language 93–94, 94–95

INDEX

Laundry. *See* Old methods
Laurel Point 111, 115
Law. *See* Occupations
Lawman. *See* Occupations
Layman
   Becky Straight 115
   Tawny. *See* Hoxter
Layman School 122
Layton
   Newt 38
Learning disability. *See* Afflictions
Leaving. *See* West Virginia
Lee
   Robert E., Gen. 95
Leeson 107
Legends. *See* West Virginia
Lesson 19, 21, 23, 32–33, 36–37, 41, 43–44, 49, 56, 59, 60, 92–93, 106, 109–110, 116–117, 119–120, 123–124
Lewellen
   Marge Waggy 67
   Steve 67
Lewis
   N. J. 100
Lewisburg 119
Ley
   C. W. 127
Lice 152
Lick Creek 152
Lick Run 126
Life. *See also* Nostalgia
   1870s 81
   1920s 31, 36, 104–105, 149, 150
   1930s 13, 20–21, 41–42, 58, 71, 84, 95, 114–115, 125–126, 129, 150
   1940s 11, 12–13, 20–21, 25, 89–90, 103–104, 107–108, 145–146
   1950s 39, 69–70, 103, 111, 118–119, 154
   1960s 24, 91
   Boom town 126
   Coal camp 5–7, 33–34, 82, **129**
   Depression, The 14, 41–42, 57, 84, 85, 114–115, 133
   Early 1900s 33–34, 55–56, 150–151
   Farm 11, 13, 25, 45, 55–56, 70–71, 83–84, 103, 107–108, 114–115, 120- 122, 123, 148, 150, 155, 158
   Late 1800s 147
   Rural 5–7, 19, 24, **25**, 32–33, **37–38**, 39, 40–41, 41–42, 60–61, 78, 89–90, 91, 103–104, 125–126, 146, 150–151, **156**, 156–157, 160
   Urban 118–119
Life events 50–51, 118–119

Anniversary 111–112
Baptism **24**
Birth 45, 71–72, 104
Birthday 61
Death 5–7, 12, 19, 22, 25, 26, 33, 35–36, 43, 65, 69, 80–81, 81, 104, 105–106, 115–116, 126–127, 153–154, **154**
Graduation
   High school 57
Marriage 90, 120–122
Starting school 56
Wedding 103–104, 114
Light
   Edward **153–154**
   Irene 153
Lilly
   Juanita Austin Dove Shepard Eades Eads. *See* Basham
   Kenneth Theadore <u>78</u>
   Tom 68
   Wilma Jean. *See* Rodes
Lindamood
   Alan 22-23
   Robyn Elliott <u>23</u>
Lindsey
   A. S. 120
Link
   Carrie 152
Linwood 95
Little Bingamon Creek 104
Little Tom's Fork 126
Litz
   Lucille. *See* Walthall
Loar
   Andy 120
   Lige 120
   Will 120
Locus Grove 120
Logan 153, 156
Lohr
   Benton 120
   Noble 120
   Strather 120
Loneliness. *See* Emotions
Loss. *See* Emotions
Loudin
   Joe 66
   Tom 66
Loughridge
   Earl 120
Love. *See* Emotions
Lover's Leap 31
Lowe
   Don <u>65</u>
Lower Run 11
Lucas
   Mabel 149
   Matt 149
Lumbering. *See* Occupations
Lutz
   Jacob 120
Lydick
   Tracy 68

Lye soap 145, 145–146, 147
Lye soap making. *See* Old methods
Lynch
   Cindy. *See* Shelton
   Dottie Ross 153
Lynchburg 85

M

Madison 41, 157
Mahaney
   Bill 66
   Mable 66
Mail delivery. *See* Occupations
Mainella
   Aida. *See* Everhart
   David, Sr. **105–106**
   Jeanette (Concetta E.) Stingo **106**
Mallett
   Barbara Parkins 49, 51
Man (WV) 145
Manley
   Katherine P. 44
Maren-Hogan
   Mesha 152
Market 126
Marks
   Richard 33
Markus
   Joe 91
   Michelle **90–91**
Marmet 31
Marquess 103
Marriage. *See* Life events
Marsh
   Betty 139
   Calvin 138
   Cleophas 120
   Floyd 139
   Gay 139
   Isaac 138
   John 138
   Kenneth 139
   Lenore 120
   Loyal 138
   Rotha 139
Marsh Fork District 83
Marshall
   Harold 21
   Mildred 21, 65
Martin
   Carl <u>34</u>
   Charles Perry 33
   Clarence <u>52</u>
   Dewey <u>34</u>
   Gertrude <u>52</u>
   Grace Kelley 33
   Helen. *See* Bainbridge
   Howard <u>52</u>
   Ollie <u>52</u>
   Ruby <u>34</u>
   Ruth <u>34</u>
Martin Beulah 120
Martinka Coal Company 5
Martinsburg 45, <u>99</u>

Maryland 123
   Baltimore 33, 138
   Cumberland 95
   Massachusetts 45
   Springfield 32
Mathena
   Carolyn 82
   Lee **82**
Matlick
   Harold 104
   Mary Lee Shriver 104
Maxey
   Clyde 82
   Lois. *See* Rosenow
Maxwell
   Charles L. 55
   Ella 67
   Ella Woofter 55
   Janis 66
Maysville 93
McCauley
   Leslie Florence. *See* Downey
McClung
   Bronson 63
McClure
   Carla Thomas 38
McComas 82
   Jessie <u>52</u>
   Julia <u>52</u>
   Lizzie <u>52</u>
   Ruth <u>52</u>
McCormick
   Ferrell <u>52</u>
   Gladys <u>52</u>
McCoy 44
McDaniel
   Claris Mitchell 115
   L. S. 120
McGee
   Rugie Fling 66
McGhee
   William C. 80
McIntire
   John 138
McIntyre
   Pat 114
McKeny
   Chantil Lee <u>50</u>
   Kaylee Jane <u>49</u>
   Missy Carpenter <u>49</u>
   William T. <u>49</u>
McLaughlin
   Evelyn Eagle 69
McMillan
   Maude Ferrell <u>14</u>
McNeely
   Bridgett Alexandra 160
   Greg 160
   Rebecca 160
McQuain
   Charlie 31
Meathouse Fork 126
Media
   Elkins Inter-Mountain 126
   Logan Banner 145
   Moundsville Daily Echo **12–13**

Name in bold indicates "Author" • Page number in bold indicates "Featured" • Underlined page number indicates "Photo"

Medicine. *See* Occupations
Meeks
  Kara Brooke 155
Memorial Day. *See* Holidays
Memories. *See* Life; Nostalgia
Men. *See* Roles
Meredith
  Frances 36
  Frank **35–36**
  Ruth 35
Methodist Protestant Church 138
Mexican War. *See* Wars
Miceli
  Rebecca 44
Mick
  Stanley 139
Middle Patch 33
Middleborne 13
Midway School 38
Midwifery. *See* Occupations
Mifflin 159
Military. *See also* West Virginia
  Army 27, 153–154
  Army National Guard **45–48**
  Medal
    Purple Heart 117–118
Mill. *See* Places
Mill Creek 160
Mill Creek Grade School 160
Miller
  Betsy 160
  Bill 160
  Bradford 120
  Clifford 42
  Clyde 42
  Edgar Roe **157–158**
  Ivan 52
  John 120
  Lummie 42
  Pearl Todd 43
  Theodore 157
  William Crichton, III 160
Miller Hill 41
Millertown 42
Milling. *See* Old methods
Mining. *See*
    Coal; Life; Occupations
Mischief. *See* Characteristics
Mitchell
  Claris. *See* McDaniel
  Daisy Moats 114–115
  John 115
  Monzel 114–115
Mitchem Ridge 83
Moats
  Daisy. *See* Mitchell
  Ellis 120
  Isaac 6
Moatsville 120
Molasses making. *See* Old methods
Mondays 158
Money. *See* Prosperity
Monfradi
  Charlie 33
  Lucille. *See* Beck

Lucy 33
Monongah 104
Monongahela National Forest 91
Monongahela River 127
Monroe
  Brent 58
  Emma 58
Montgomery 34, 84
Montgomery Hill 25
Moonshine 14, 157
Moore
  Darlene 23
  Dorothy 129
  J. D. 82
  Lillie. *See* Richman
  Paul 155
  Ruthie **158**
Moran
  Margaret 121
Morgan
  Ben 127
  Evan 11
  Jeremiah 11
  Jerry 11
  Mary Waters 11
  Morgan 11, 45
  Patricia Kiger 124, 125
  Ruth Gaynell. *See* George
Morgan's Ridge 122
Morgantown 23, 59, 89, 93, 95, 104, 106, 109, 111, 115, 118, 119, 124, 127, 129, 130
Morgantown High School 90, 130
Morris
  Frances 61
  Susan 21
Mother. *See* Family
Moundsville 47
Mountain lion. *See* Animals
Mountain state. *See* West Virginia
Mountaineers. *See* West Virginia
Mountains. *See* West Virginia
Movies. *See* Recreation
Mt. Nebo 61
Mt. Olivet 138
Mt. View 120
Mud Fork 154
Mudlick School **20–21**
Mulberries. *See* Food
Mule. *See* Animals
Mullins
  Andrew 156
  Barbara. *See* Parsons
  James L. **85**
  Matthew 155
  Okey E. **69-70**
Murphy
  Artie 58
  Frank 58
Murphytown 19
Murray
  Elizabeth. *See* Deitz

Mushrooms. *See* Food
Music 71
  Shape notes 43

N

Napier 56
National Guard. *See* Military
National Register of Historic Places. *See* Places
Native Americans 51
Nature *See also* West Virginia 32, 37–38, 90–91
  Rocks 145
Nay-Hess 104
Neal
  Betty Walkup **81**
  Ester 81
  Everette 81
  Richard Benjamin **81**
  Troy 81
Nedrow
  Clarence E. **110**
  James Edward 110
  Lloyd A. 110
Nestorville United Methodist Church **138–139**
Nestor
  Bill 138
  Delmer 120
  Faye 120
  Fred 120
  George 138
  Hazel 120
  Hulda 138
  Jacob 138
  James S. 138
  John 120
  John W. 120
  Jonas 138
  Nellie 120
  William 138
Nestorville 120, 138
Nevada
  Las Vegas 91
New England 130
New Era School 22
New Hill 109
New Martinsville 12
New York 27, 35, 56, 91, 129
  Newburgh 117
Newcomer. *See* West Virginia
Newton 23
Nicholas County Fair 159
Nicholas County High School 58
Nida
  Ruth Ann 24
Nolan
  Mervin 20
  Thelma Davis 20
North Bend State Park 23
North Carolina 38
  Bolivia 70
  Charlotte 31, 138
  Salisbury 96
Nostalgia. *See also* Life

13, 19, 20, 22–23, 23, 25, 31, 36, 37–38, 39, 40–41, 42, 50–51, 60–61, 64, 65–69, 70–71, 71, 79–80, 80, 82, 82–83, 83–84, 91, 103, 107–108, 114–115, 118–119, 122–123, 123, 126, 126–127, 131–132, 145–146, 146, 146–147, 147, 149, 150, 150–151, 153, 156–157, 157, 158, 159–160, 160
Notter
  Russel 52
Nottingham
  Lowell 52
  Tom 52
Nutter
  Bob 25
Nutter Fort 126
Nuzum
  Eldora Bolyard 126

O

Occupations
  Babysitting 109–110
  Carpentry 85
  Coal mine owner 133–134
  Coal mining 5–7, 79, 105–106, 111
  Ditcher 6
  Ice man 129
  Journalism 12
  Law 133–134
  Lawman 44
  Lumbering 51, 147
  Mail delivery 94, **125–126**
  Medicine 59
  Midwifery 153
  Plumbing 35–36
  Pumper 15
  Railroad tie making **147**
  Repairman 25-26
  Sales **24**, 117
  Tailor 27
  Teaching 15, 22, 43–44, 52, 65, 84, 104–105
  Writing 86
O'Dell
  Christina. *See* Hughes
Ohio 152
  Akron 27, 70
  Gallipolis 52
  Marion 25
  Newark 56
Ohio River 22
Old methods
  Haying **13**
  Ink making 149
  Laundry **145–146**
  Lye soap making **145, 147**
  Milling 154
  Molasses making **60–61, 151**
  Shaving 27–28
Ona 52

INDEX

Organ (pump) 81
Osage 116
Osborne
   Danny R. 23
Outhouse. *See* Places
Overbaugh 58
Overbey
   Robert 80

P

Packsville 83
Paden City 16
Paint Creek 33, 58
Painting. *See* Skills
Pancake **89**
Panther. *See* Animals
Parade 122–123
Paradise 51
Parents. *See* Family
Parker
   Brett Russell 134
   Brooks Edward 134
   Diane Hutchinson 132, 134, 135
   Edith. *See* Griffith
   Jan Carpenter 134
   Paul Edward, III 134
   Paul Edward, Jr. 132, 134, 135
   Sylvia E. 135, 138
   William G. 27–28
Parkersburg 19, 25, 56, 123
Parkins
   Bada Lee Garten 49, 50
   Barbara. *See* Mallett
   Ralph Ranson 49
Parsons 104
   Barbara Mullins 70
Passion. *See* Emotions
Patience. *See* Characteristics
Patterson
   Malcolm "Pat" 40
   Sally L. 40, 42
Pawn shop 99
Peck
   Ned 154
Pecks Mill **154**, 157, 160
Peed
   Brooks Hutchinson 134
   George Pullen 134
   George Pullen, III 134
   Robert Fleming 134
Pefley
   Lucinda Gumbert 133
   Peter J. 133
   Ray. *See* Hutchinson
Pennsylvania 63, 139
   Harrisburg 19
   Philadelphia 105
   Pittsburgh 16, 109, 114, 138
   Washington 82
Pennsylvania State University 110
Pete Dalton Rock 149
Peters 125
Pets. *See also* Animals
   Bear 69–70
   Cat 80–81
   Dog 12, 157–158, **159**
   Skunk 105
Pettry
   James R. 83
Phares
   Sally A. 91, 92
Philippi 5, 115, 119, 120
Phillips
   Aaron 138
   Elijah 138
   Ruth 11
Phillips Run 58
Photographs 38, 145
Pickens
   Macel G. *See* Gear
Picklesimer
   Brandon John 154
   Margaret 154
   Mike 154
Picnics. *See* Recreation
Pierce
   Billie Marie. *See* Straight
   Bondolyn Jackson 115
   Charles 115
Pig. *See* Animals
Pinch 44, 154
Pine Grove 11
Pipestem 150
Pipestem State Park 157
Pity. *See* Emotions
Pitzer
   Laura F. *See* Ross
Places
   Appalachia **78**, 110–111
   Barn 42, **70–71**
   Birth place 61
   Cabin 50–51, **90–91**
   Church 55, 81, 111–112, 127–129, 138–139
   Company store 5–7, 156
   Garden 110–111
   Historic Landmark 138–139
   Historic Register 55, 127-129
   Hollow 31, 58
   Home 25, 86, 118–119, 134–138
   Hotel 126
   House **153**
   Mill 154
      Grist 72–73
   Outhouse 32, 89, 145, 158
   Restoration 61
   Road 104
   Sawmill 62–63
   School 43
   Swimming hole 64
Play. *See* Recreation
Plumbing. *See* Occupations
Poar
   Lea 52
Pocatalico 160
Poetry 24–25, 25–26, 78, 99, 99–100, 105–106, 123–124, 124–125
Polin

Melvin 120
Poling
   Belva 120
   Blanch 120
   Dora. *See* Wilson
   Roselee 120
Poor. *See* Poverty
Porto Rico 126
Poston
   Basil 52
   Everette 52
   Grace 52
   Wilford 52
Poverty 37–38, 41–42, 43–44, 44, 69, 99
Practical. *See* Knowledge
Prank. *See* Characteristics
Pratt
   Katie 41
Prayer **21**
Preserving food. *See* Food; Skills
Price
   Elmus G. 121
Pride. *See* Characteristics; Emotions; West Virginia
Princeton 41, 82, 84, 85
Procious 69
Prohibition 14
Prosperity 55–56, 134–138
Proud. *See* Characteristics
Proudfoot
   Clementa 139
Pt. Pleasant Baptist Church 6
Puerto Rico 44
Pullen
   George. *See* Peed
Pure. *See* Characteristics
Purgetsville 89
Pursglove 113
Puzzle Hole 51

Q

Queen
   Martha. *See* Spry
Quick
   Rose 38
Quilting. *See* Skills

R

Rabbit. *See* Animals
Radabaugh
   Bob 68
   Mary Ann 66, 69
Radio. *See* Technological advances
Rain 23, 70–71
Rainelle 31
Randolph
   Jennings 55
Randolph-Macon College 86
Rationing 125, 152–153
Ratliff
   Alex 160

Ruby Barker **160**
Rattlesnake. *See* Animals
Rawson
   Jim **91**
Recreation. *See also* Life; West Virginia
   Auctions **108–109**
   Bicycling **149**
   Camping 90–91, 157
   Ice skating 147
   Movies 80
   Picnics 19, **149**
   Play 5–7, 15, **22–23**, **36**, 42, 158
   Rock climbing 92–93
   Sleigh riding 146–147
   Socials 20–21, 121–122, 158
   Swimming 64, 90–91
Reedy Creek 24–25
Reinhart
   Minnie. *See* Ringgold
Religion. *See* Characteristics; Church
Repairman. *See* Occupations
Reppert
   Clarence 121
Resourcefulness. *See* Characteristics
Respected. *See* Characteristics
Restoration. *See* Places
Retirement. *See* West Virginia
Returning. *See* West Virginia
Reunion. *See* Family
Reynolds
   Charles Bonar 19
   Christiana 19
   Evelyn. *See* Carr
   George F. **19**
Reynoldsville 107
Rhodes
   Belva 57
   Lafe 56–57
Richman
   Lillie Moore 120
Richwood 60, **62–63**, 64, 69, 71
Riddle
   Ada 66, 68
   George B. 66
   Lucille 67
   Lyde 66
Ridenour 104
   John Wesley 139
Righman
   Albert 138
   Andrew 138
   Andrew Jackson 138
   Charles 138
   Clifford 119, 138
   Dana Ann Swartz 119
   Ethel Louise 118
   Jesse L. 138
   John Lee 120
   Louise 138
   Ronnie 139
Ringgold
   Minnie Reinhart 133

Name in bold indicates "Author" • Page number in bold indicates "Featured" • Underlined page number indicates "Photo"

Ripley 22
Risko
  Nancy 154
Ritter
  Harold 120
Roads. *See* Places;
    West Virginia
Roberts
  Linda 21
Robinson
  Anne 66, 68
Rock climbing. *See* Recreation
Rock Creek 41
Rockefeller
  Jay, Sen. 48–49
Rockenstein
  Anne 111
  Walter H., Rev. 111
Rodes
  David Austin 77
  Wilma Jean Lilly 77, 78
Rogers
  J. Therin 67
Rohrbough
  Nate 67
Roles
  Female 5–7, **26–27**
  Male 5–7, **36–37**
Romance. *See* Emotions
Romney 86, 123
Romney High School 90
Ronceverte 24
Rood
  Nora Alice 32
Roosevelt
  Franklin D. 85
Rose
  Alma 52
Rosenow
  Lois Maxey 83
Ross
  Dottie. *See* Lynch
  James 153
  Jerry O. 153
  Laura F. Pitzer **153**
Round town. *See* Sports
Roundhouse. *See* Sports
Roush
  Dewey Lee 37
  Hattie Pearl Short 37
  Herbert L., Sr. 26
  Lorena Mae. *See* Siders
Rowlesburg 104
Rumble
  Darlie Rebecca 120
  Dorothea Cyrena. *See* King
  Gertrude Elizabeth Gibson
    120–122
  Thomas Benton 120
  William Alexander **120–122**
Rural. *See* Life
Rush Run 123
Ryan
  Pat 120

S

Sadness. *See* Emotions
Sales. *See* Occupations
Samples
  Abner Jehu "Hooge" 69
  Laura "Alice" Dodd 69
  Patricia. *See* Workman
Sams
  Ann. *See* Grimm
Sandy Hollow School 89
Sandyville 22
Sardis 5
Satisfaction. *See* Emotions
Saw Mill Hollow 152
Sawmill. *See* Places
School. *See also* Education;
    History; Occupations;
    Places; Schoolhouse;
    Teacher
  20–21, 43, 65–69,
  104–105, 120, 120–122,
  149, **150–151**, 158
Schoolhouse. *See also*
    History; School
  One-two room 20–21,
    43, 57, 65,
    89, 146, **149**, 150,
    150–151, 156, 158
  Other 15
Scott
  Jeff 157
Scotts Run 113
Scott's Run Settlement House
  116
Seasons
  Autumn 25, 104, 131–132
  Spring 25
  Summer 25, 57–58
  Winter 25, **145**, **146**, 146–
    147, 148
Secret 45
Security. *See* Emotions
Self-sufficiency.
    See Characteristics
Seneca Rocks 92
Service. *See* Community
Sewing. *See* Skills
Shack Presbyterian Church 113
Shame. *See* Emotions
Sharp
  L. D. 96
  Luther David, Jr. 96
  Rachael Dilley 95
  Silas 96
  William 95
Sharples 145, 149, 153, 158
Shaver
  Joy Elizabeth 131
  Mark 131
  Pauline Wilson, Col.
    130–131
Shaver's Fork 90
Shaving 27–28
Shaw
  Ena 120

John C. 120
Sam 13
Shaw's Run 104
Shelton
  Cindy Lynch 126
  William H. D. 126
Shepard
  Billy Earl 78
  Juanita Austin Dove. *See*
    Basham
Shepherd
  Edwin, Dr. 35
  Polly 25
Shepherdstown 99
Shinnston 110, 116, 132
Shively 156
Shopping 89
Short
  Hattie Pearl. *See* Roush
Shriver 109
  Mary Lee. *See* Matlick
Shuman
  Francis Ellsworth 123
  Helen 123
  John 123
  Norabelle. *See* Corra
  Willis 123
Siders
  Jack T. 38
  Lorena Mae Roush 38
Sielen
  Rae Jean 109, 114
Silvius
  Carole 85
  Wendell **84–85**
Simpson 126
Simpson Creek Collieries 5
Simpson Hotel **126**
Sissonville 42, 145, 148, 153,
    154, 157, 158, 159
Sister. *See* Family
Sizemore
  Cathy A. *See* Helms
  Isaac **83–84**
  Pheobe Tetter **83–84**
Skidmore
  Ed 120
Skills. *See also* Knowledge
  Baking 37
  Canning 154–155
  Ceramics 116
  Gardening 159
  Painting 12
  Quilting 91–92, 148
  Sewing 15, 91–92, 116
Skunk. *See* Animals; Pets
Slab Fork 34
Slatyfork 95
Sleigh riding. *See* Recreation
Smith
  Alan 154
  Amber 153
  Barbara 7
  Craig Ancel **13–16**
  Donna Ellen. *See* Davis
  Jacob 154
  Jennifer 154

John Samuel 16
Louis W. 123
Peggy June Ferrell **13–16**
Vicki 154
Smoot High School 152
Smutko
  Billy 159
  Michael 159
Snider
  Clara 67
Snowhill 158
Soccer. *See* Sports
Socials. *See* Recreation
Somerville
  Isa James 21
Sonnencroft **134–138**
South Carolina
  Inman 81
  Myrtle Beach 39
Spangler
  Crystal Dawn 147
  Janie 147
Spanish-American War. *See*
    Wars
Spanishburg 82
Sparks
  Alisha Dawn 157
Spears 19
  Madge 43
Spencer 25
  Ernest 31
  Sterling 63
Spinks 58
Sports
  Baseball 42
  Basketball 82
  Round town 149
  Roundhouse 150–151
  Soccer 148
Spriggs
  Robert L. **95**
Spring (water) 20
Spring Hill 19
Springston
  Albert 67
  Emma 67
Springton 79
Sprout 19
  Esrom 121
Spry
  Ira 154
  Martha Queen 154
Squirrel. *See* Animals
St. Albans 35, 36, 38, 45, 57,
    119, 126
Stalnaker
  Frank 67
Stauber
  Renaud 92–93
Steam engines **84–85**
Stemple
  Blaine 120
Stevenson
  Amy 90–91, 91
Stewart
  Archie 13
Stewart's Run 111

INDEX

Stingo
 Jeanette (Concetta E.). See Mainella
St. John's EUB Church 139
St. Louis
 Kenneth 109, 114
 Melinda 109
St. Louis World's Fair 56
St. Mary's School of Nursing 130
Stone
 Dorothy M. **31–32**
Stonestreet
 Leatha. See Carroll
Stories. See also Family; History
 Family 13–16, 38, 41, 44, 51, 56–57, 62, 81, 82–83, 83, 119, 132–138, 156, 157–158, 158–159
 Ghost 126
 Headless Horseman 56–57
 Humorous 32, 52, 57–58, 60, 69–70, 79, 80, 81, 82, **94–95**, 105, 117, 150, 153, 154, 158–159, **159–160**
 Tall tales 23–24
 Witch's spell 69
Stout
 L. Meigs 126
 Loutellus 126
Stowers
 Belva 160
 Clarence 160
 Nancy 160
Straight
 Becky. See Layman
 Billie Marie Pierce **115–116**
 Robert 115
Stratton
 Erica L. 95
Strength. See Characteristics
Strike. See Coal
Stump
 Carl 31
 Ethel 42
 Harold L. 42
 Jesse 42
Sturm
 Lula Coffman 120
Sugar Creek 94
Sugar Grove 111, 115
Sugar Grove Church **111–112**
Summer. See Seasons
Summers
 Robert 120
Summers County High School. 77
Summersville 58, 59, 72, 148
Suncrest Junior High School 130
Surprise 145, 154
Swartz
 Dana Ann. See Righman
Swearingen
 Brooks. See Hutchinson
Swick
 Gerald D. 117
 Howard Harold, Sr. **116–117**
Swimming. See Recreation
Swimming hole. See Places
Sych
 Judith. See Walters
Sympathy. See Emotions

T

Tackette
 Virgil James **146–147**
Tad 39
Tailor. See Occupations
Tall tales. See Stories
Tanner 55, 65
Tanner Creek 68
Tanner School 65, **65–69**
Taylor
 Iva Margaret Campbell 58
 Mary Sue. See Cottle
 Wilbur Wade 58
Teacher. See also Education; Occupations; School; Schoolhouse 20–21, 43–44, 52, 56, 65, 89, 91–92, 109–110, 152
Teaching. See Occupations
Technological advances
 Radio 7, 14
 Television 111
Television. See Technological advances
Temple
 Margaret Louise Eads 78
Tenderness. See Emotions
Tennessee 79
Teter Creek 138
Tetter
 Pheobe. See Sizemore
Texas
 Tyler 99
Thanksgiving. See Holidays
Thaxton
 Mable 155
 Okey **155**
Thomas 58
 Carla. See McClure
Thompson
 "Hob" 120
 James 127
Thornhill 131
 Melissa 132
Thrifty. See Characteristics
Tichner
 Vivian. See Carpenter
Tincher
 Francis. See Hughes
Todd
 Pearl. See Miller
Tolerance. See Characteristics
Tom's Fork 126
Tornado. See Disasters
Trace Fork 68
Trains 38–39, 84–85

Traits. See Characteristics
Travels 24, **31**, 38–39, 149
Treasure
 Buried 83
Trees
 Mulberry 103
Tripplett 60
Truck. See Vehicles
Tunnelton 105
Twistabout Ridge 69
Tygart Valley River 125
Tygart's Valley 94
Tyree
 Ed 58
 Hester 58
 Oat 58
 Sarah Martha 58

U

Uncle. See Family
United Brethren Church 139
United Methodist Church 114, 139
Upper Trace School 146
Urban. See Life
Utah 38

V

Vacations 31
Valley Furnace 120
Values. See Characteristics; Community; Family; West Virginia
Van Camp
 Isaac 127
Van Schaik
 Debbie 12
VanCamp
 DesDemona 68
 Diane Lynn 68
 Harlen 68
Vande Linde
 Otto "Dick" Vernon, Jr. **41–42**
 Stacey 42
Varney
 Ashley Jeanette 156
Vehicles
 Automobile 31, 107–108
 Truck 22–23
Victory High School 107
Vincent
 Stanley 122
Virginia 45
 Richmond 83, 96
 Staunton 94
 Woodstock 90
Volk
 Jessie 129
Voltz
 Mary 13

W

Waggy

 Marge. See Lewellen
Wagner
 Jean **5**
Walkers Crick 19
Walkup
 Betty. See Neal
Walnut Hill 109
Walters
 Emily Gray 160
 Judith Sych **160**
Walthall
 Gayle. See Wise
 Lucille Litz 84
Walton
 Charles 13
 Marian 13
War (WV) 79
War of 1812. See Wars
Ware
 Blackburn 120
 Edith 132
Warfield
 Eloise Davis 56
Warren
 Carol 62
 Isabelle Hanna "Izzy" 62
 J. T. 62
Wars. See also Military
 1812 46
 Civil 46, 83, 85–86, 95–96
 French and Indian 45
 Korean 47
 Mexican 46
 Spanish-American 47
 World War I 47, 117–118
 World War II 33, 47, 125, 152–153, 153–154, 159
Washington
 George, Gen. 117
Washington, D.C. 38
Waterman
 William R. 25
Waters
 Herbert 139
 Mary. See Morgan
Watkins
 Lyda. See Hutchinson
Watoga State Park 149
Wealth. See Prosperity
Weatherholt
 Elizabeth. See Brake
Webb
 Anna 52
 Ella 52
 John L. 51
Webster
 Olive 66
Webster Springs 51
Wedding. See Life events
Welch 82
Wells
 Jeremy 151
West Fork River 72
West Grade School 146
West Union 14

Name in bold indicates "Author" • Page number in bold indicates "Featured" • Underlined page number indicates "Photo"

West Virginia. *See also* Counties
　Beauty 62–63, 90–91,
　　99–100, 110–111,
　　130–131, 151
　Dialect **93–94**, 94–95
　Heritage 26–27, 45, 51,
　　60–61, 72–73, 86, 93
　Hills 40–41, 79–80
　History
　　31, 45, 55, 78, 83, **95–96**
　Home 58, 89, 130–131
　Homecoming 55
　Industry 62–63
　Leaving 19
　Legends 83
　Mountain state 112–114
　Mountaineers **82**, 129–130
　Mountains **151**
　National Guard **45–48**
　Newcomer 27, 31–32,
　　32, 84-85, 91, **112-114,
　　129–130**, 159
　Pride 39–40, 45–48, 48–49,
　　79–80, 94–95, **99–100**
　Recreation 62–63, 108–109
　Retirement **39–40**
　Returning 19, 79–80,
　　99–100
　Roads **23**
　Values 55, 89, 89–90,
　　108–109, 129–130
West Virginia Institute of
　Technology 84

West Virginia University
　16, 129, 130, 132, 133
West Virginia Wesleyan College
　130
Westwood Middle School 127
Wheeling 33, 89
White
　B. 65
　Inez 160
　Nesta 160
White Sulphur Springs 80, 81
Whitman 145, 156
Whitt
　Leva. *See* Barker
Whyte
　Jennifer Nicole 127
Wiblin
　Clay 58
Wild Cat Cut 31
Williams
　Donald 37
　Phyllis. *See* Jarvis
　Ralph 43, 51
Williamson 47
Wilmington High School. 105
Wilson
　Allen Chambers "Chame"
　　139
　Arthur 139
　Dora Poling 139
　Hallie 66
　Inez 130
　James 120

Paul 130
Pauline. *See* Shaver
Tillie 11
William H. 112
Wilt
　Gail 66
　Mable 66
Winifrede Junction 31
Winter. *See* Seasons
Wise
　Gayle Walthall 85
Wiseman
　Anna 61
　Bowling 61
　Emma. *See* Bryant
Withrow
　Dustin Brock 50
　Kara Beth 50
　Krista Jean 50
Wolfe
　Dallas 120
　Dorwin 120
　Hazel 120
　Ira 120
　Oliver 120
Women. *See* Roles
Wood
　Bryan 91
Woodford
　Lorena 68
　Robert 68
　Teresa Jo 68
Woofter

　Ella. *See* Maxwell
　Elma Jean 66
　Lona 55
Work. *See*
　　Characteristics; Occupations
Workman 58
　Alicia 152
　Bennie 152
　Linda 152
　Lori. *See* Carter
　Mark 82
　Patricia Samples 61
　Wade 152
World War I. *See* Wars
World War II. *See* Wars
Wright
　Betty 66
Writing. *See* Occupations
Wynne
　Geneva Anderson 86
　James B. 86
　Joseph Anderson 86
　Stephen Lee 86

Y

Yoho
　Clyde, Sr. **52**
　Denver C. 52
Young
　Kay. *See* Hill
　Lewis Otho **22**
Yugoslavia 48

About The Editors

Rae Jean Sielen is president and co-founder of Populore Publishing Company. She was born and raised on the West Coast, but now lives in the Scotts Run area of Monongalia County in West Virginia with her husband Ken St. Louis. Rae Jean's fascination with language and languages led to a Bachelor of Arts degree in linguistics and a Master of Science degree in speech and hearing sciences. Her involvement with Populore is a natural result of this interest coupled with her business experience, love of words and graphics, and a delight in people's stories — the *real* stories of people from all walks of life and in their own language. Ken and Rae Jean developed the Populore approach to story preservation to offer everyday folks the opportunity to share in the joys of seeing their stories in print and knowing those stories won't be lost.

Amy Stevenson is a project manager and senior writer for Populore Publishing Company. Her enthusiasm for story preservation comes from a strong sense of history, a family tradition of storytelling and journal writing dating back to the mid-1800s, and a shared sense of accomplishment and discovery with Populore contributors. She was previously the English editor of a bilingual business magazine in St. Petersburg, Russia. While getting out on the streets to hear stories from all sorts of people, she developed a soft spot for tales of endurance and overcoming hardship. Amy was also a member of the management team for a monthly industrial publication out of Ohio. She holds a Bachelor of Arts degree in International Studies and German from West Virginia University. She resides in her hometown of Morgantown, West Virginia.

Mountain State Stories Of The People

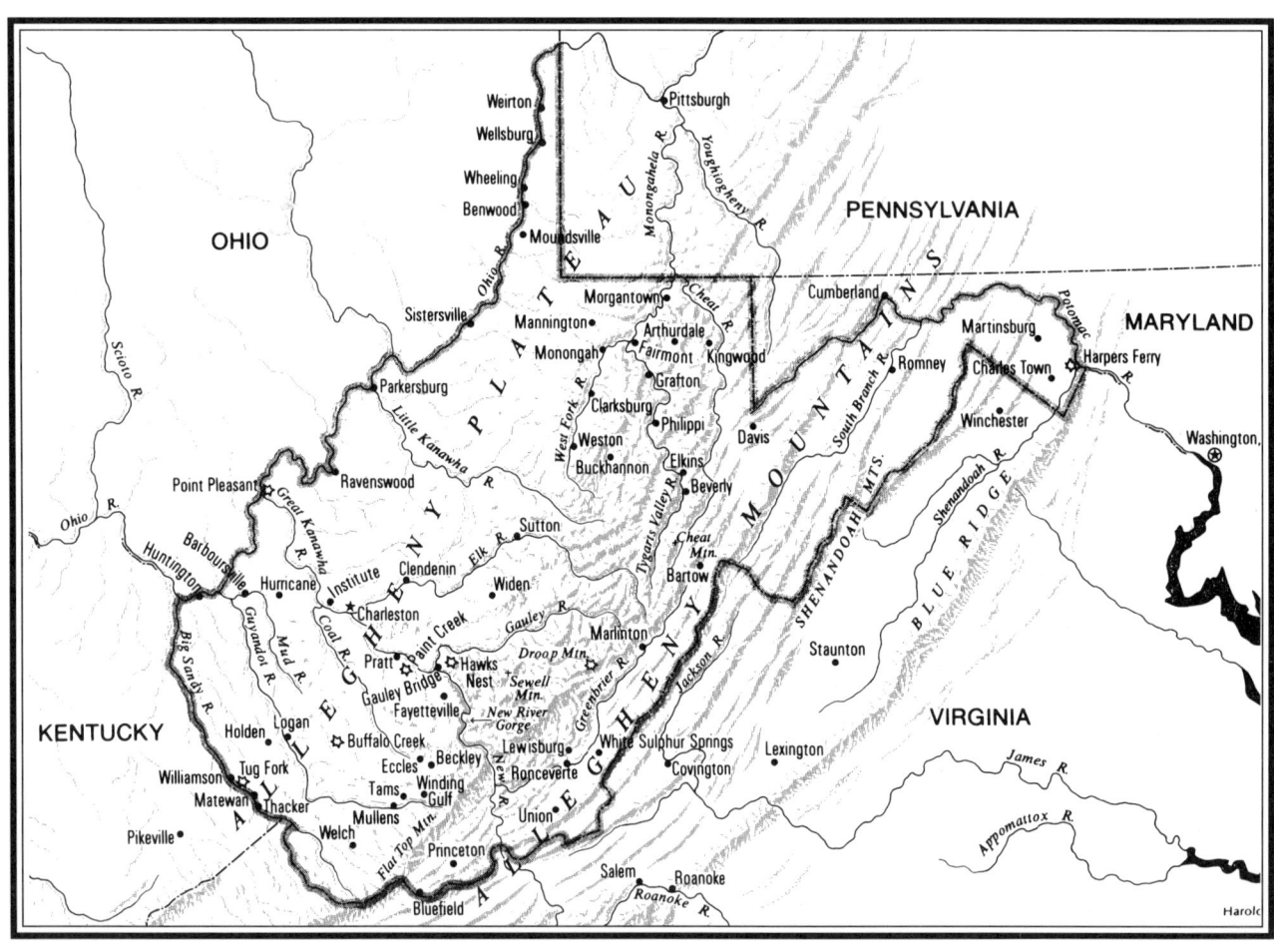